SWEET TOOTH

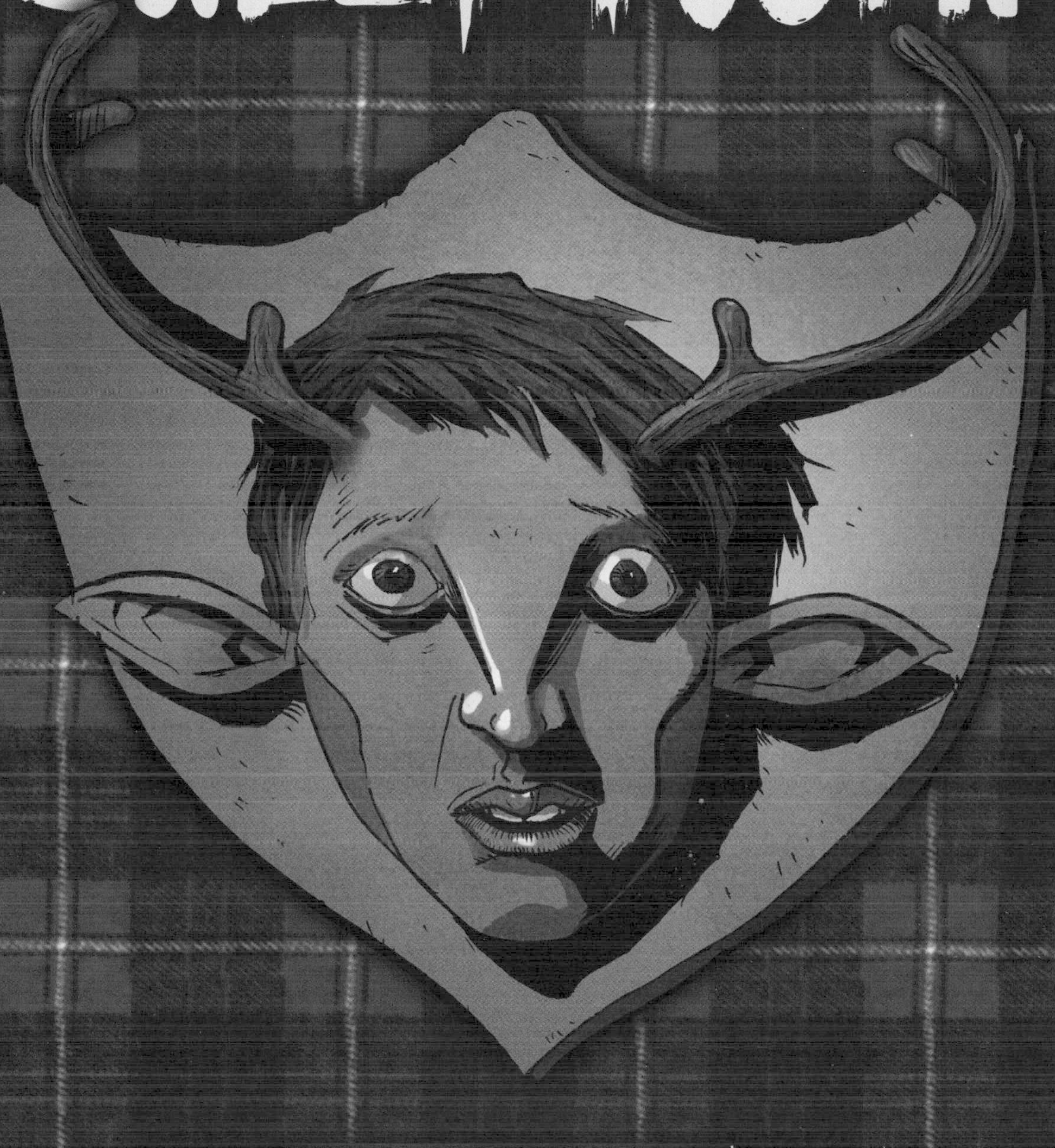

Out of the DEEP WOODS

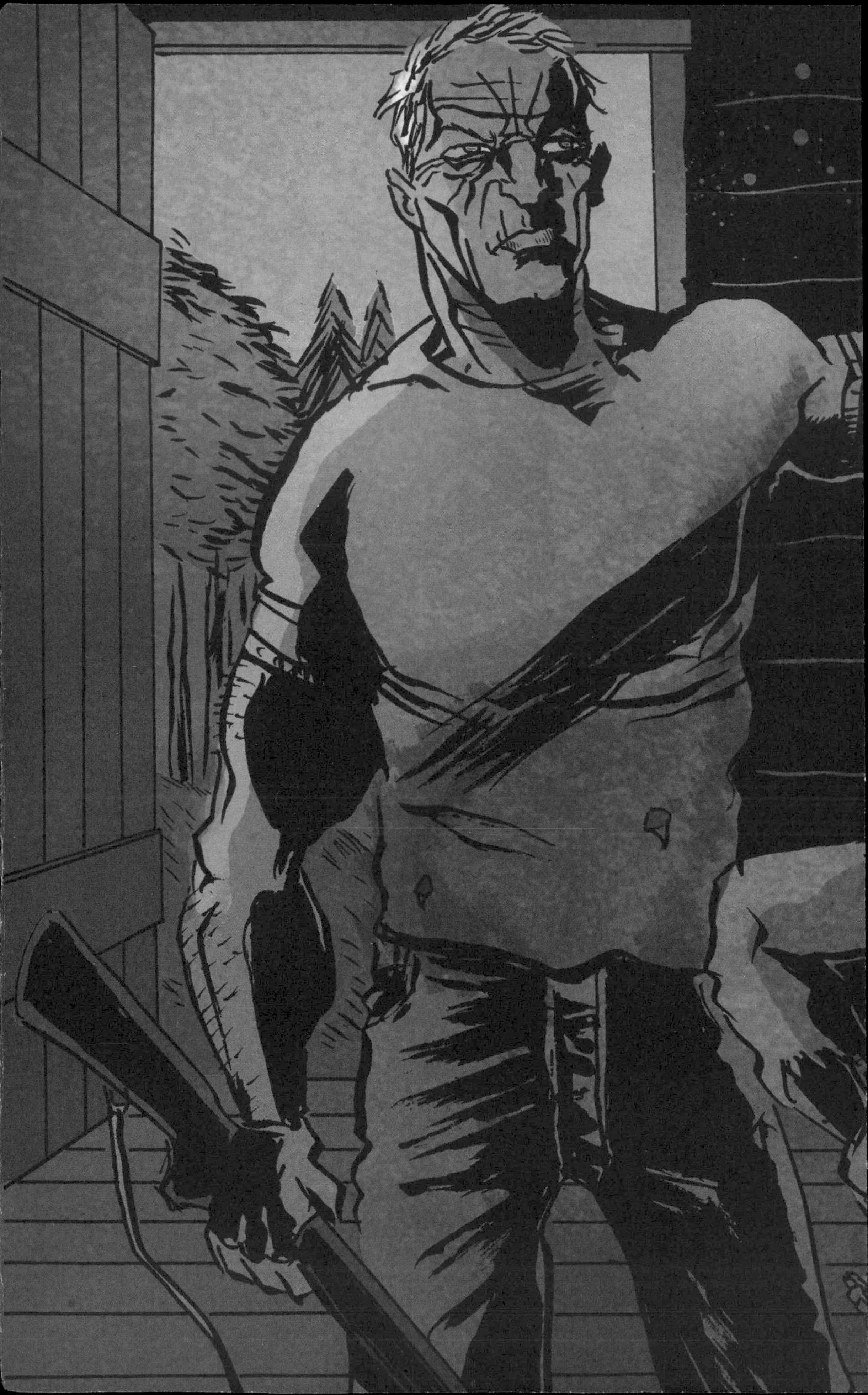

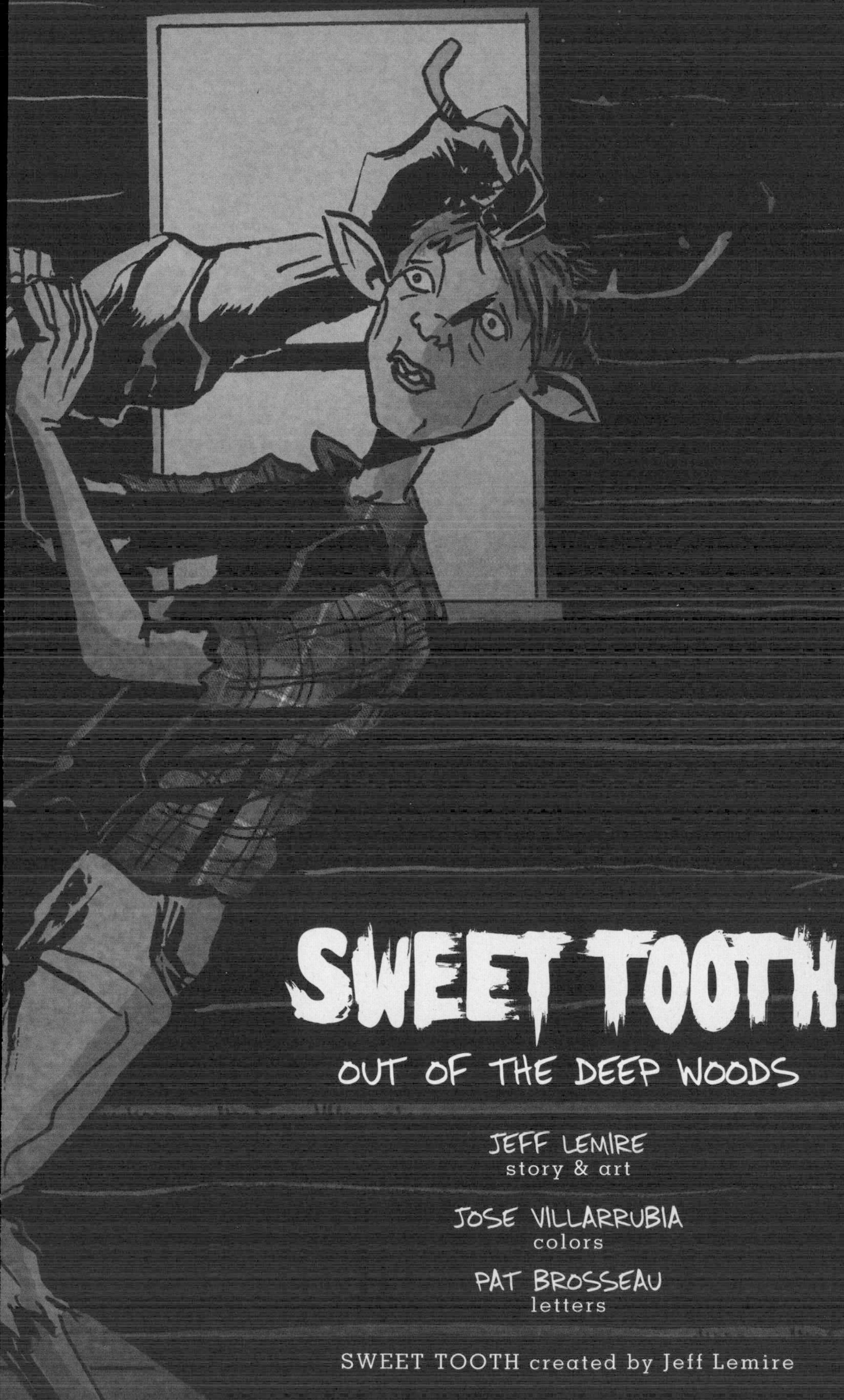

SWEET TOOTH

OUT OF THE DEEP WOODS

JEFF LEMIRE
story & art

JOSE VILLARRUBIA
colors

PAT BROSSEAU
letters

SWEET TOOTH created by Jeff Lemire

Cover by Jeff Lemire with Jose Villarrubia

SWEET TOOTH: OUT OF THE DEEP WOODS
Published by DC Comics. Cover, text and
compilation Copyright © 2010 DC Comics.
All Rights Reserved.

Originally published in single magazine
form as SWEET TOOTH 1-5. Copyright ©
2009, 2010 Jeff Lemire. All Rights Reserved.
VERTIGO is a trademark of DC Comics. All
characters, their distinctive likenesses and
related elements featured in this publication
are trademarks of DC Comics. The stories,
characters and incidents featured in this
publication are entirely fictional. DC Comics
does not read or accept unsolicited submissions
of ideas, stories or artwork.

DC Comics, 1700 Broadway, New York, NY 10019
A Warner Bros. Entertainment Company
Printed in the USA.
Fifth Printing.
ISBN: 978-1-4012-2696-1

Library of Congress Cataloging-in-Publication Data

Lemire, Jeff.
  Sweet tooth : out of the deep woods / Jeff Lemire.
    p. cm.
  "Originally published in single magazine form as
SWEET TOOTH 1-5."
  ISBN 978-1-4012-2696-1 (alk. paper)
  1. End of the world--Comic books, strips, etc. 2. Animal
mutation--Comic
books, strips, etc. 3. Graphic novels. I. Title. II. Title: Out
of the deep woods.

  PN6733.L45S95 2012
  741.5'973--dc23
                              2012017902

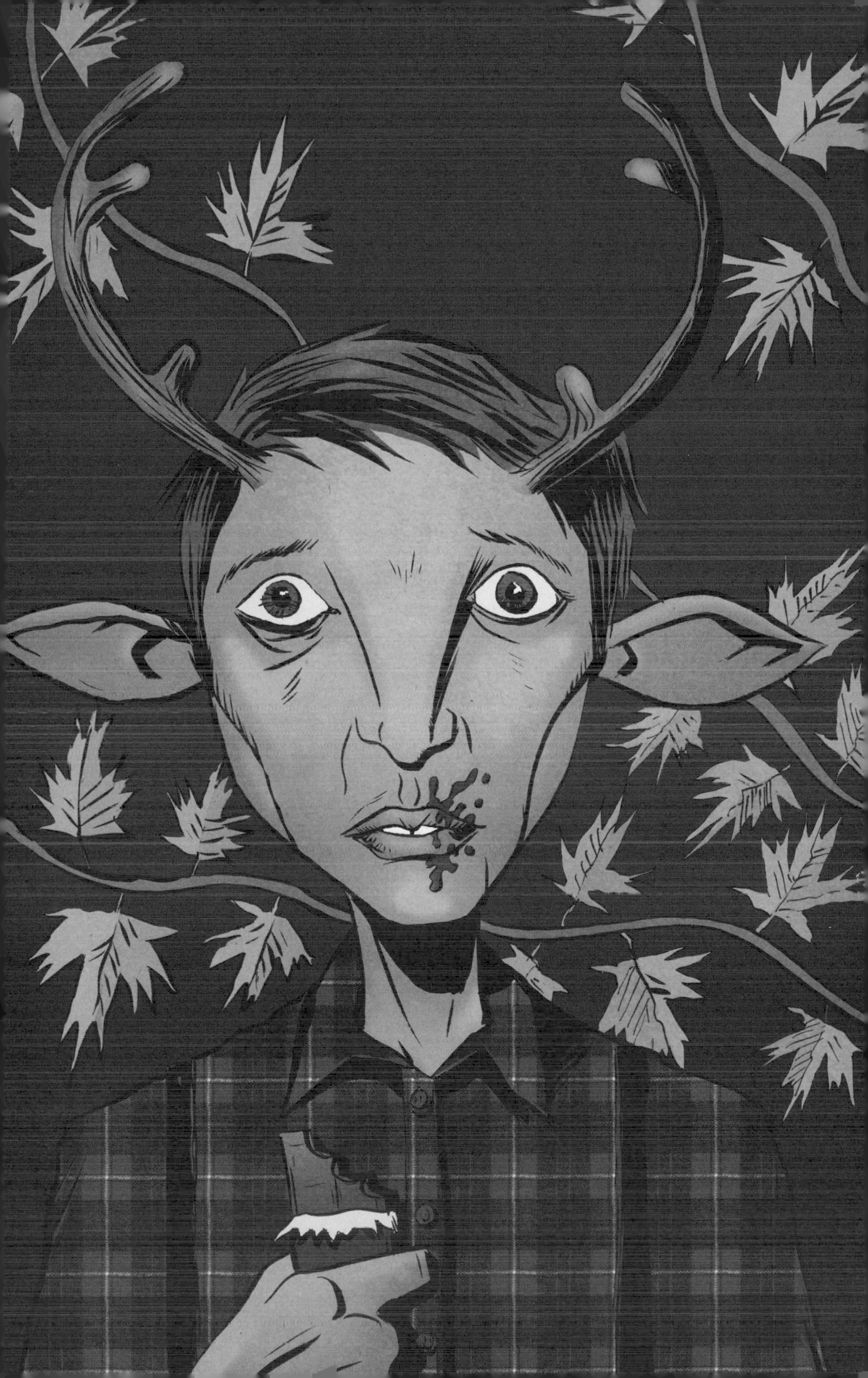

I SEEN HIS FACE AGAIN WHEN I WAS SLEEPING.

THE BIG MAN...HE'S JUST LOOKING DOWN AT ME WITH THEM COLD EYES.

AND I RUN. I RUN FASTER THAN I EVEN THOUGHT I COULD, 'CAUSE BEHIND ME IS FIRE AND HELL AND BAD STUFF.

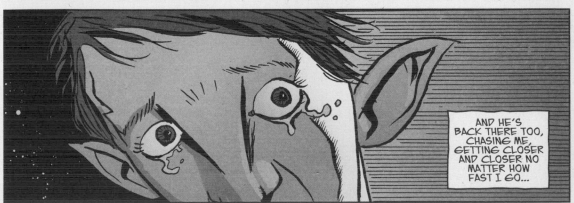

AND HE'S BACK THERE TOO, CHASING ME, GETTING CLOSER AND CLOSER NO MATTER HOW FAST I GO...

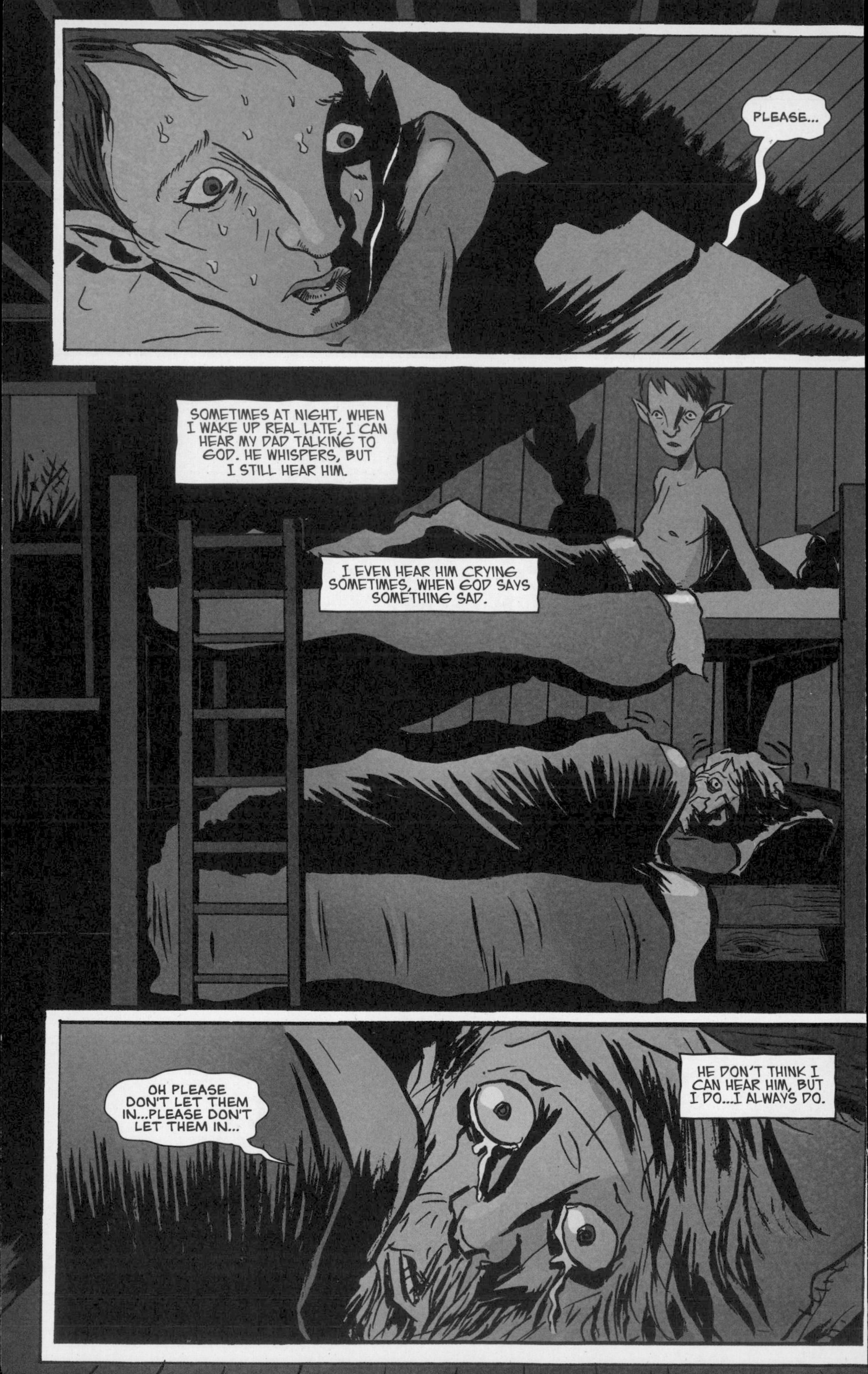
PLEASE...
SOMETIMES AT NIGHT, WHEN I WAKE UP REAL LATE, I CAN HEAR MY DAD TALKING TO GOD. HE WHISPERS, BUT I STILL HEAR HIM.
I EVEN HEAR HIM CRYING SOMETIMES, WHEN GOD SAYS SOMETHING SAD.
HE DON'T THINK I CAN HEAR HIM, BUT I DO...I ALWAYS DO.
OH PLEASE DON'T LET THEM IN...PLEASE DON'T LET THEM IN...

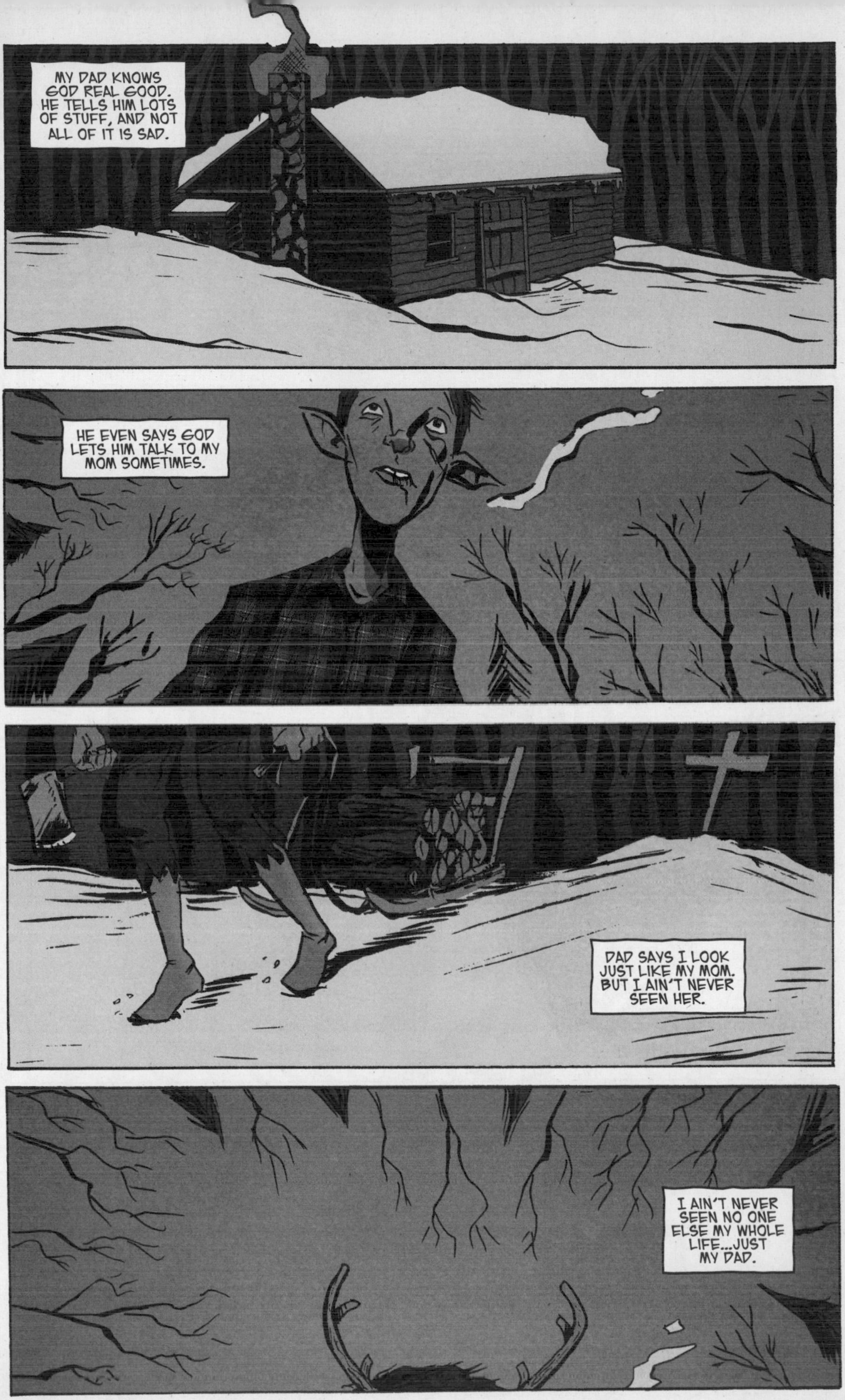
MY DAD KNOWS GOD REAL GOOD. HE TELLS HIM LOTS OF STUFF, AND NOT ALL OF IT IS SAD.
HE EVEN SAYS GOD LETS HIM TALK TO MY MOM SOMETIMES.
DAD SAYS I LOOK JUST LIKE MY MOM. BUT I AIN'T NEVER SEEN HER.
I AIN'T NEVER SEEN NO ONE ELSE MY WHOLE LIFE...JUST MY DAD.

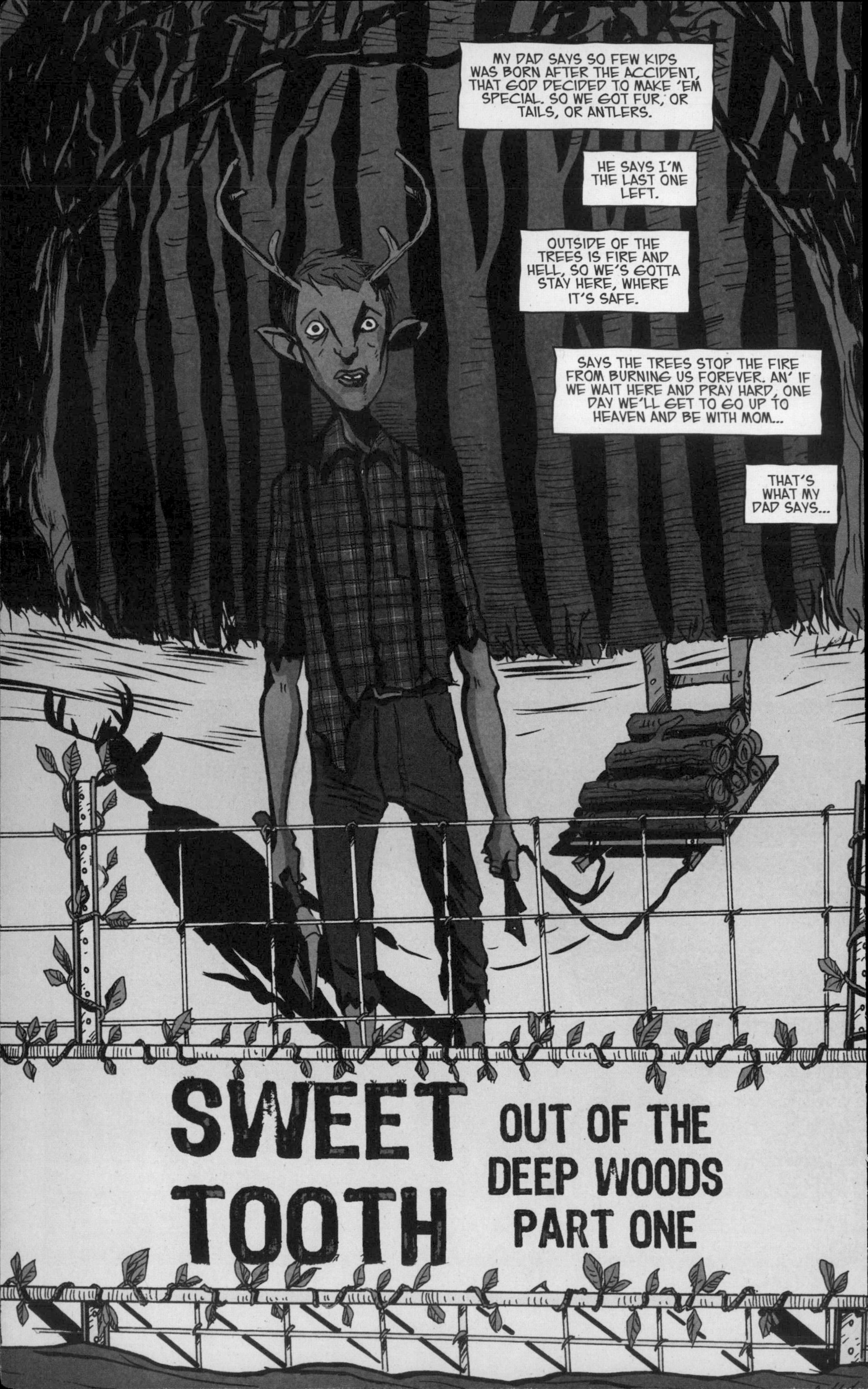
MY DAD SAYS SO FEW KIDS WAS BORN AFTER THE ACCIDENT, THAT GOD DECIDED TO MAKE 'EM SPECIAL. SO WE GOT FUR, OR TAILS, OR ANTLERS.
HE SAYS I'M THE LAST ONE LEFT.
OUTSIDE OF THE TREES IS FIRE AND HELL, SO WE'S GOTTA STAY HERE, WHERE IT'S SAFE.
SAYS THE TREES STOP THE FIRE FROM BURNING US FOREVER. AN' IF WE WAIT HERE AND PRAY HARD, ONE DAY WE'LL GET TO GO UP TO HEAVEN AND BE WITH MOM...
THAT'S WHAT MY DAD SAYS...
SWEET TOOTH
OUT OF THE DEEP WOODS PART ONE

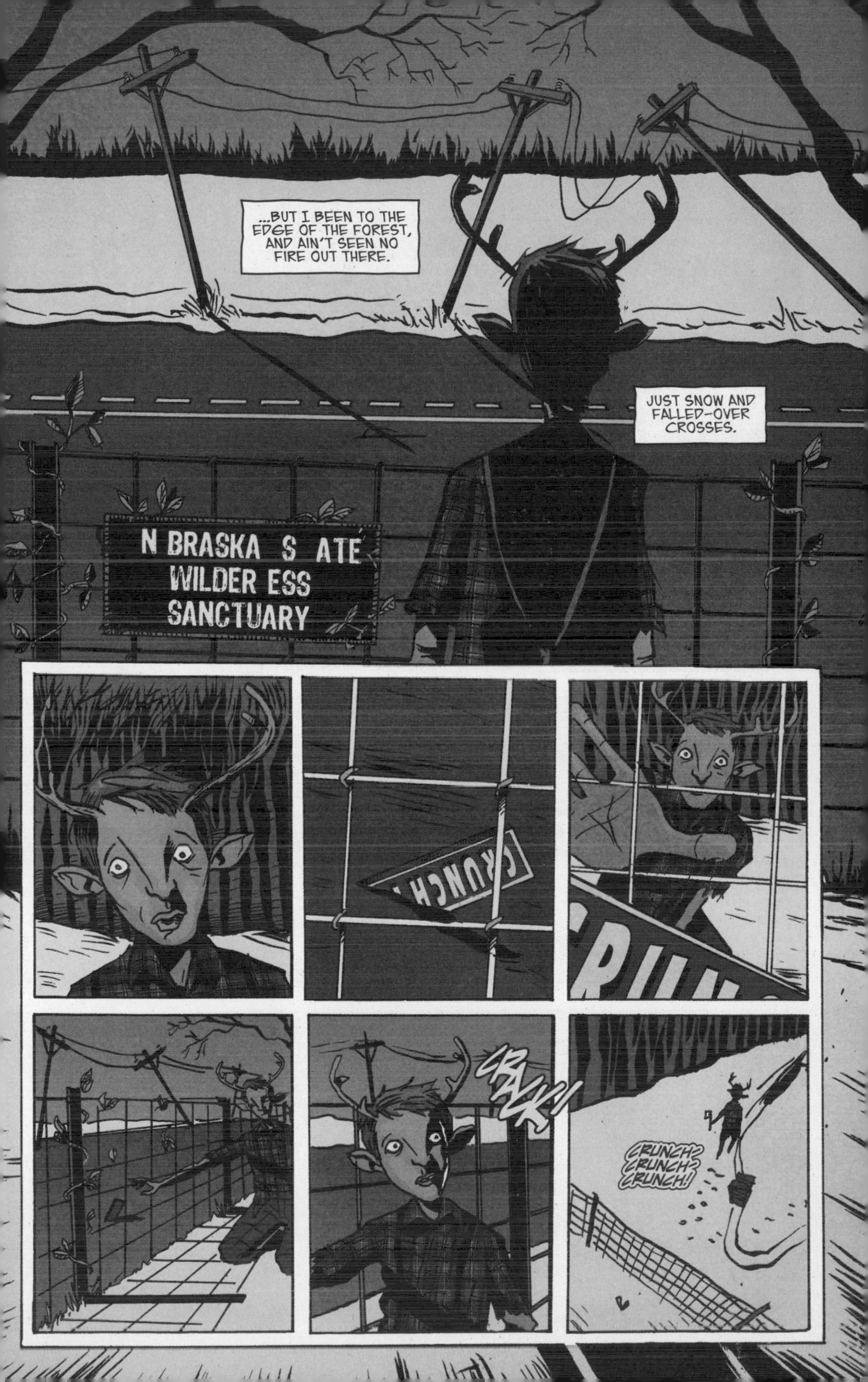
...BUT I BEEN TO THE EDGE OF THE FOREST, AND AIN'T SEEN NO FIRE OUT THERE.
JUST SNOW AND FALLED-OVER CROSSES.
N BRASKA S ATE WILDER ESS SANCTUARY
CRUNCH
CRACK!
CRUNCH- CRUNCH- CRUNCH!

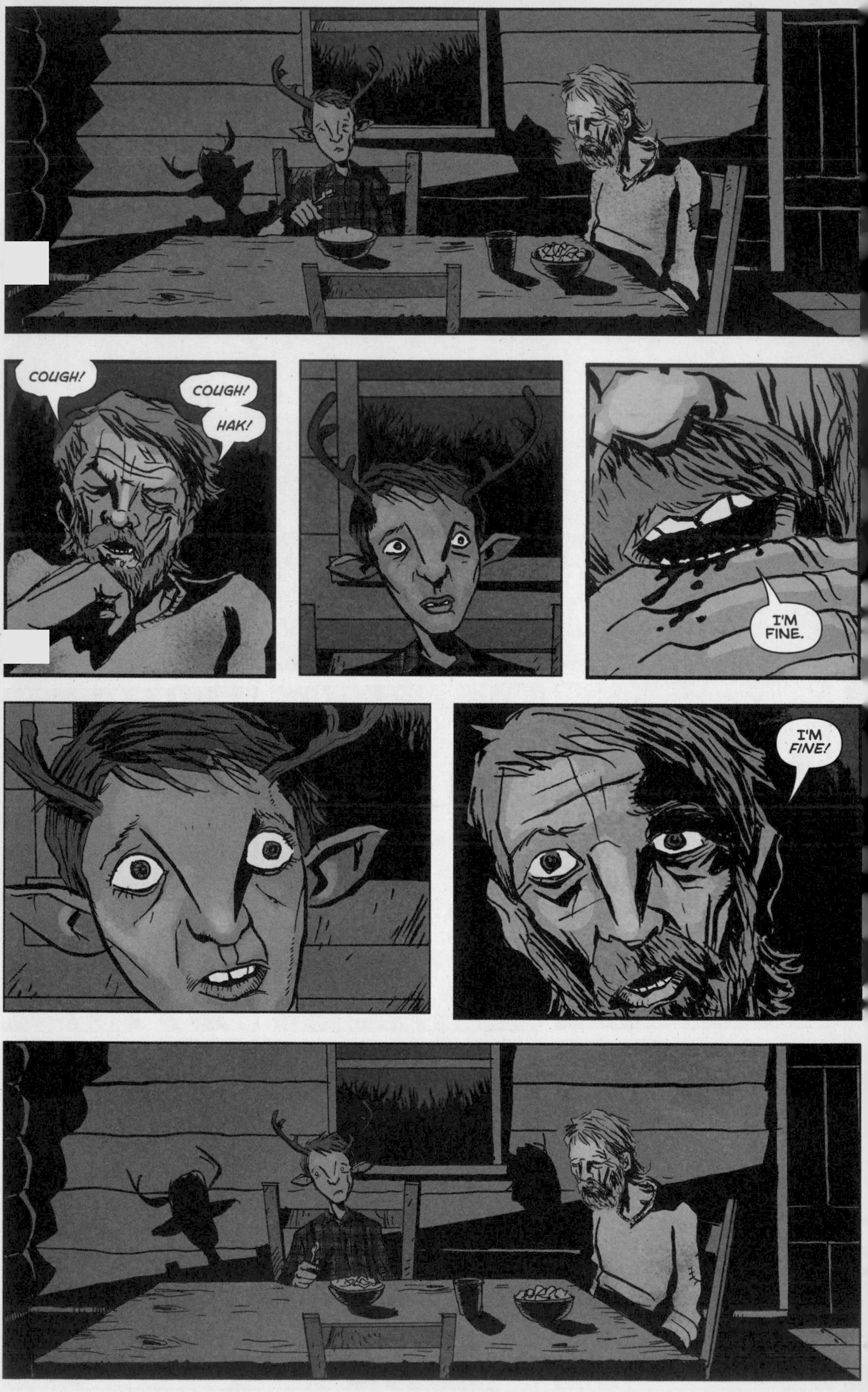
COUGH!
COUGH!
HAK!
I'M FINE.
I'M FINE!

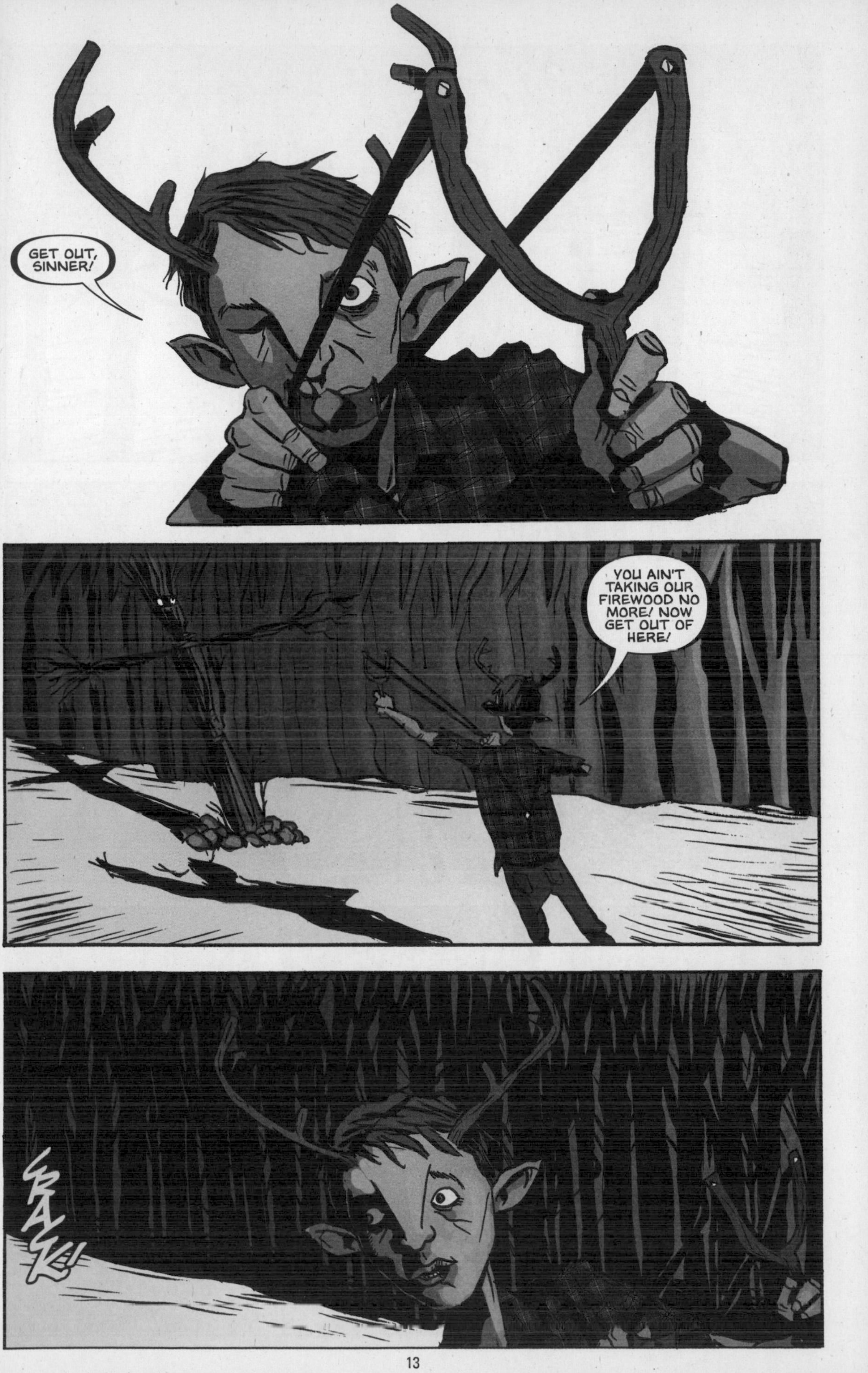
GET OUT, SINNER!
YOU AIN'T TAKING OUR FIREWOOD NO MORE! NOW GET OUT OF HERE!
CRACK!

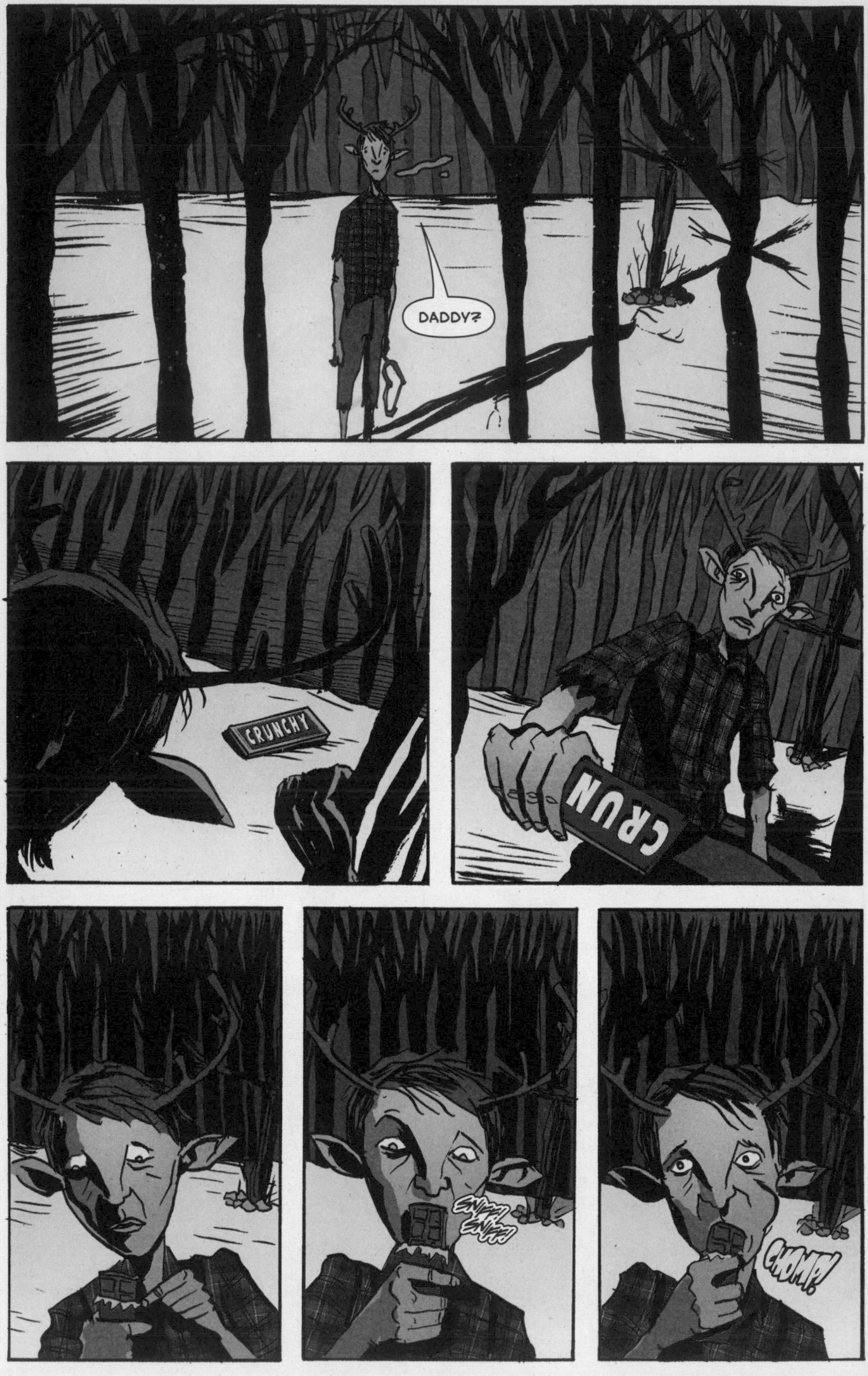

DADDY?
CRUNCHY
CRUN
SNIFF! SNIFF!
CHOMP!

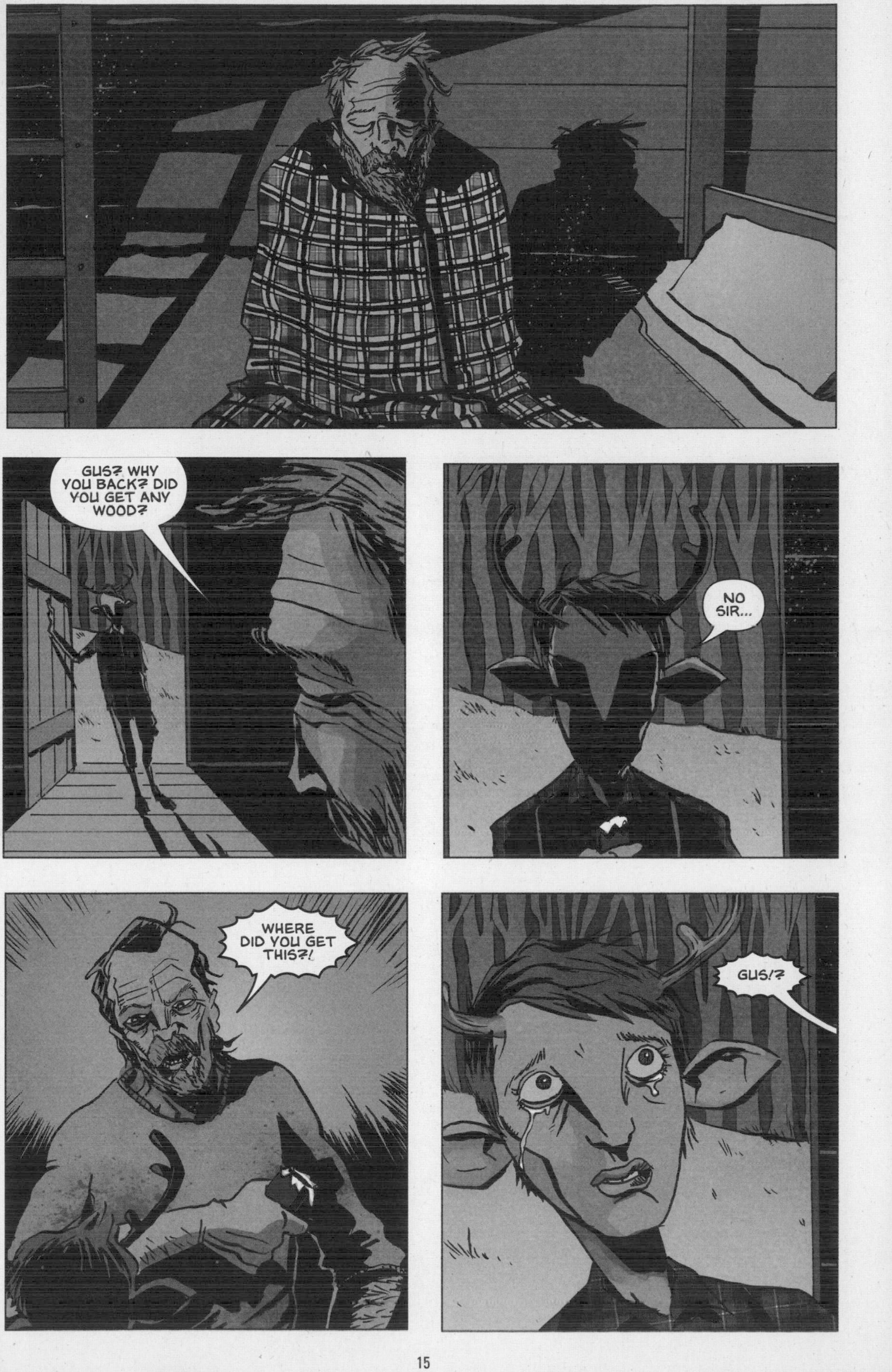
GUS? WHY YOU BACK? DID YOU GET ANY WOOD?
NO SIR...
WHERE DID YOU GET THIS?!
GUS!?

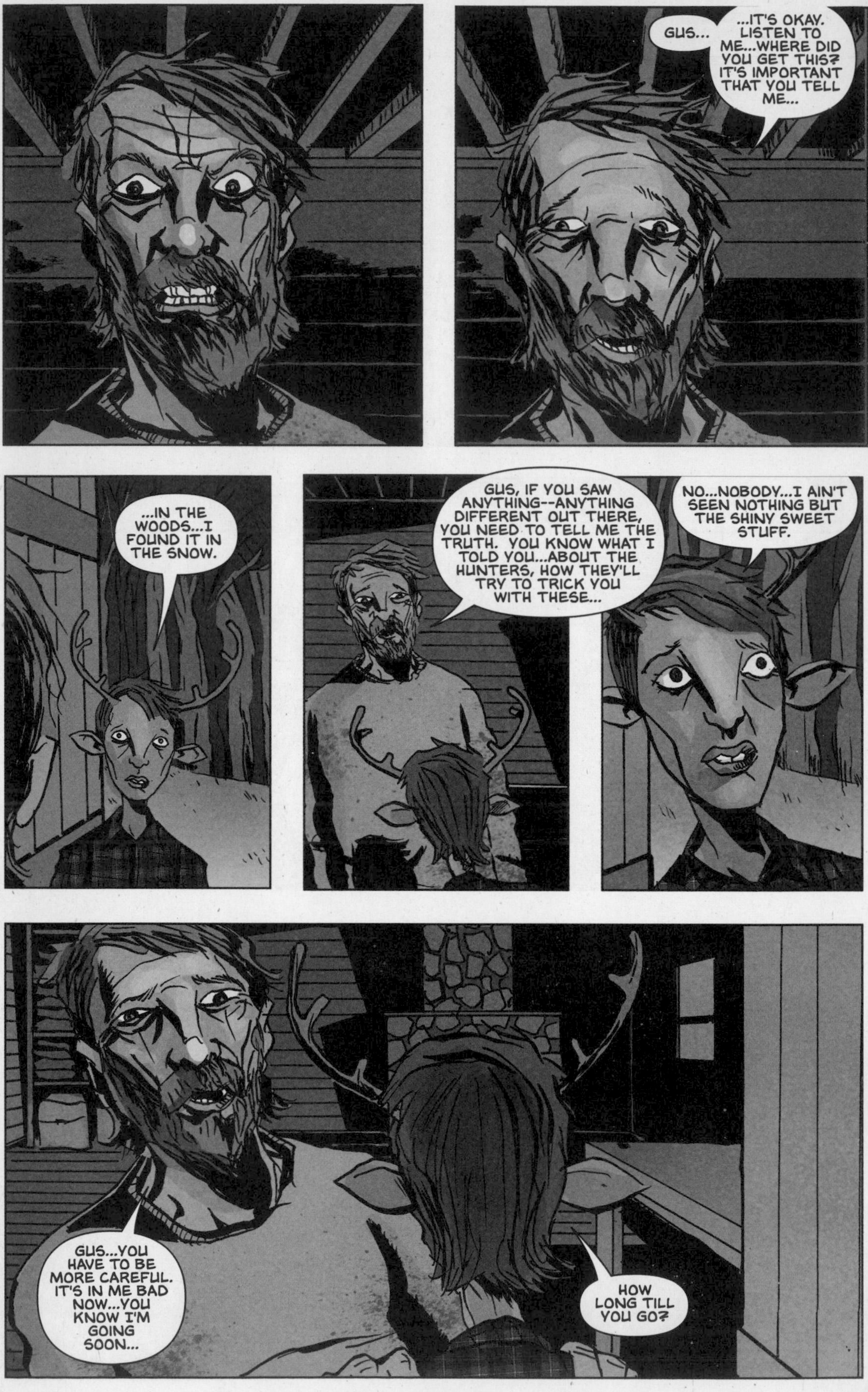
GUS...
...IT'S OKAY. LISTEN TO ME...WHERE DID YOU GET THIS? IT'S IMPORTANT THAT YOU TELL ME...
...IN THE WOODS...I FOUND IT IN THE SNOW.
GUS, IF YOU SAW ANYTHING--ANYTHING DIFFERENT OUT THERE, YOU NEED TO TELL ME THE TRUTH. YOU KNOW WHAT I TOLD YOU...ABOUT THE HUNTERS, HOW THEY'LL TRY TO TRICK YOU WITH THESE...
NO...NOBODY...I AIN'T SEEN NOTHING BUT THE SHINY SWEET STUFF.
GUS...YOU HAVE TO BE MORE CAREFUL. IT'S IN ME BAD NOW...YOU KNOW I'M GOING SOON...
HOW LONG TILL YOU GO?

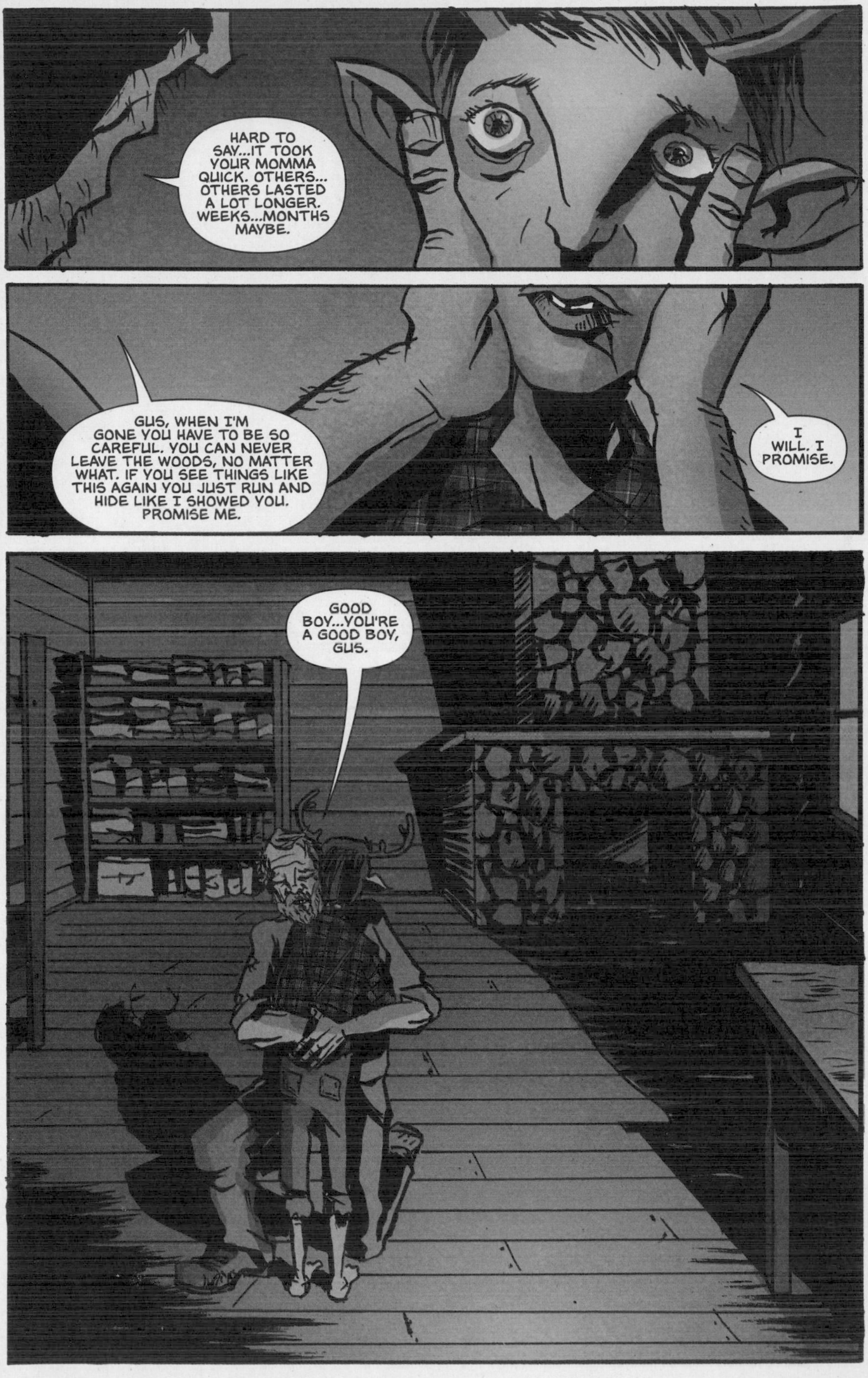
HARD TO SAY...IT TOOK YOUR MOMMA QUICK. OTHERS... OTHERS LASTED A LOT LONGER. WEEKS...MONTHS MAYBE.
GUS, WHEN I'M GONE YOU HAVE TO BE SO CAREFUL. YOU CAN NEVER LEAVE THE WOODS, NO MATTER WHAT. IF YOU SEE THINGS LIKE THIS AGAIN YOU JUST RUN AND HIDE LIKE I SHOWED YOU. PROMISE ME.
I WILL. I PROMISE.
GOOD BOY...YOU'RE A GOOD BOY, GUS.

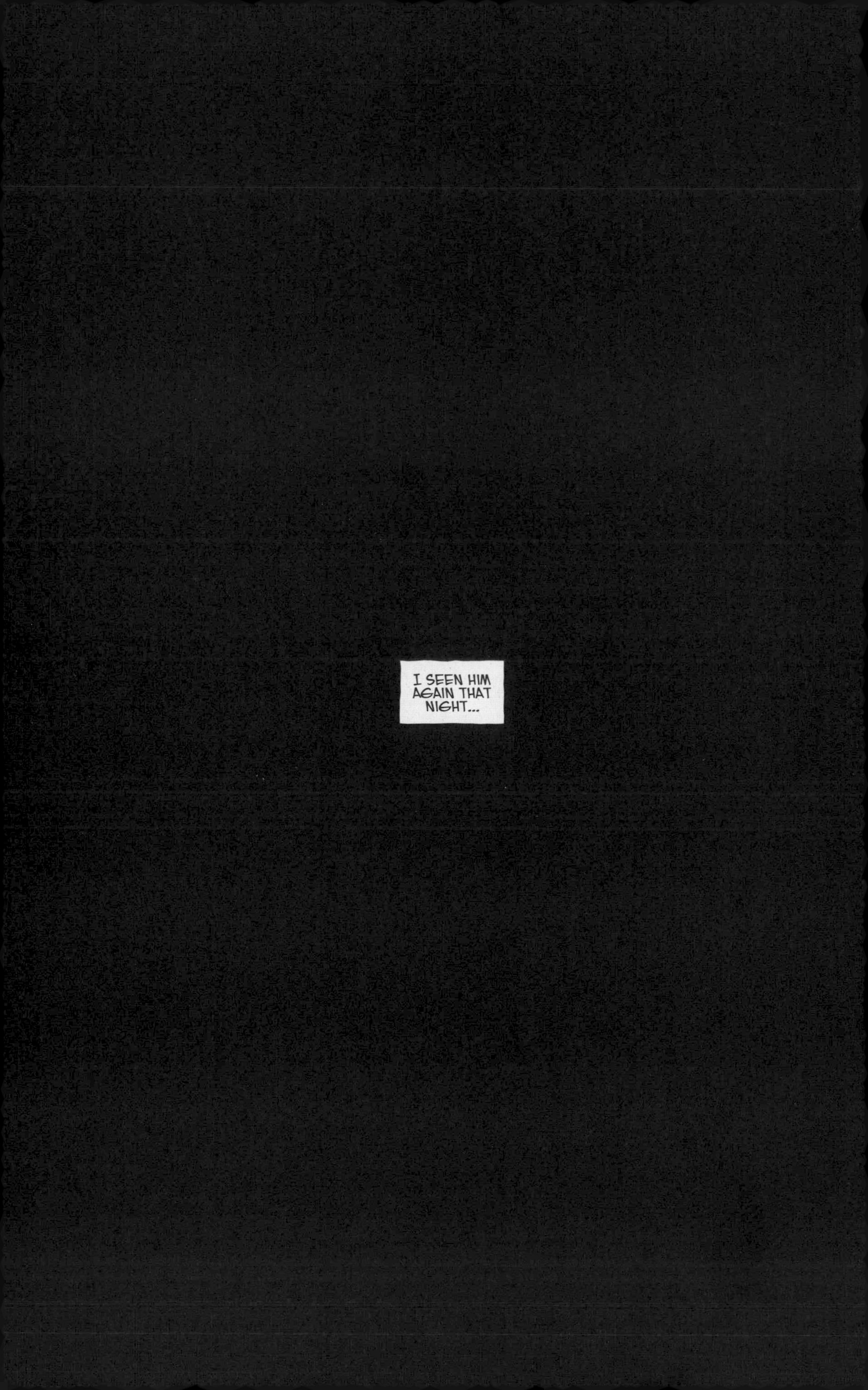
I SEEN HIM AGAIN THAT NIGHT...

...STARING AT ME WITH THEM BAD EYES.

BUT THIS TIME I DON'T RUN, I JUST STARE BACK AT HIM.

GUS...

GUS?

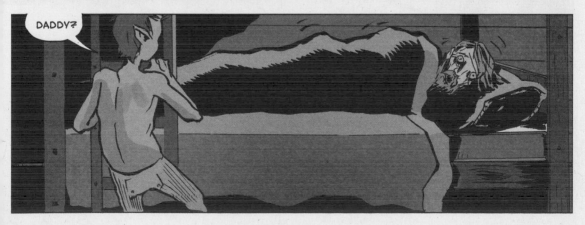

DADDY?

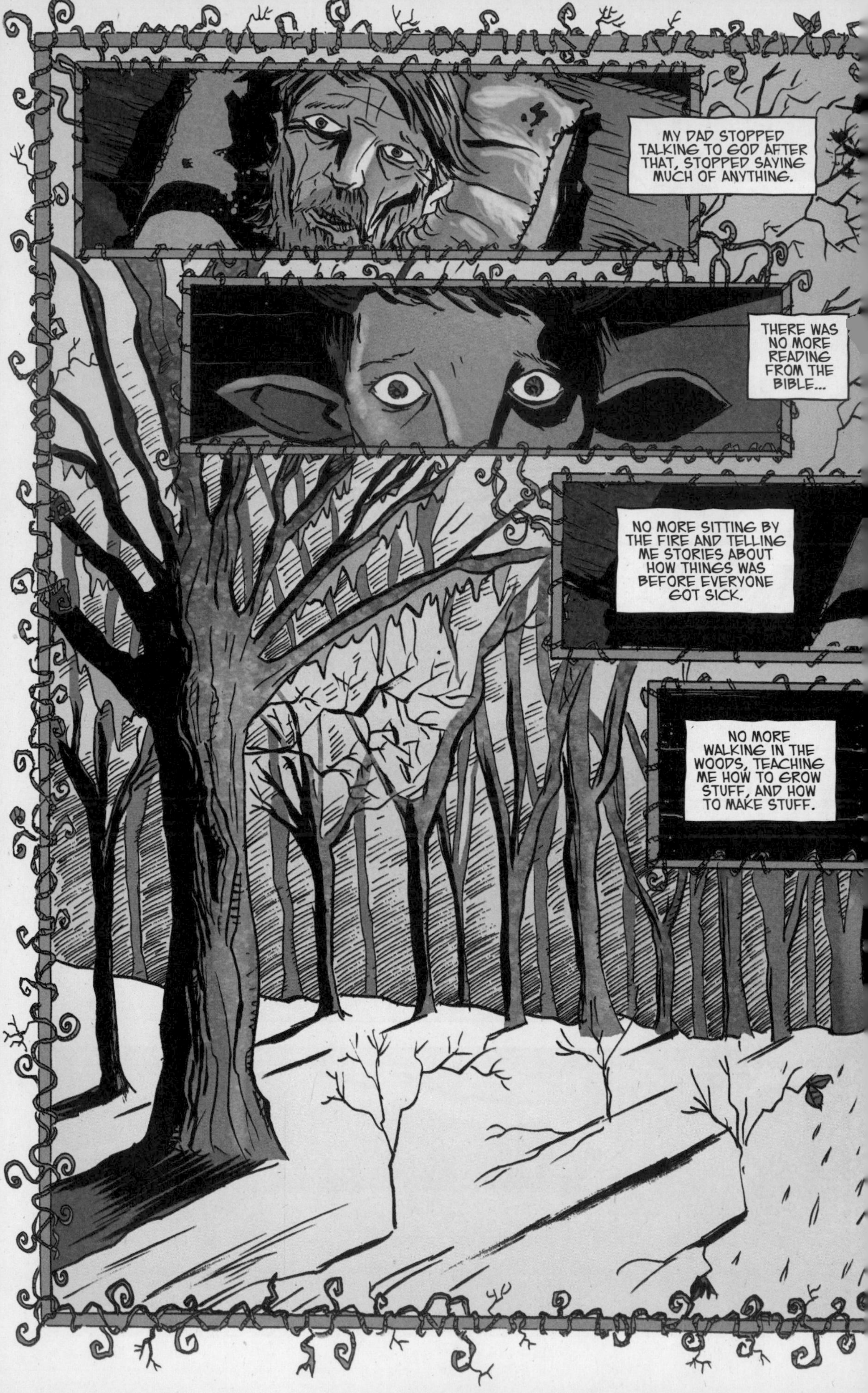
MY DAD STOPPED TALKING TO GOD AFTER THAT, STOPPED SAYING MUCH OF ANYTHING.
THERE WAS NO MORE READING FROM THE BIBLE...
NO MORE SITTING BY THE FIRE AND TELLING ME STORIES ABOUT HOW THINGS WAS BEFORE EVERYONE GOT SICK.
NO MORE WALKING IN THE WOODS, TEACHING ME HOW TO GROW STUFF, AND HOW TO MAKE STUFF.

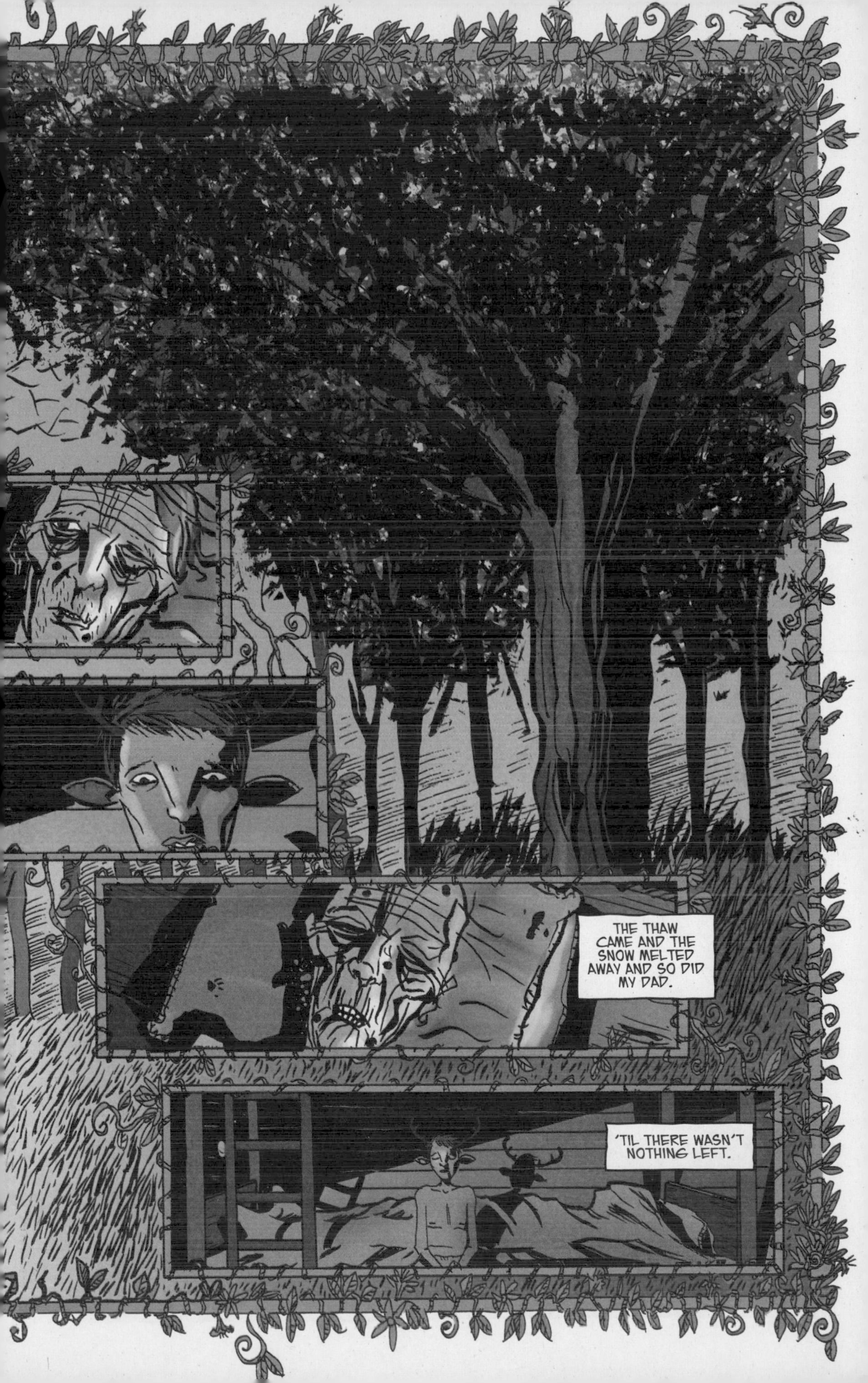
THE THAW CAME AND THE SNOW MELTED AWAY AND SO DID MY DAD.
'TIL THERE WASN'T NOTHING LEFT.

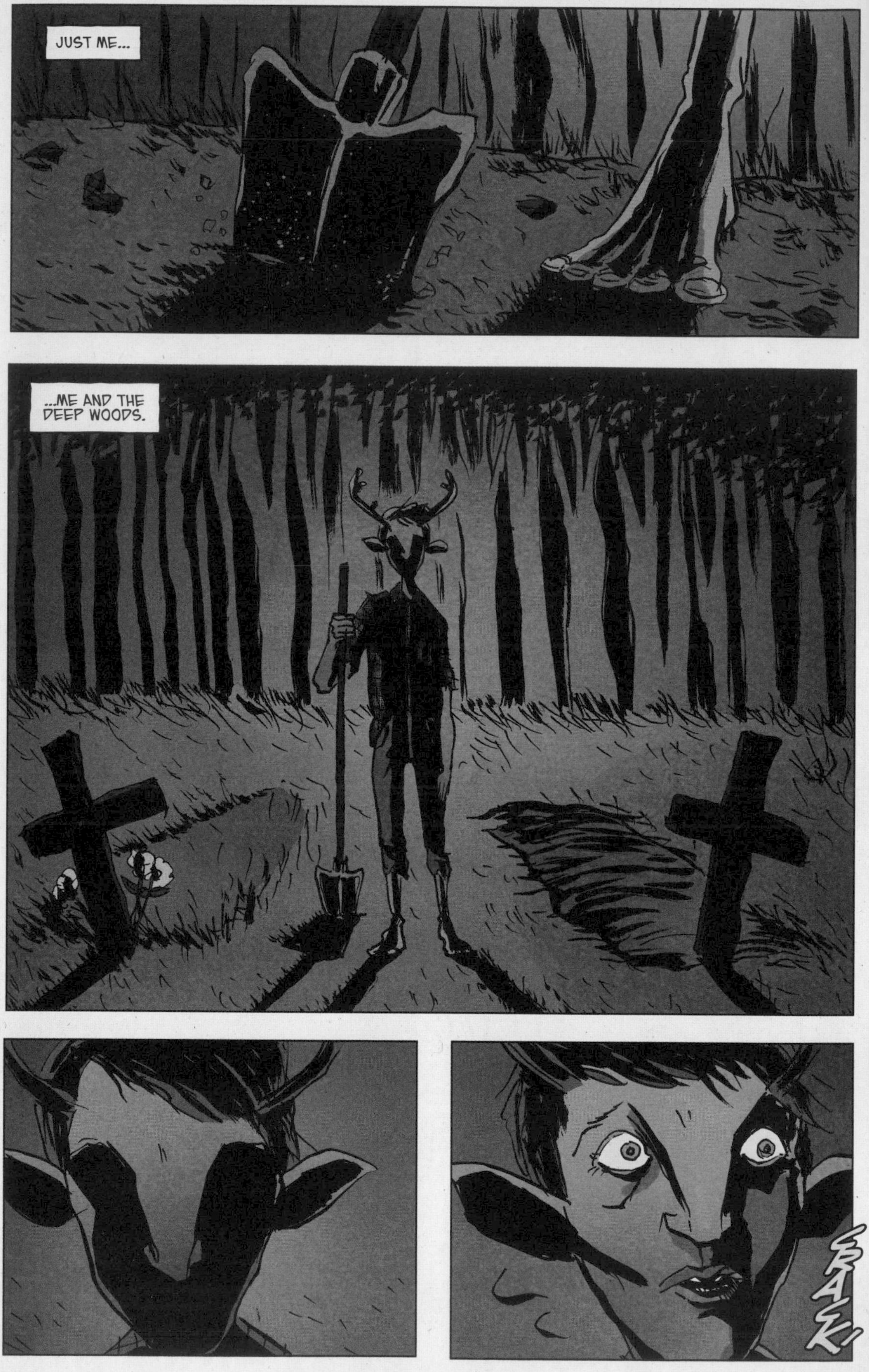
JUST ME...
...ME AND THE DEEP WOODS.
CRACK!

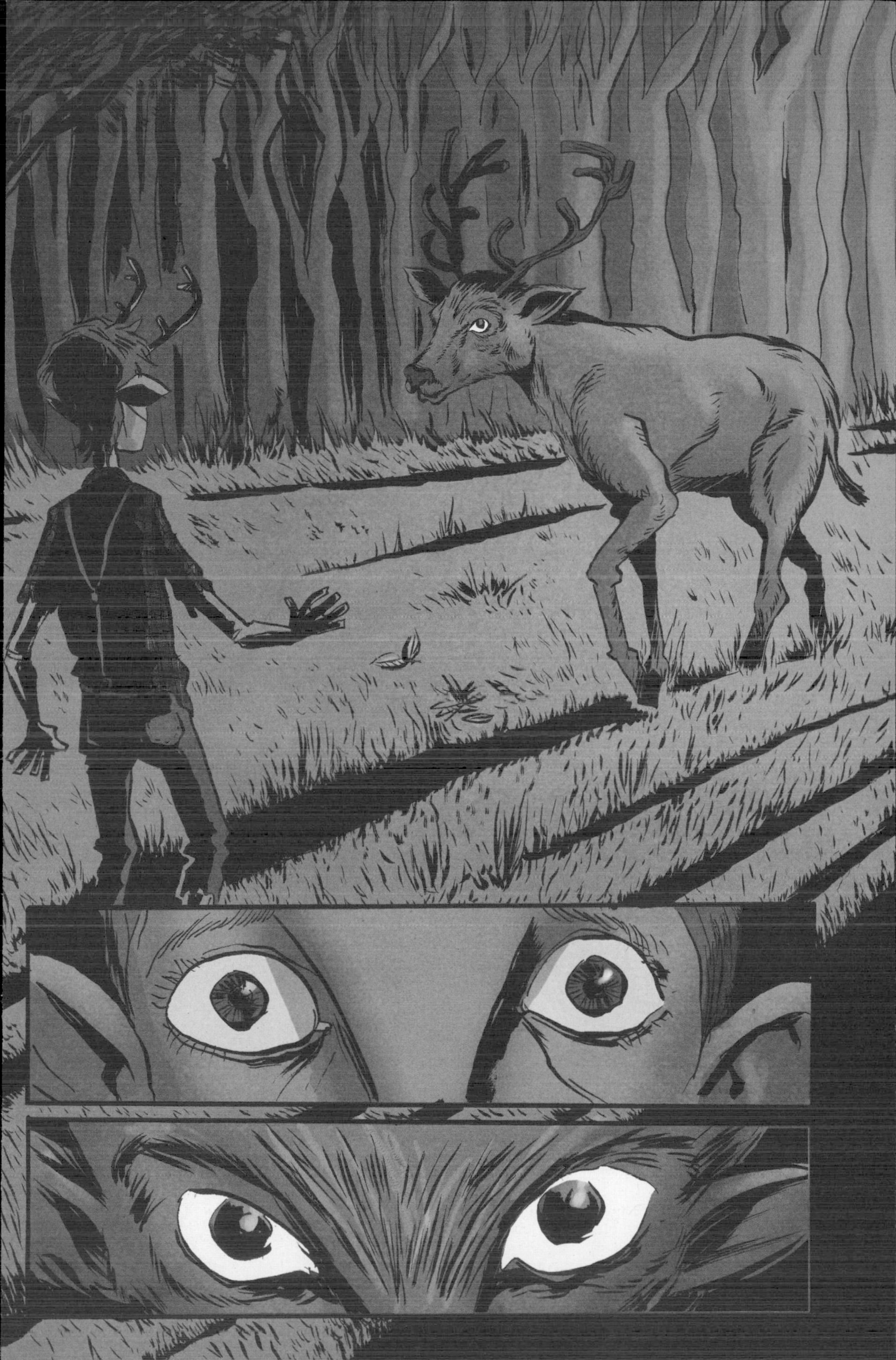

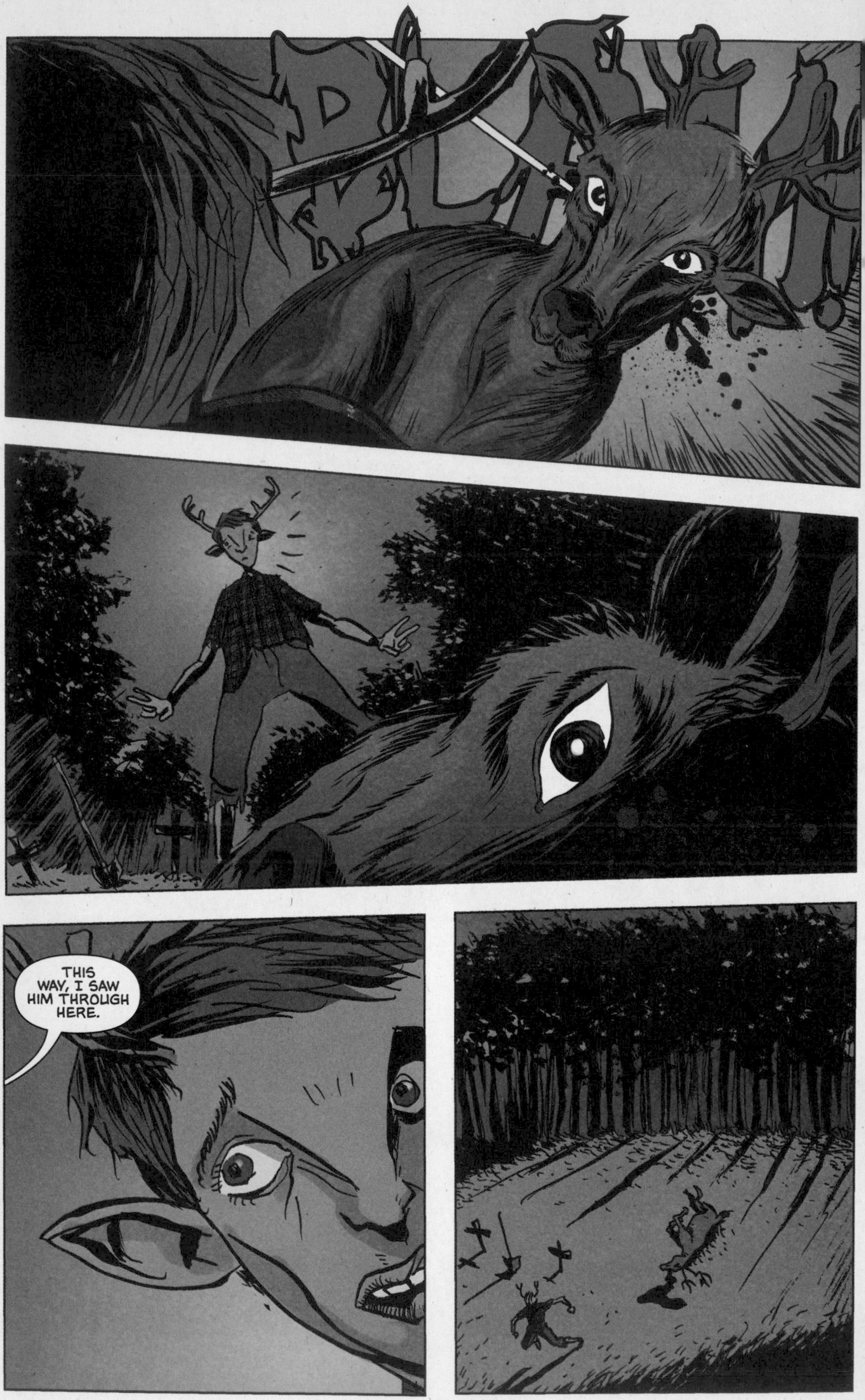
THIS WAY, I SAW HIM THROUGH HERE.

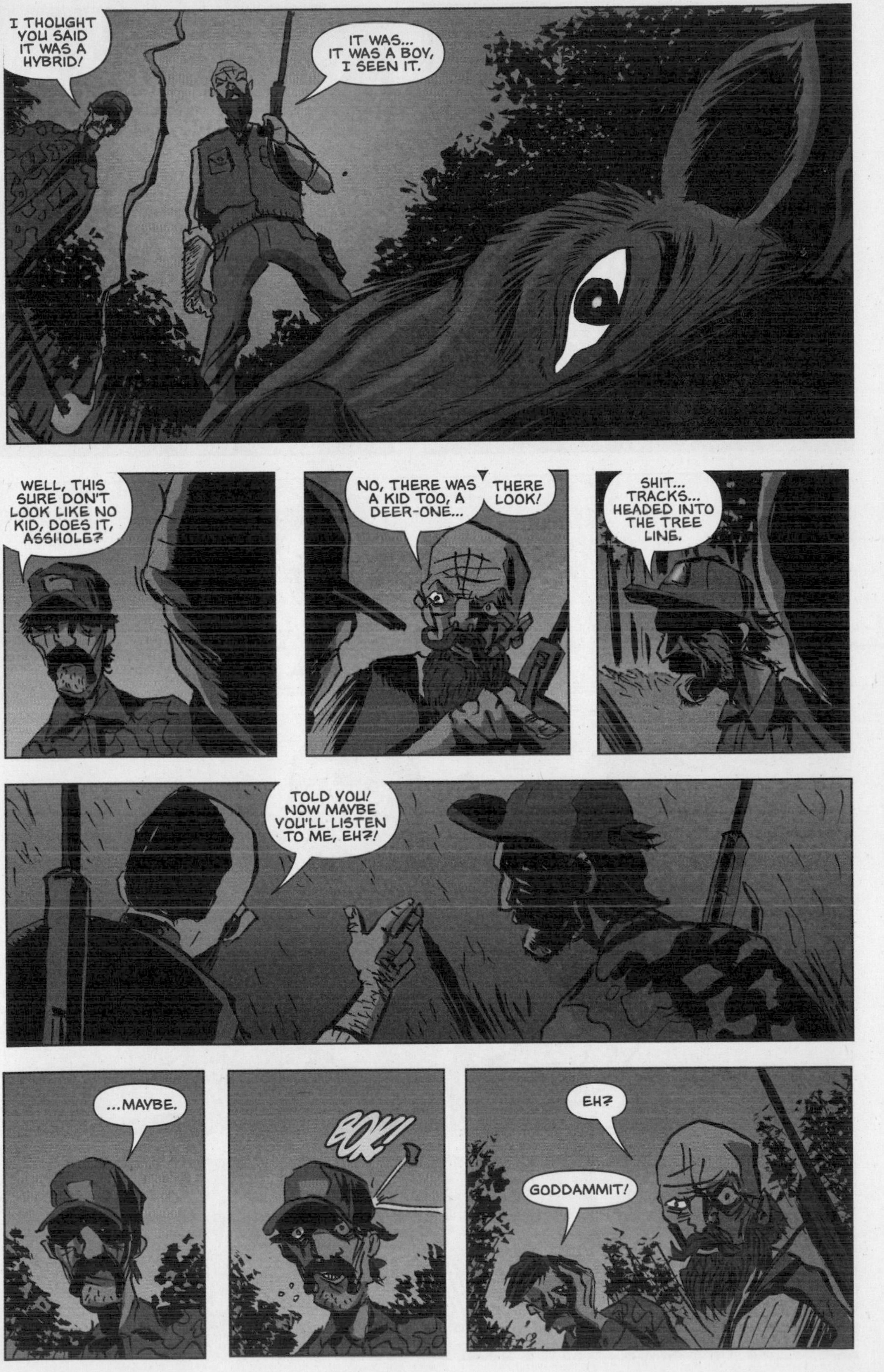
I THOUGHT YOU SAID IT WAS A HYBRID!
IT WAS... IT WAS A BOY, I SEEN IT.
WELL, THIS SURE DON'T LOOK LIKE NO KID, DOES IT, ASSHOLE?
NO, THERE WAS A KID TOO, A DEER-ONE...
THERE LOOK!
SHIT... TRACKS... HEADED INTO THE TREE LINE.
TOLD YOU! NOW MAYBE YOU'LL LISTEN TO ME, EH?!
...MAYBE.
EH?
GODDAMMIT!

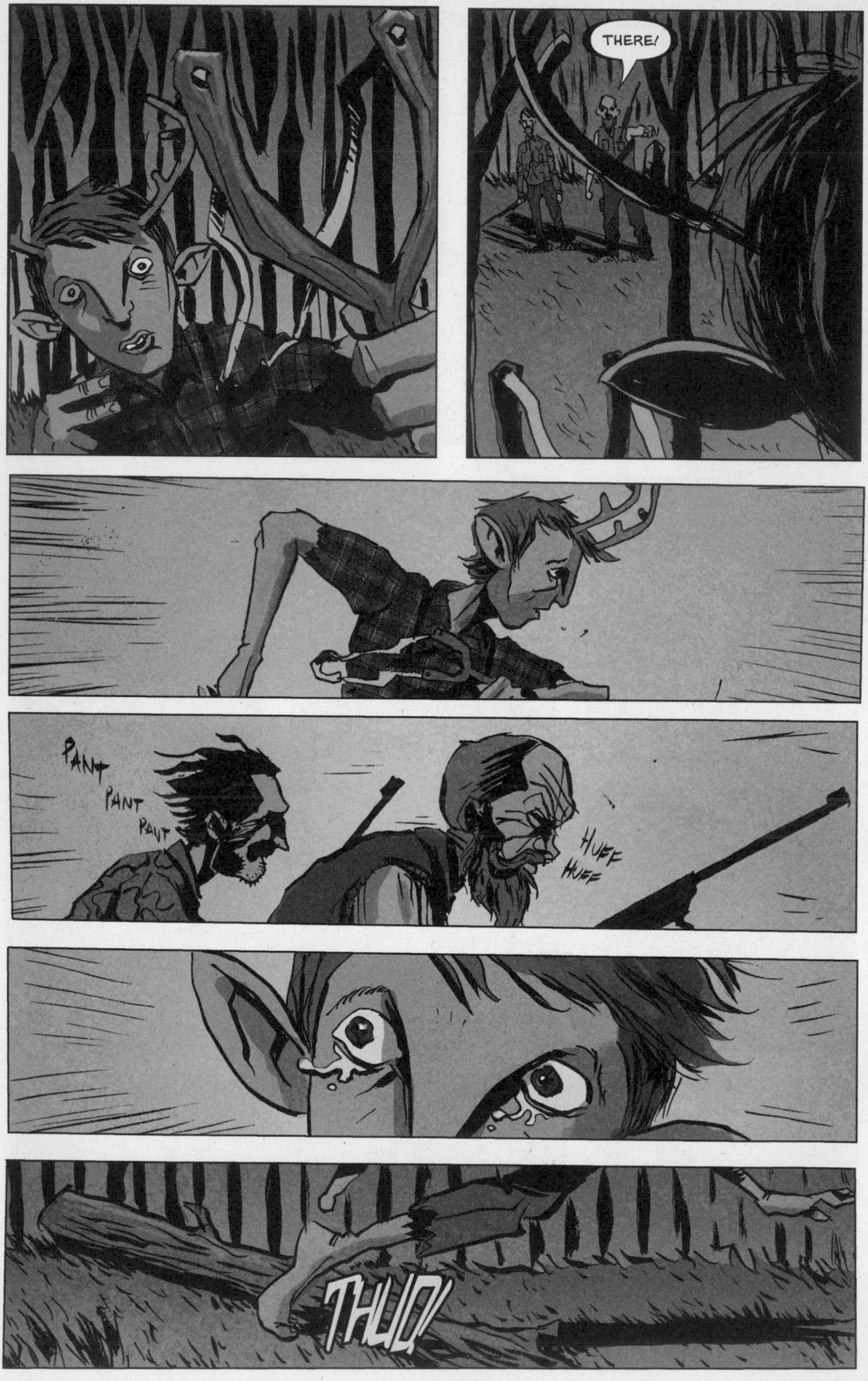
THERE!
PANT
PANT
PANT
HUFF
HUFF
THUD!

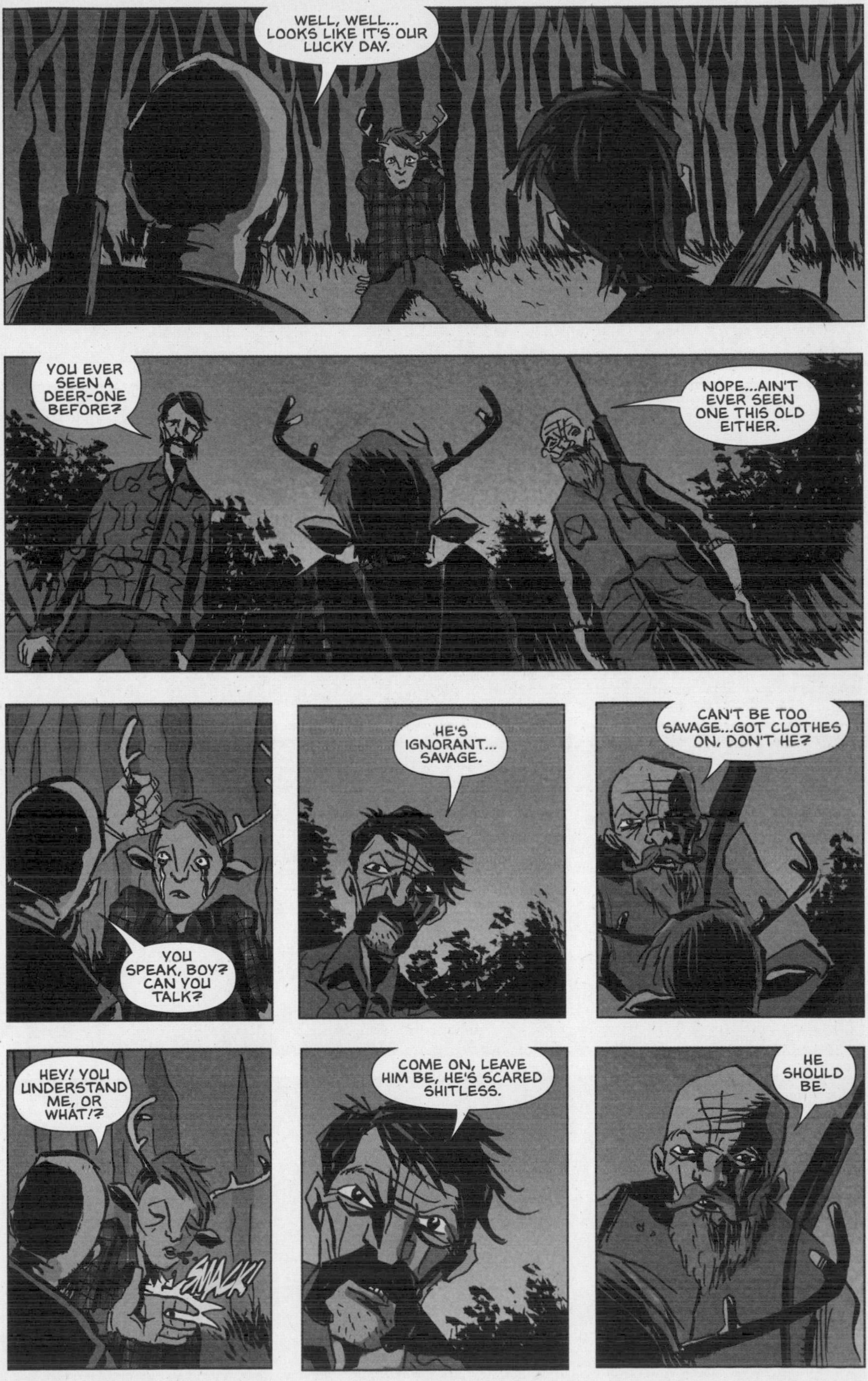
WELL, WELL... LOOKS LIKE IT'S OUR LUCKY DAY.
YOU EVER SEEN A DEER-ONE BEFORE?
NOPE...AIN'T EVER SEEN ONE THIS OLD EITHER.
YOU SPEAK, BOY? CAN YOU TALK?
HE'S IGNORANT... SAVAGE.
CAN'T BE TOO SAVAGE...GOT CLOTHES ON, DON'T HE?
HEY! YOU UNDERSTAND ME, OR WHAT!?
SMACK!
COME ON, LEAVE HIM BE, HE'S SCARED SHITLESS.
HE SHOULD BE.

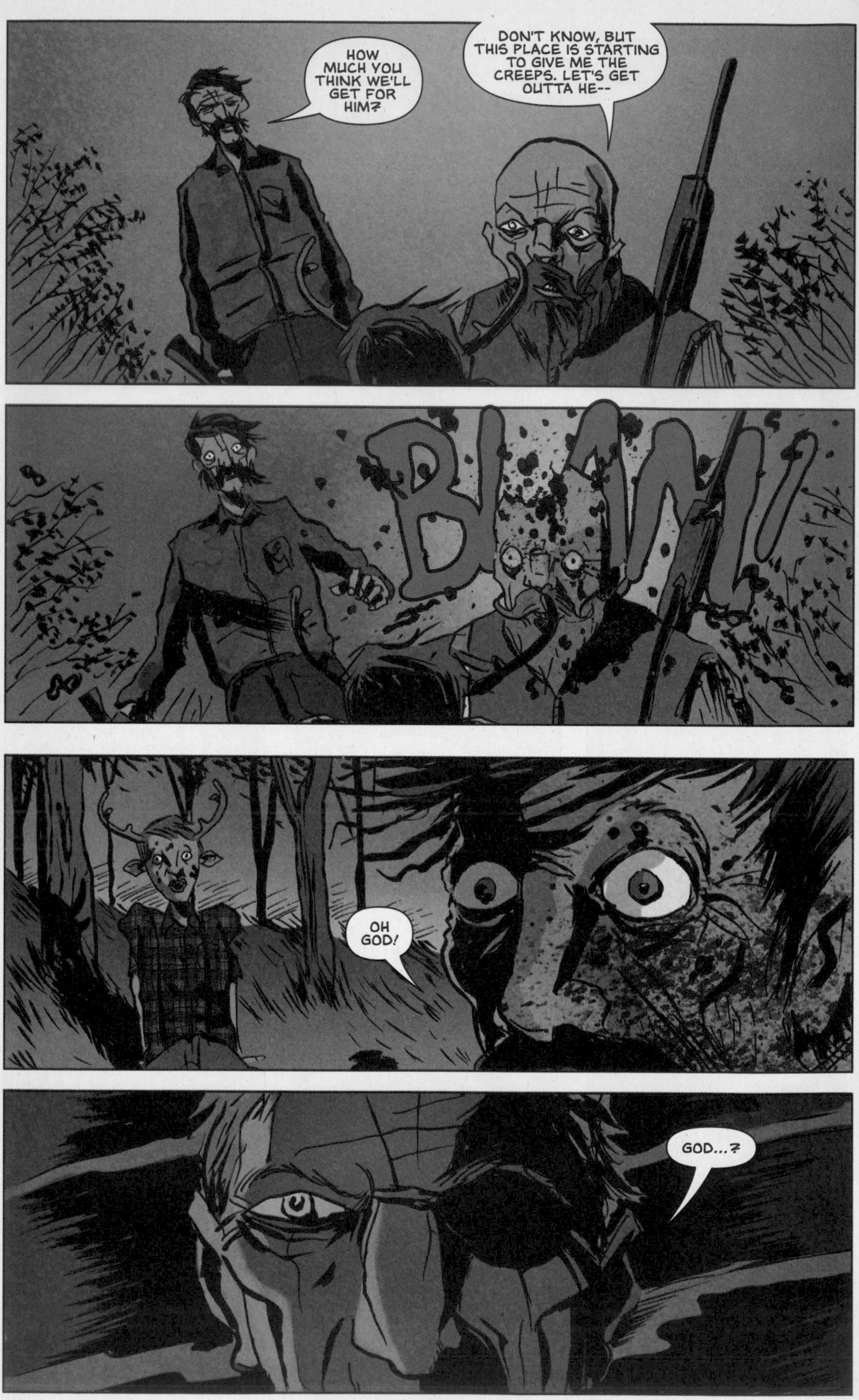
HOW MUCH YOU THINK WE'LL GET FOR HIM?
DON'T KNOW, BUT THIS PLACE IS STARTING TO GIVE ME THE CREEPS. LET'S GET OUTTA HE--
BLAM!
OH GOD!
GOD...?

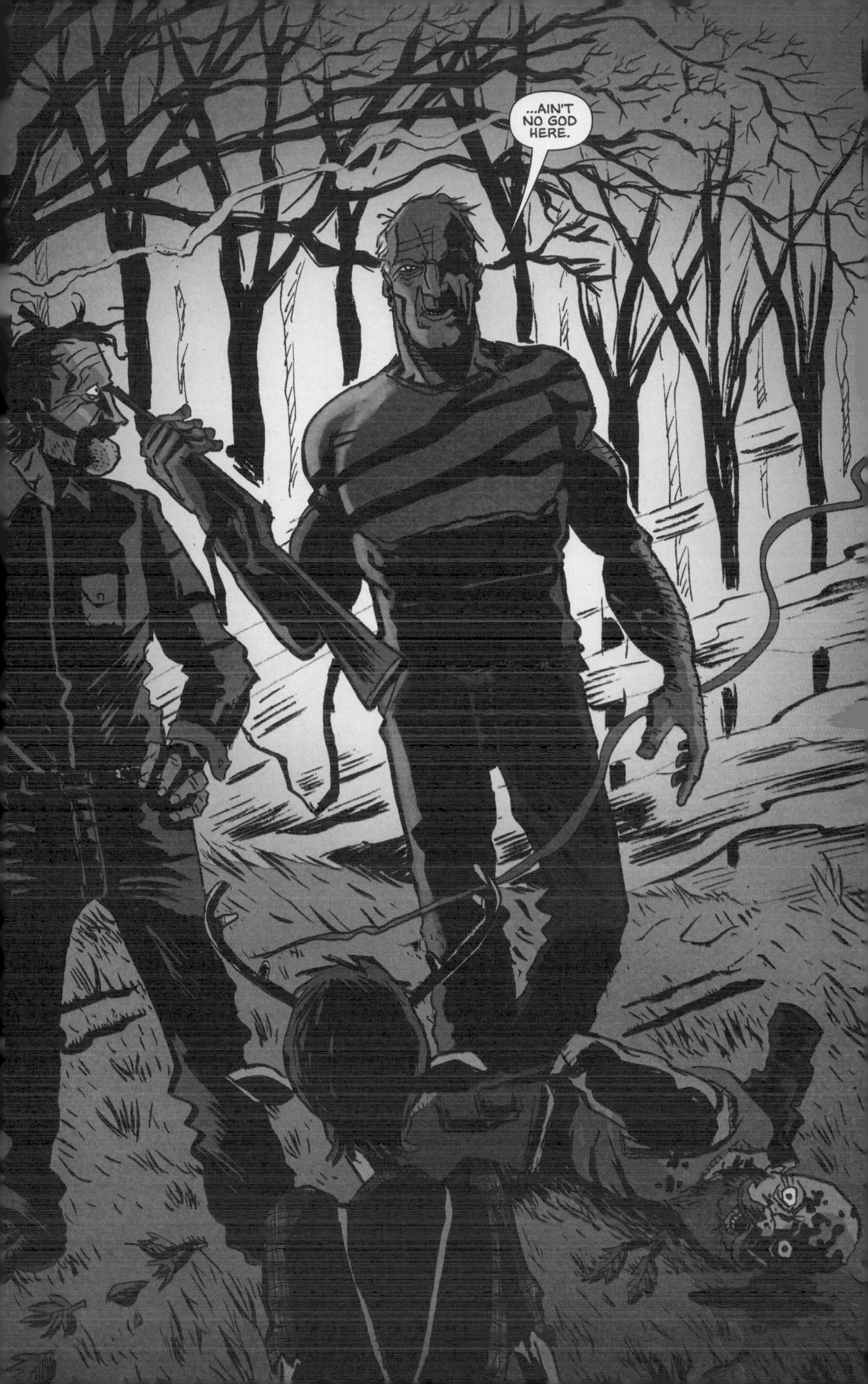
...AIN'T NO GOD HERE.

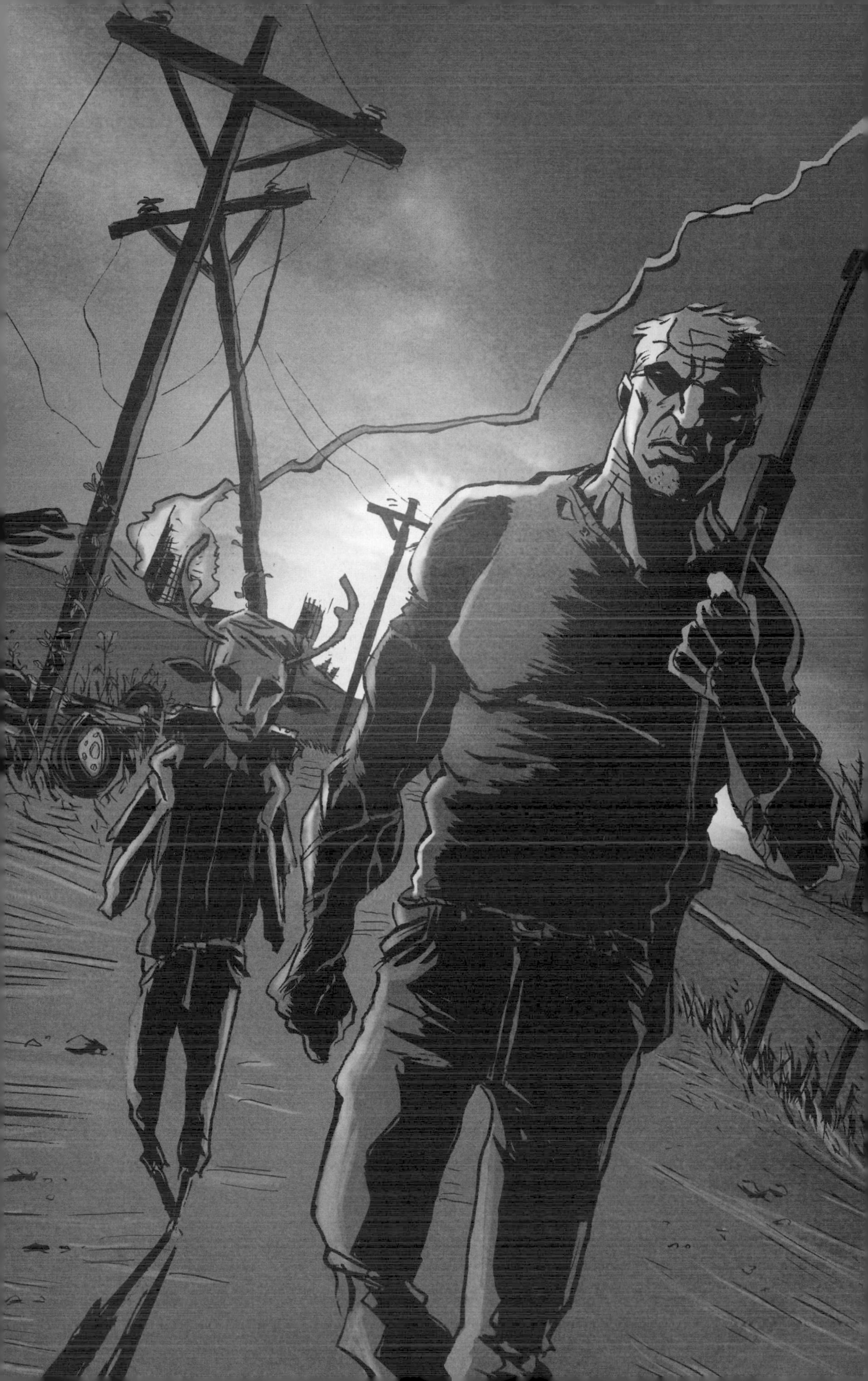

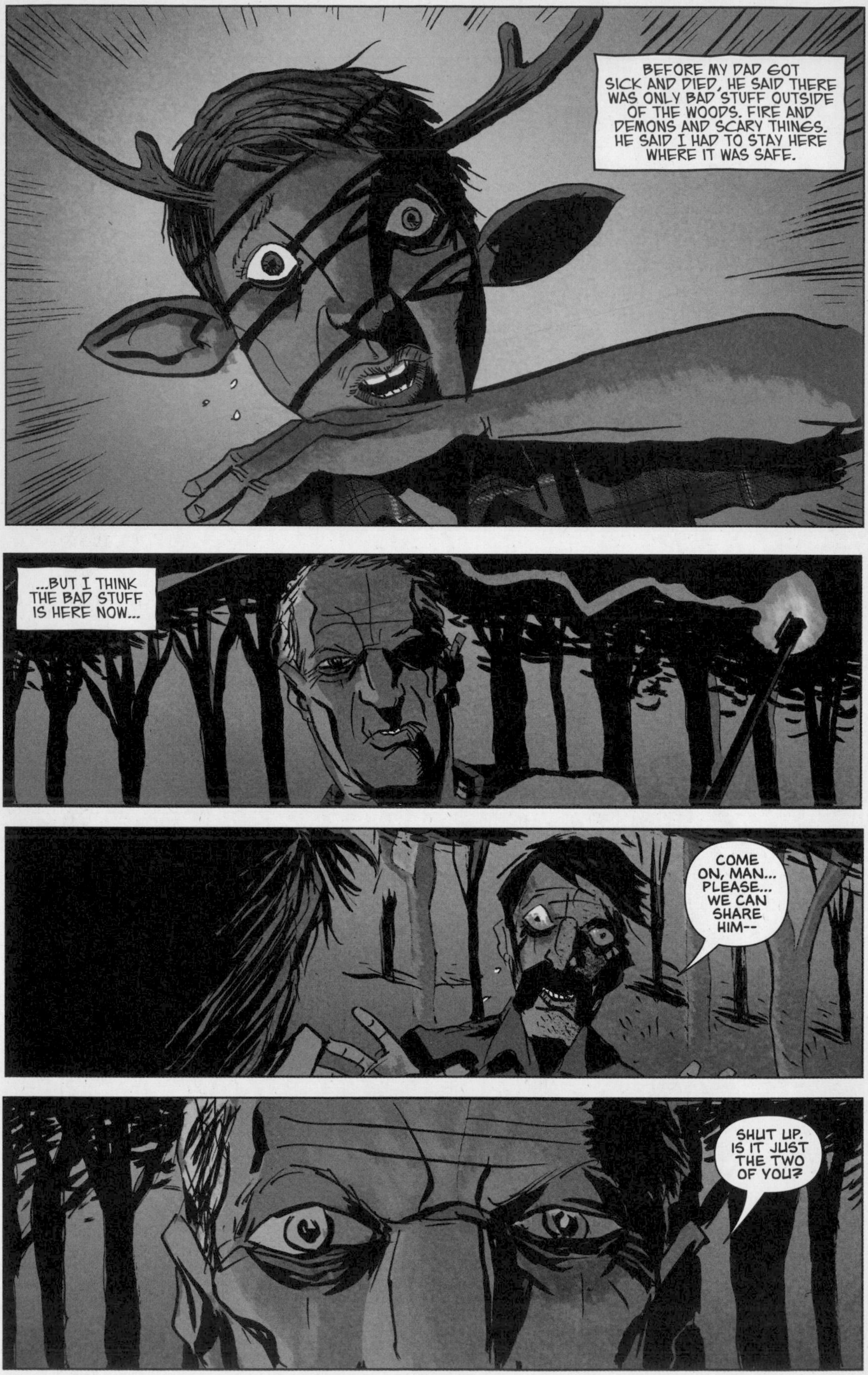
BEFORE MY DAD GOT SICK AND DIED, HE SAID THERE WAS ONLY BAD STUFF OUTSIDE OF THE WOODS. FIRE AND DEMONS AND SCARY THINGS. HE SAID I HAD TO STAY HERE WHERE IT WAS SAFE.
...BUT I THINK THE BAD STUFF IS HERE NOW...
COME ON, MAN... PLEASE... WE CAN SHARE HIM--
SHUT UP. IS IT JUST THE TWO OF YOU?

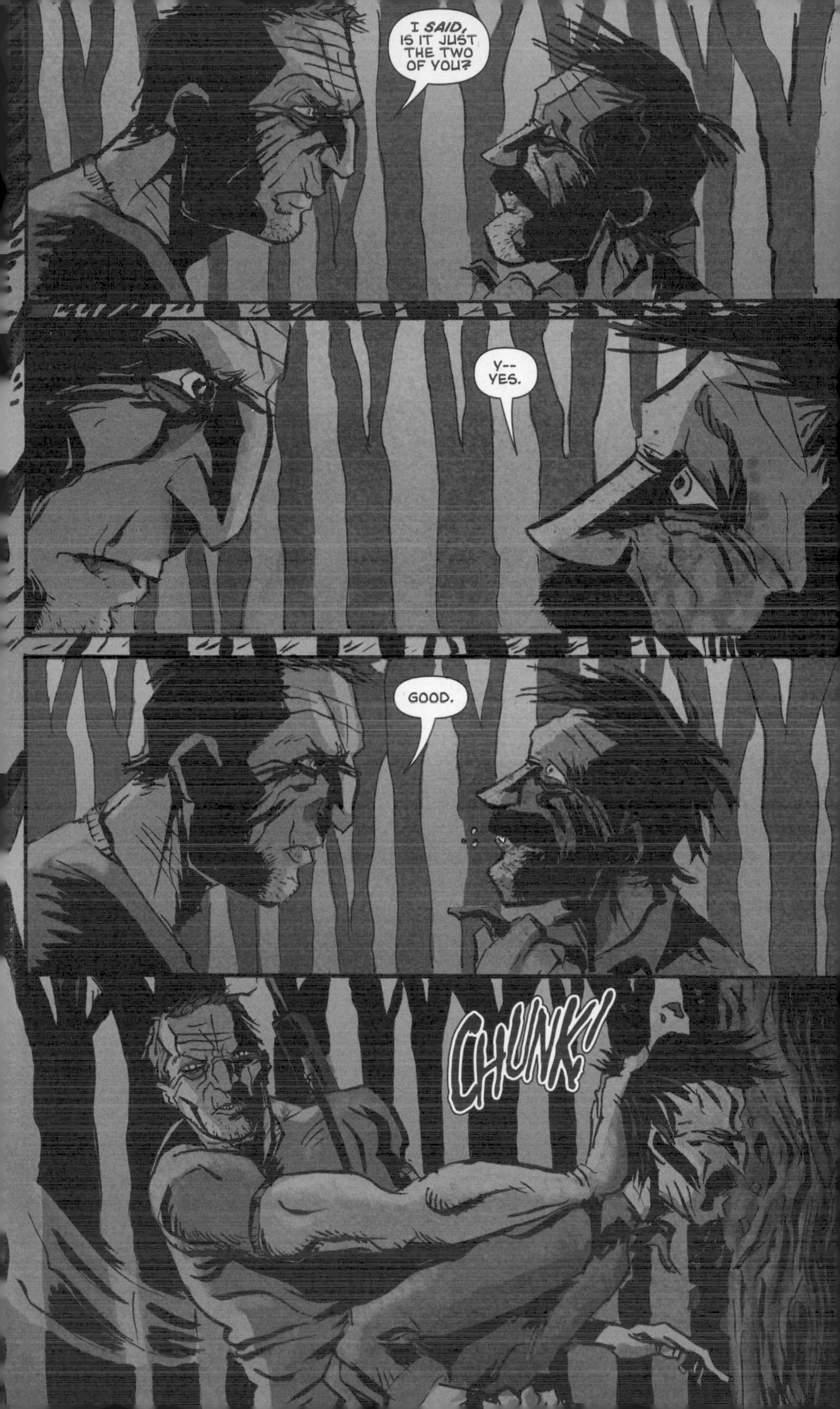
I SAID, IS IT JUST THE TWO OF YOU?
Y-- YES.
GOOD.
CHUNK!

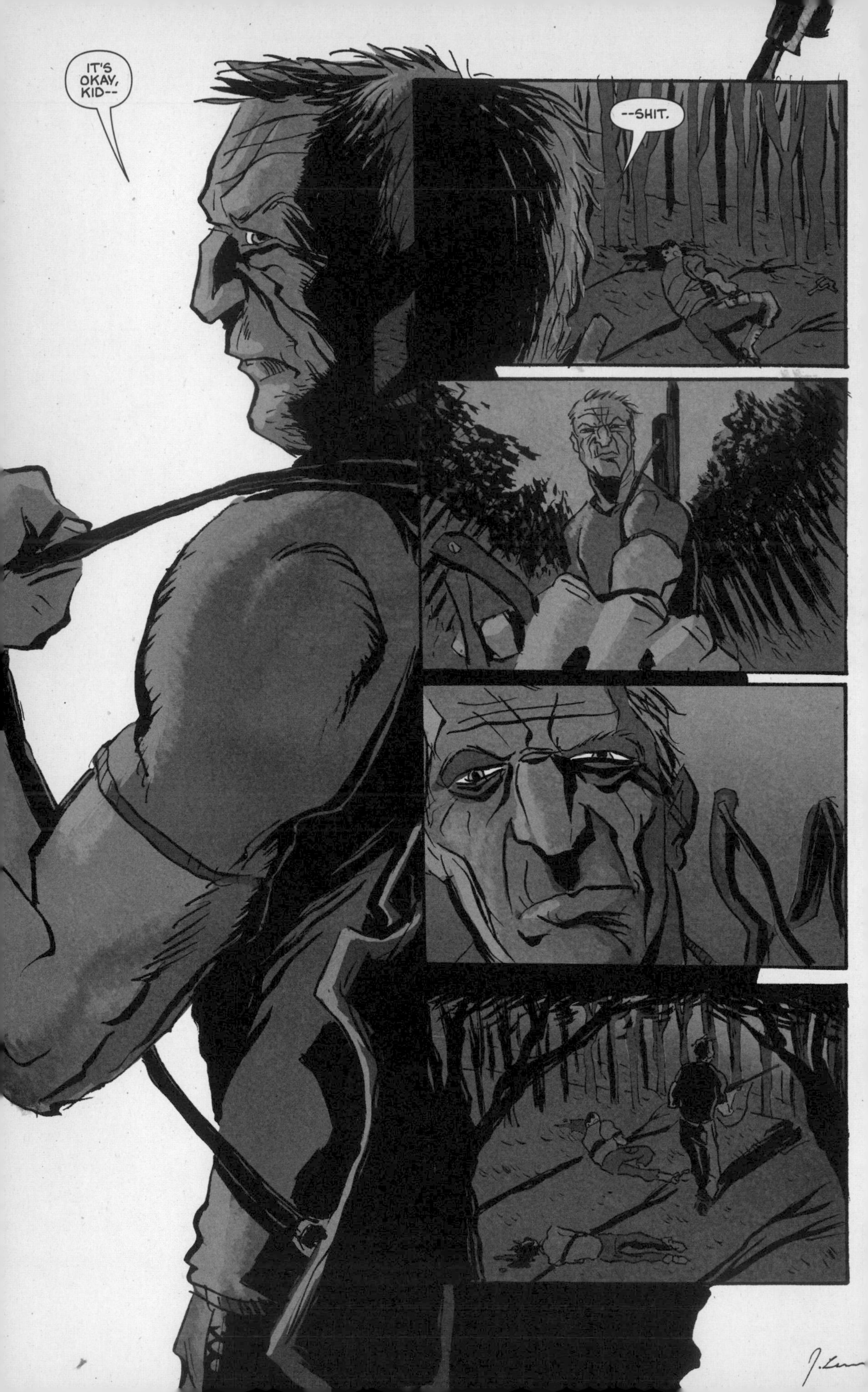
IT'S OKAY, KID--
--SHIT.

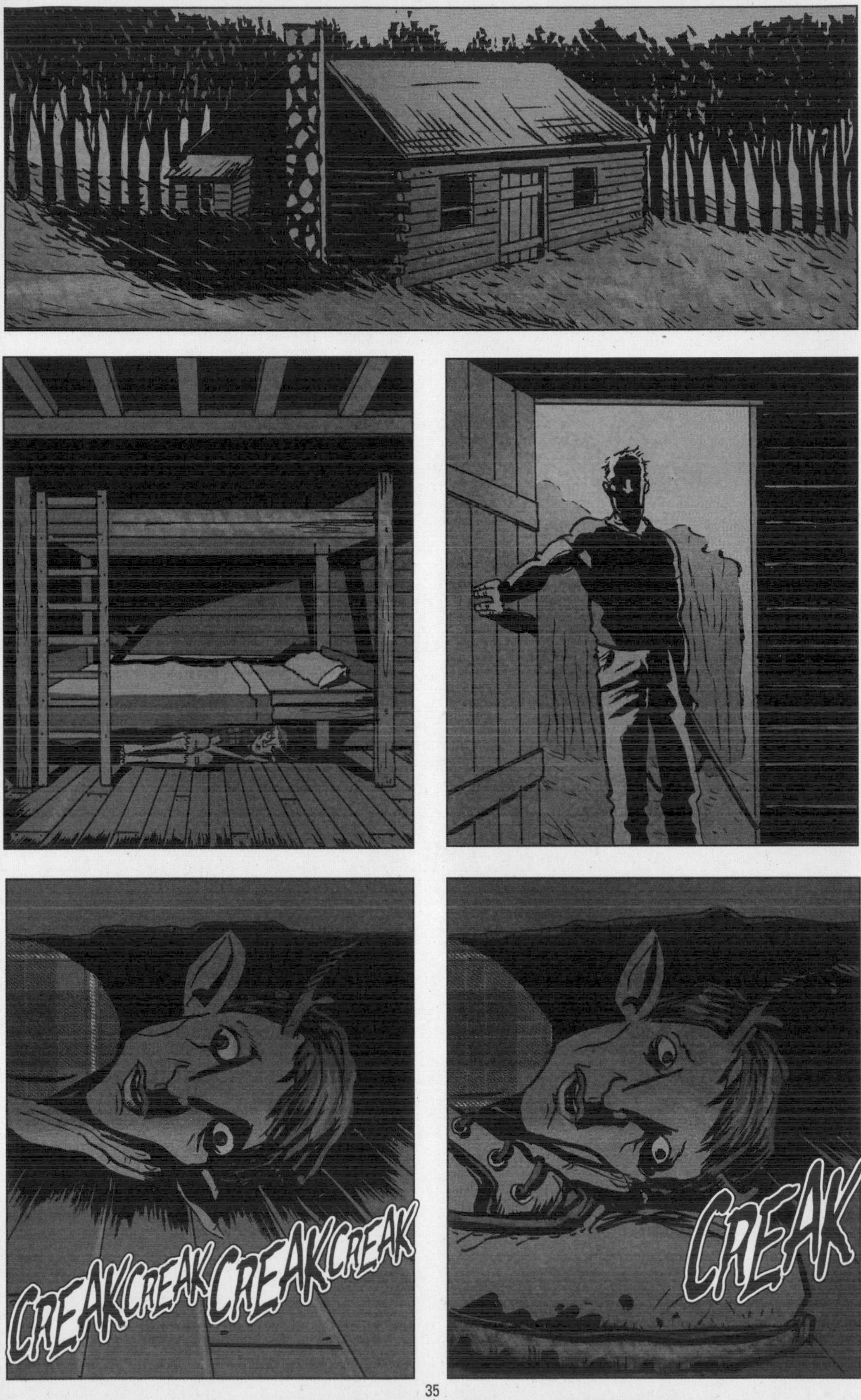
CREAK CREAK CREAK CREAK
CREAK

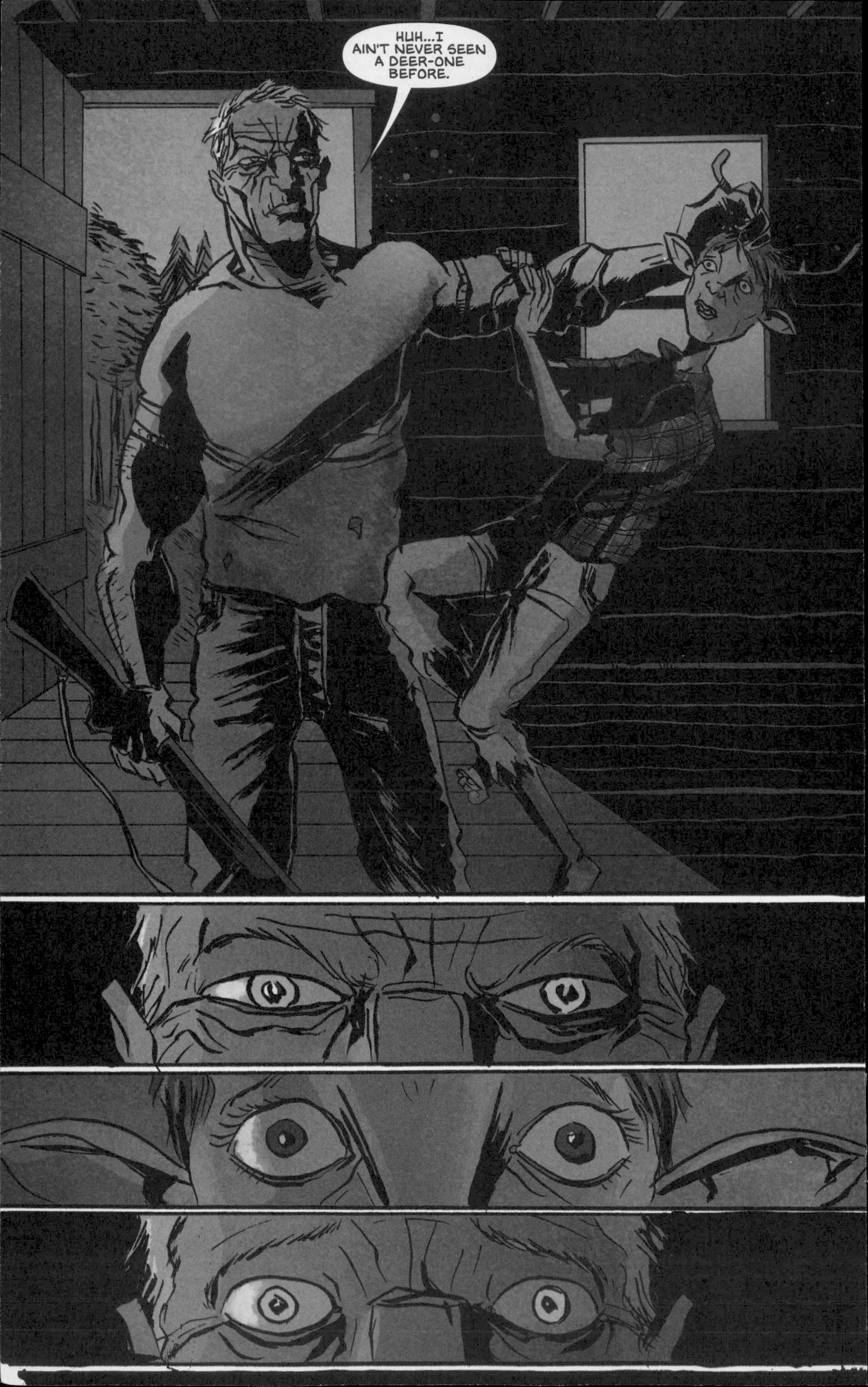
HUH...I AIN'T NEVER SEEN A DEER-ONE BEFORE.

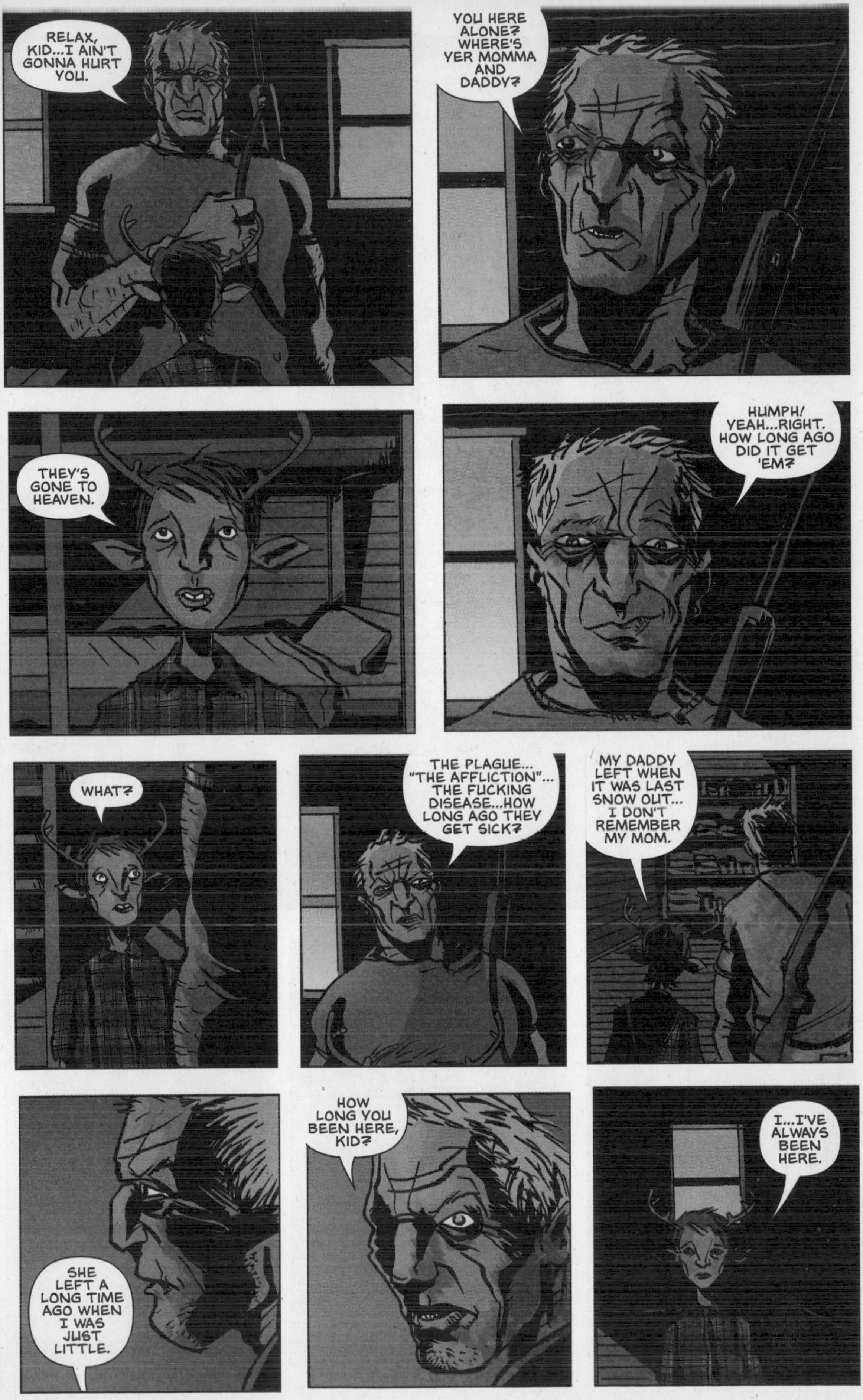
RELAX, KID...I AIN'T GONNA HURT YOU.
YOU HERE ALONE? WHERE'S YER MOMMA AND DADDY?
THEY'S GONE TO HEAVEN.
HUMPH! YEAH...RIGHT. HOW LONG AGO DID IT GET 'EM?
WHAT?
THE PLAGUE... "THE AFFLICTION"... THE FUCKING DISEASE...HOW LONG AGO THEY GET SICK?
MY DADDY LEFT WHEN IT WAS LAST SNOW OUT... I DON'T REMEMBER MY MOM.
SHE LEFT A LONG TIME AGO WHEN I WAS JUST LITTLE.
HOW LONG YOU BEEN HERE, KID?
I...I'VE ALWAYS BEEN HERE.

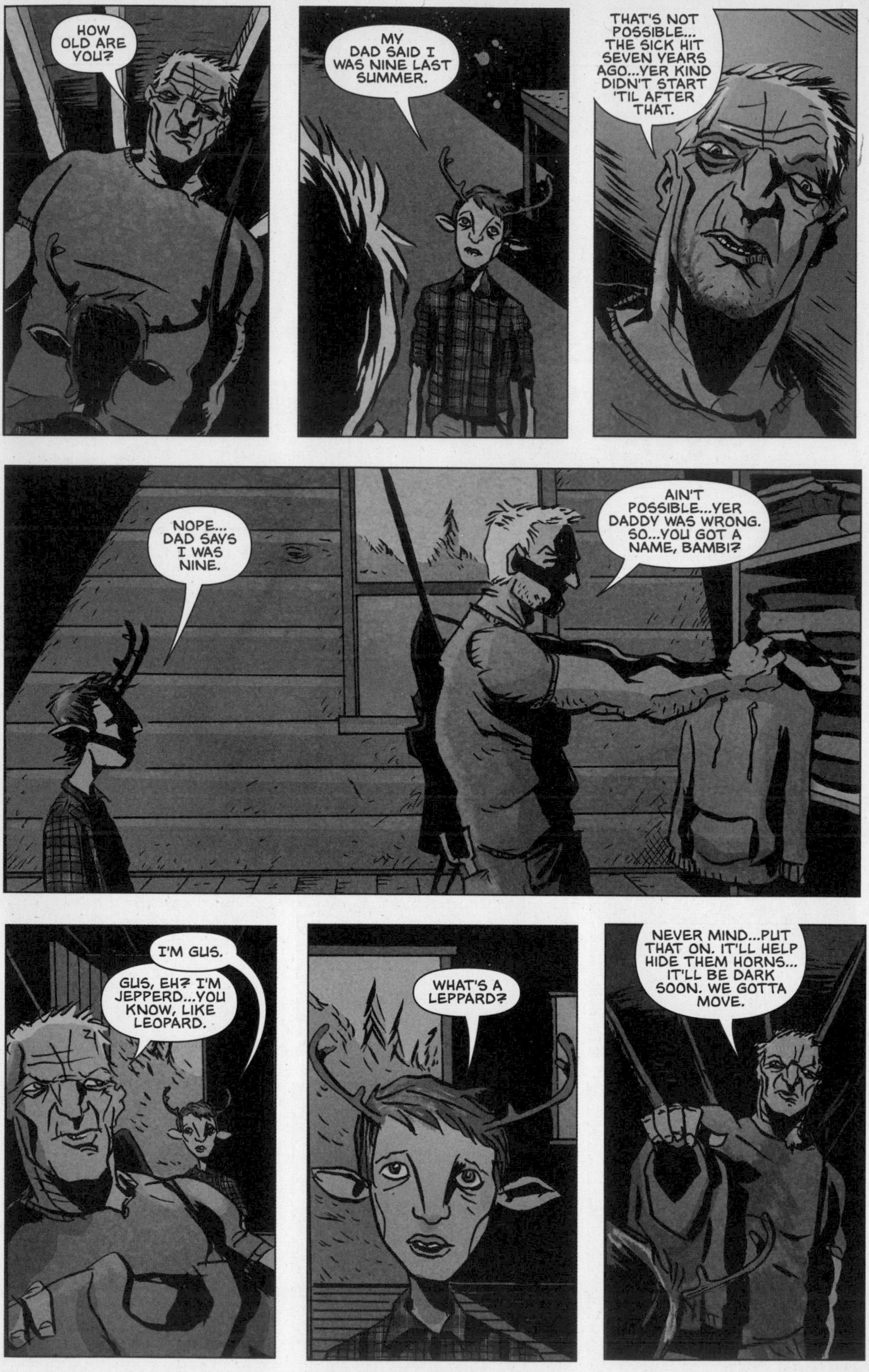
HOW OLD ARE YOU?
MY DAD SAID I WAS NINE LAST SUMMER.
THAT'S NOT POSSIBLE... THE SICK HIT SEVEN YEARS AGO...YER KIND DIDN'T START 'TIL AFTER THAT.
NOPE... DAD SAYS I WAS NINE.
AIN'T POSSIBLE...YER DADDY WAS WRONG. SO...YOU GOT A NAME, BAMBI?
I'M GUS.
GUS, EH? I'M JEPPERD...YOU KNOW, LIKE LEOPARD.
WHAT'S A LEPPARD?
NEVER MIND...PUT THAT ON. IT'LL HELP HIDE THEM HORNS... IT'LL BE DARK SOON. WE GOTTA MOVE.

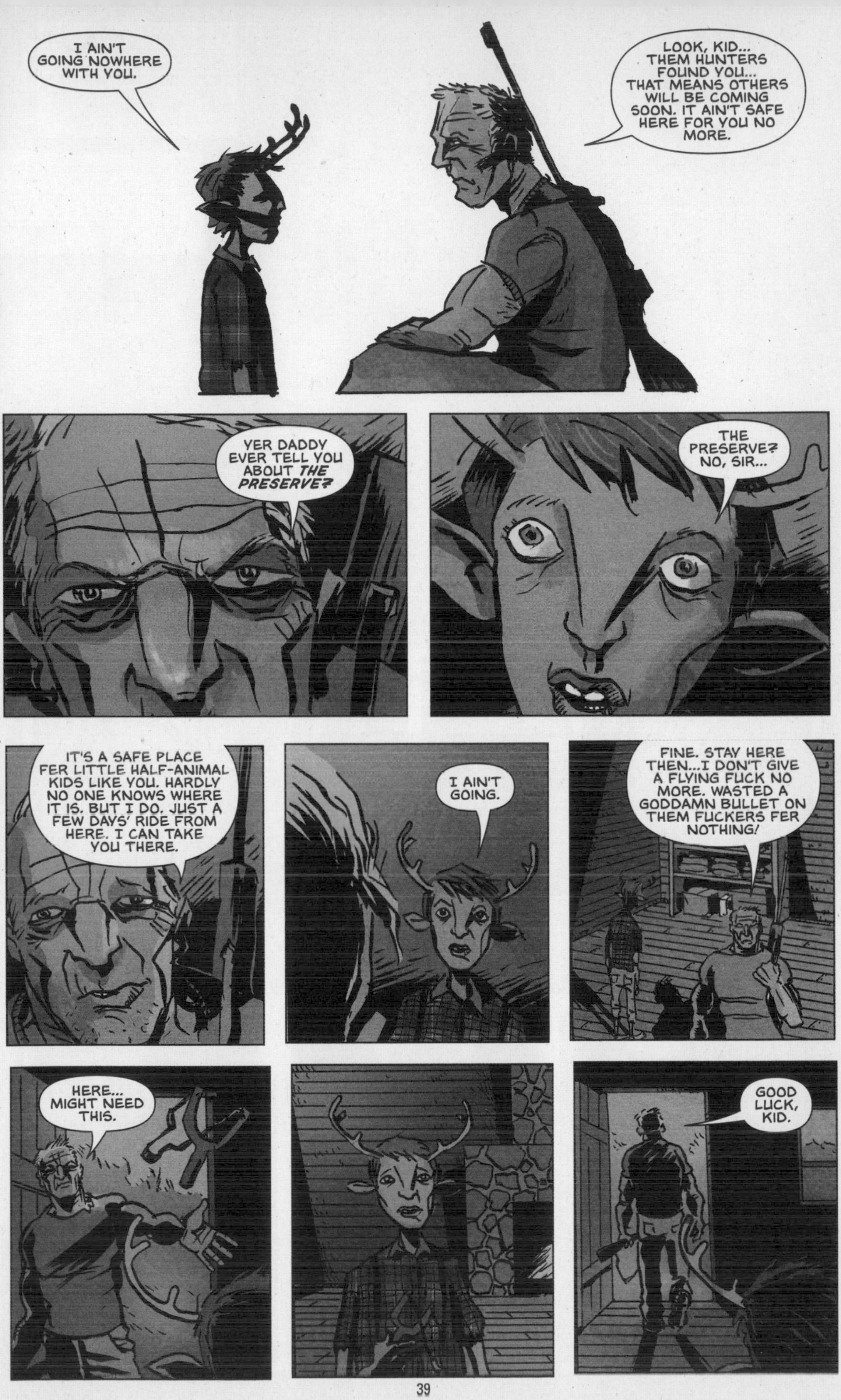
I AIN'T GOING NOWHERE WITH YOU.
LOOK, KID... THEM HUNTERS FOUND YOU... THAT MEANS OTHERS WILL BE COMING SOON. IT AIN'T SAFE HERE FOR YOU NO MORE.
YER DADDY EVER TELL YOU ABOUT *THE PRESERVE?*
THE PRESERVE? NO, SIR...
IT'S A SAFE PLACE FER LITTLE HALF-ANIMAL KIDS LIKE YOU. HARDLY NO ONE KNOWS WHERE IT IS. BUT I DO. JUST A FEW DAYS' RIDE FROM HERE. I CAN TAKE YOU THERE.
I AIN'T GOING.
FINE. STAY HERE THEN...I DON'T GIVE A FLYING FUCK NO MORE. WASTED A GODDAMN BULLET ON THEM FUCKERS FER NOTHING!
HERE... MIGHT NEED THIS.
GOOD LUCK, KID.

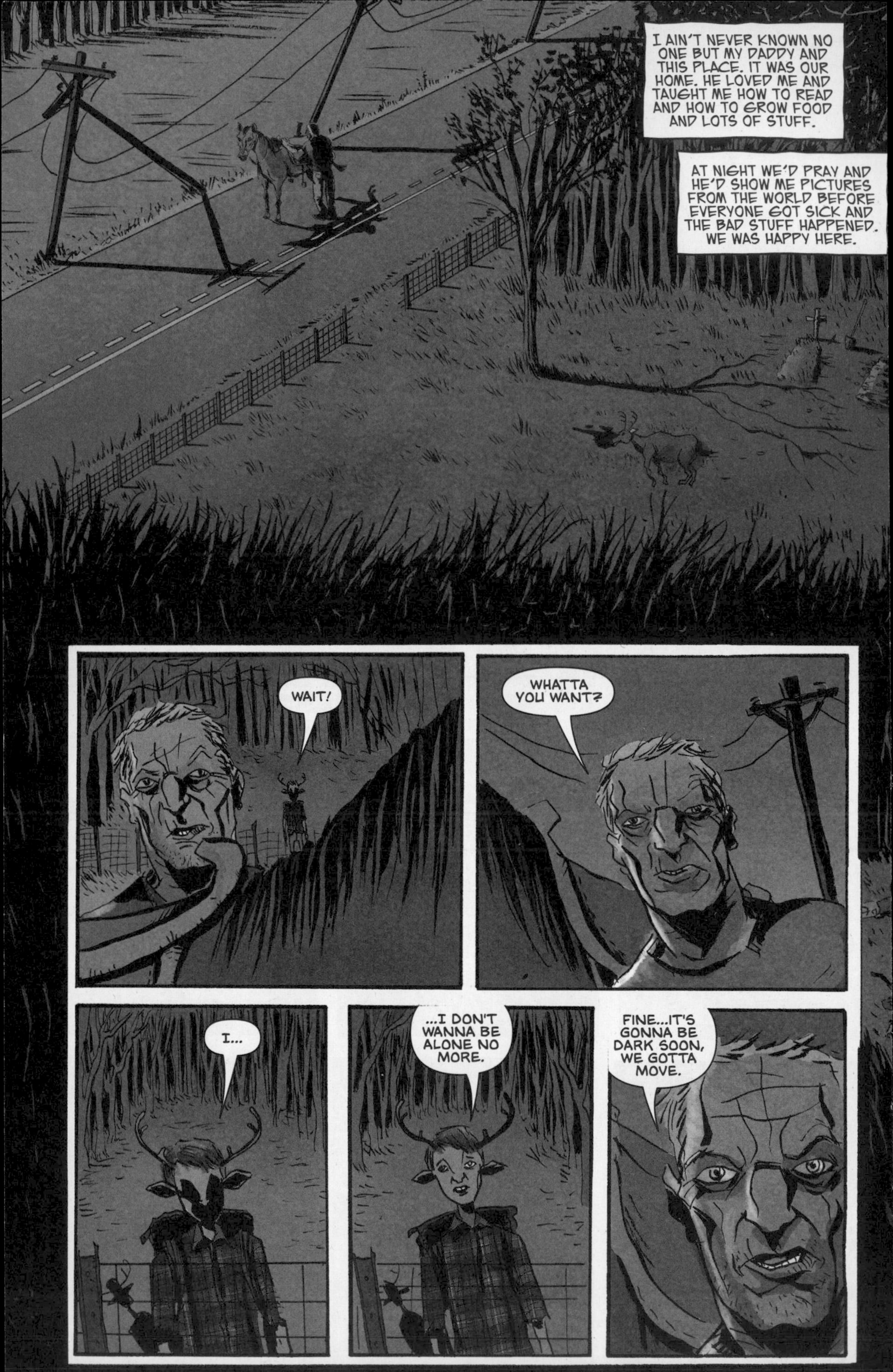
I AIN'T NEVER KNOWN NO ONE BUT MY DADDY AND THIS PLACE. IT WAS OUR HOME. HE LOVED ME AND TAUGHT ME HOW TO READ AND HOW TO GROW FOOD AND LOTS OF STUFF.
AT NIGHT WE'D PRAY AND HE'D SHOW ME PICTURES FROM THE WORLD BEFORE EVERYONE GOT SICK AND THE BAD STUFF HAPPENED. WE WAS HAPPY HERE.
WAIT!
WHATTA YOU WANT?
I...
...I DON'T WANNA BE ALONE NO MORE.
FINE...IT'S GONNA BE DARK SOON, WE GOTTA MOVE.

MY DAD SAID I AIN'T NEVER SUPPOSED TO LEAVE THE WOODS.

SAID IF I DID, I'D CATCH FIRE AND BURN UP FOREVER.

SAID I'D BE SAFE IN THE TREES, THAT OUTSIDE WAS ONLY SINNERS AND PAIN AND HELL.

MY DAD SAID A LOT OF THINGS.

BUT MY DADDY AIN'T HERE NO MORE...

NOW IT'S JUST ME...

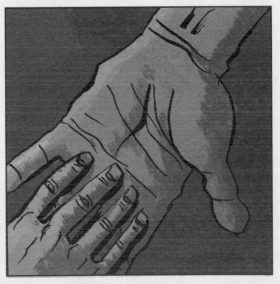

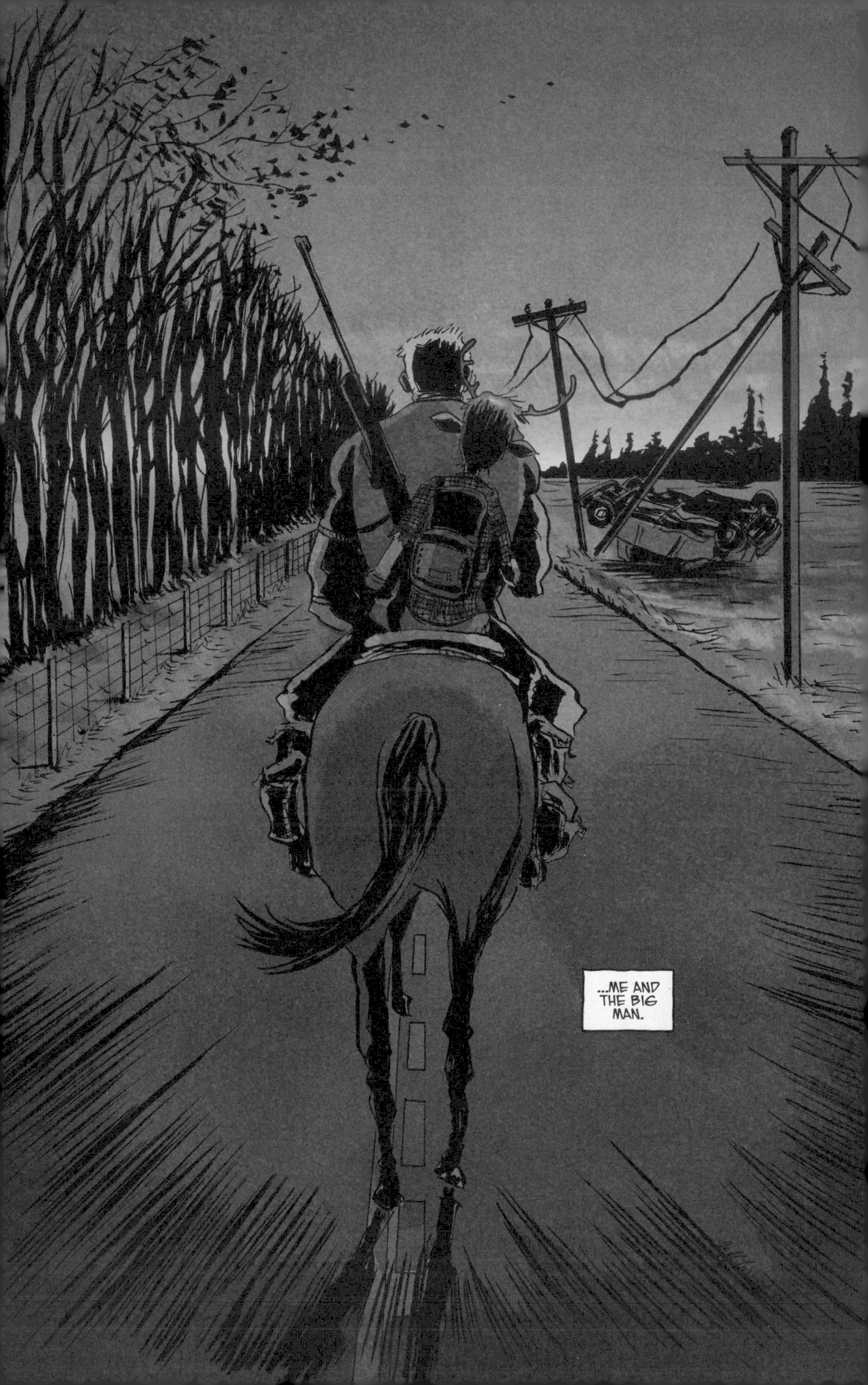
...ME AND THE BIG MAN.

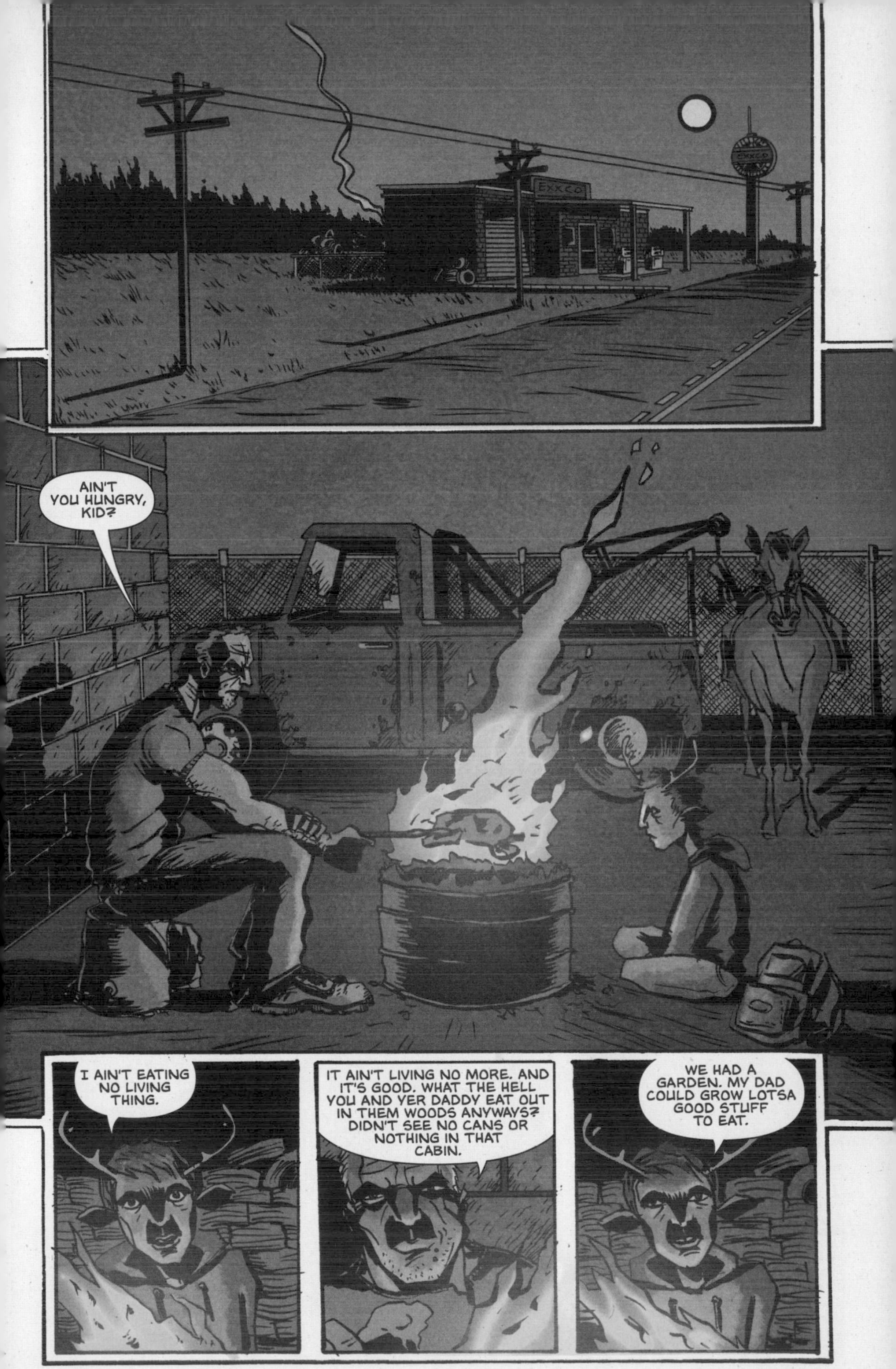

EXXCO
EXXCO
AIN'T YOU HUNGRY, KID?
I AIN'T EATING NO LIVING THING.
IT AIN'T LIVING NO MORE. AND IT'S GOOD. WHAT THE HELL YOU AND YER DADDY EAT OUT IN THEM WOODS ANYWAYS? DIDN'T SEE NO CANS OR NOTHING IN THAT CABIN.
WE HAD A GARDEN. MY DAD COULD GROW LOTSA GOOD STUFF TO EAT.

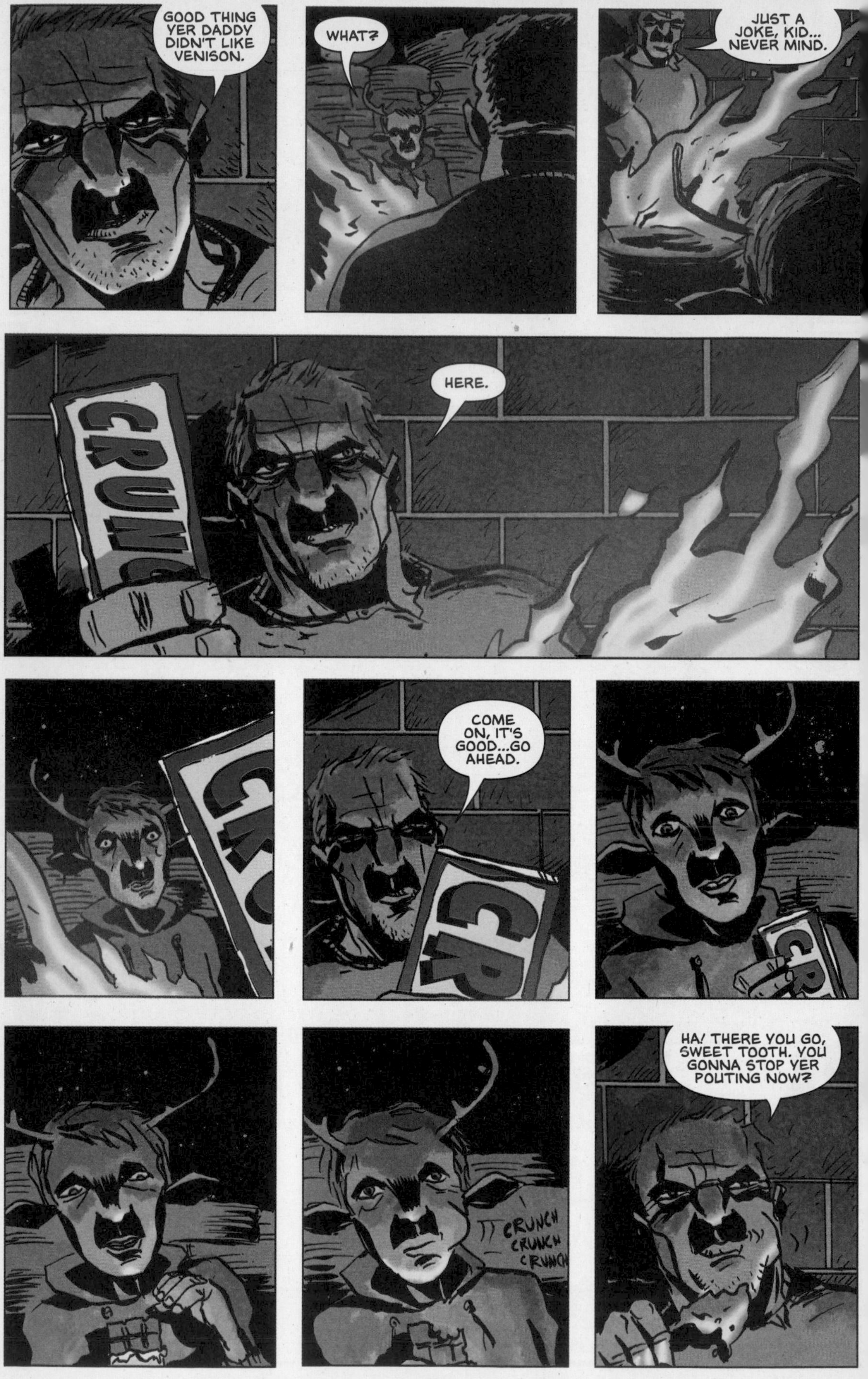
GOOD THING YER DADDY DIDN'T LIKE VENISON.
WHAT?
JUST A JOKE, KID... NEVER MIND.
HERE.
COME ON, IT'S GOOD...GO AHEAD.
CRUNCH CRUNCH CRUNCH
HA! THERE YOU GO, SWEET TOOTH. YOU GONNA STOP YER POUTING NOW?

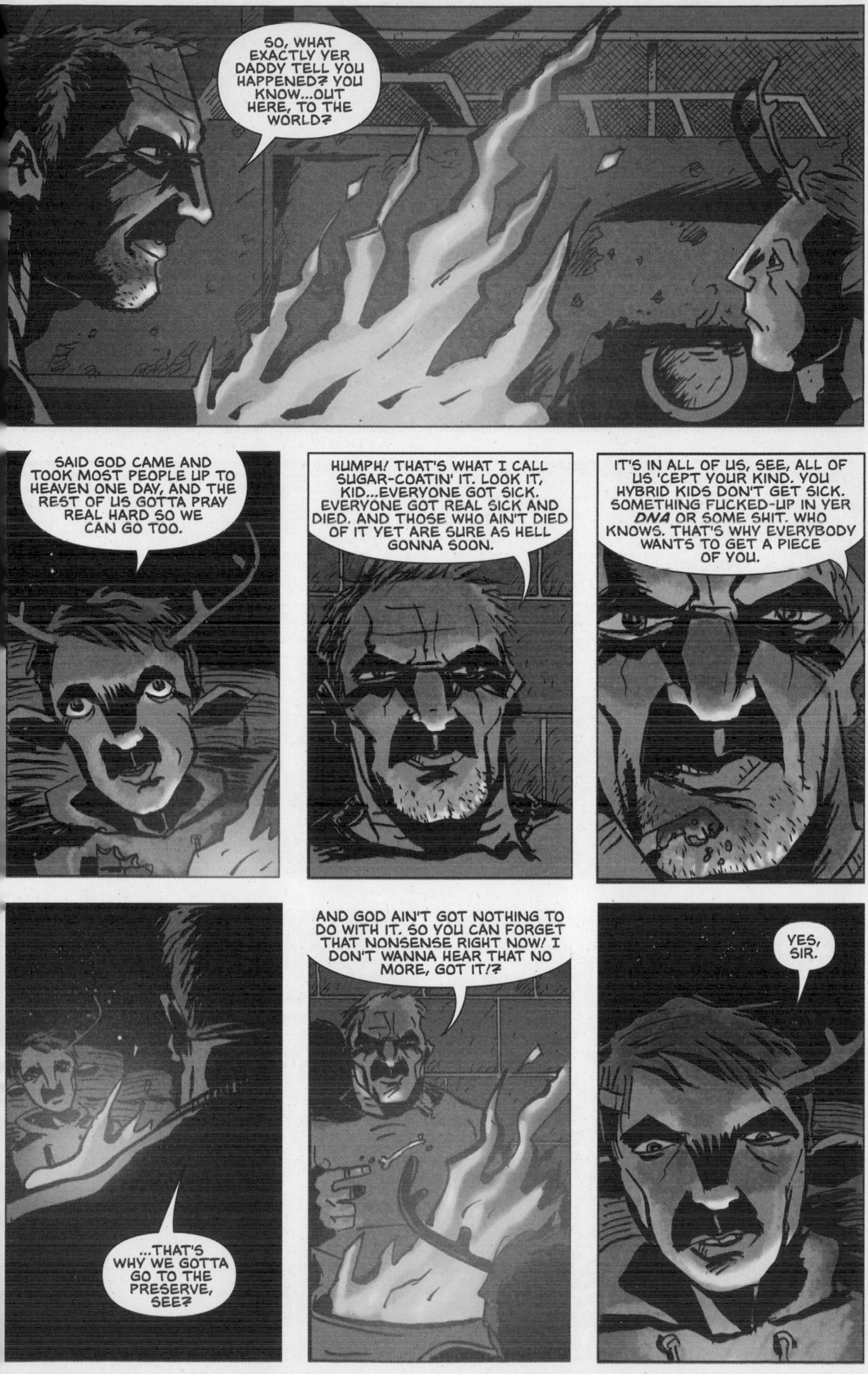
SO, WHAT EXACTLY YER DADDY TELL YOU HAPPENED? YOU KNOW...OUT HERE, TO THE WORLD?
SAID GOD CAME AND TOOK MOST PEOPLE UP TO HEAVEN ONE DAY, AND THE REST OF US GOTTA PRAY REAL HARD SO WE CAN GO TOO.
HUMPH! THAT'S WHAT I CALL SUGAR-COATIN' IT. LOOK IT, KID...EVERYONE GOT SICK. EVERYONE GOT REAL SICK AND DIED. AND THOSE WHO AIN'T DIED OF IT YET ARE SURE AS HELL GONNA SOON.
IT'S IN ALL OF US, SEE, ALL OF US 'CEPT YOUR KIND. YOU HYBRID KIDS DON'T GET SICK. SOMETHING FUCKED-UP IN YER *DNA* OR SOME SHIT. WHO KNOWS. THAT'S WHY EVERYBODY WANTS TO GET A PIECE OF YOU.
...THAT'S WHY WE GOTTA GO TO THE PRESERVE, SEE?
AND GOD AIN'T GOT NOTHING TO DO WITH IT. SO YOU CAN FORGET THAT NONSENSE RIGHT NOW! I DON'T WANNA HEAR THAT NO MORE, GOT IT!?
YES, SIR.

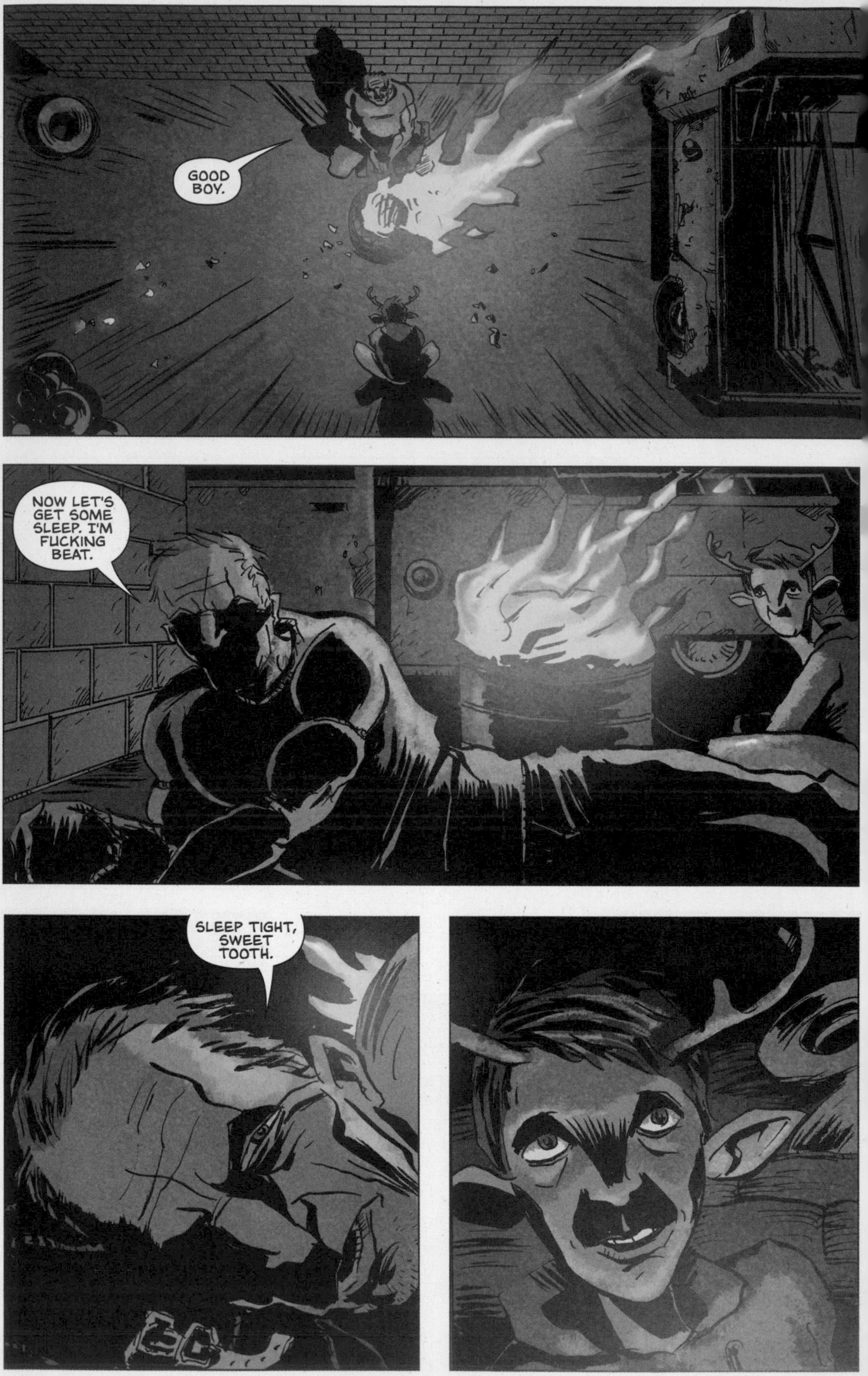
GOOD BOY.
NOW LET'S GET SOME SLEEP. I'M FUCKING BEAT.
SLEEP TIGHT, SWEET TOOTH.

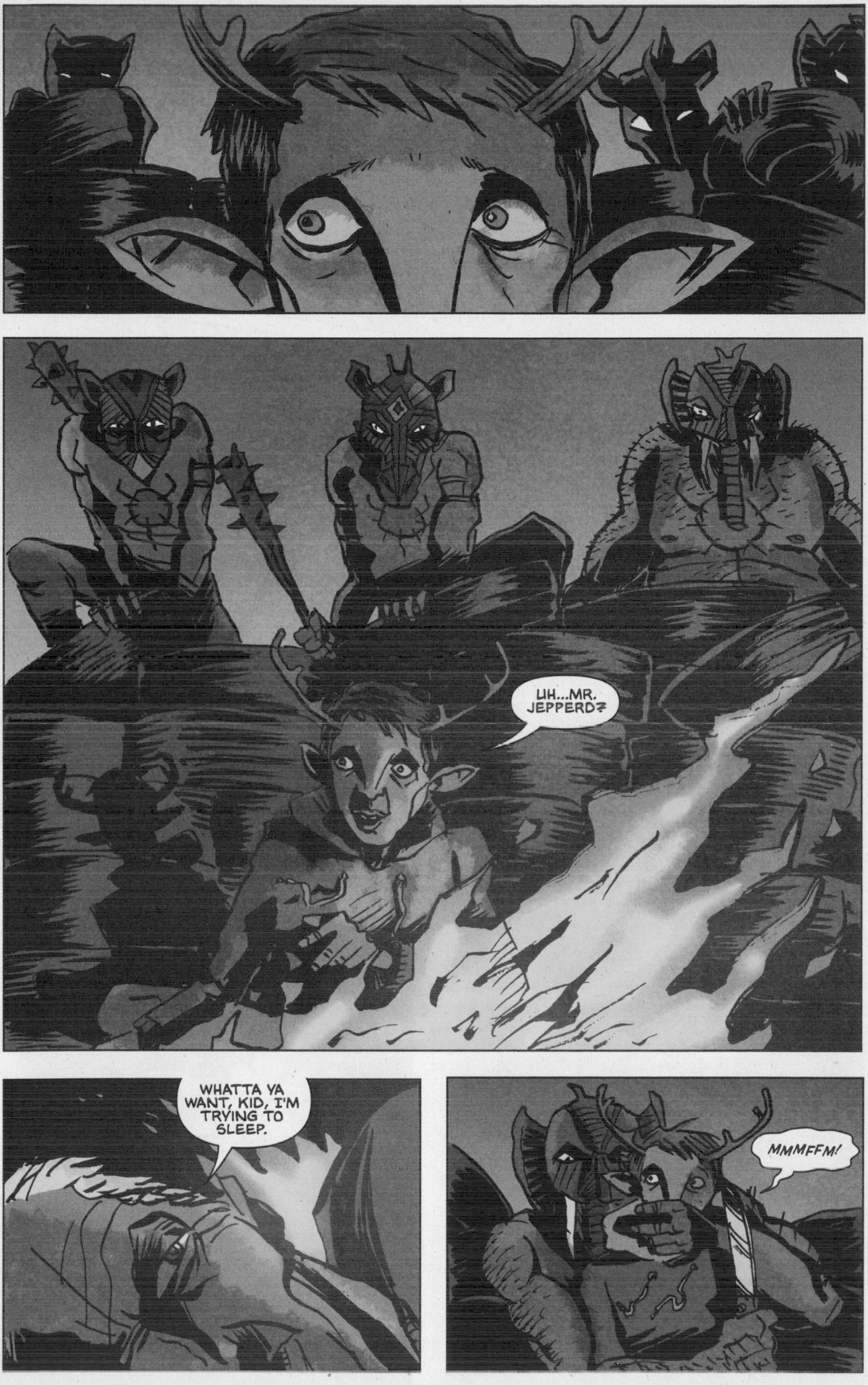
UH...MR. JEPPERD?
WHATTA YA WANT, KID, I'M TRYING TO SLEEP.
MMMFFM!

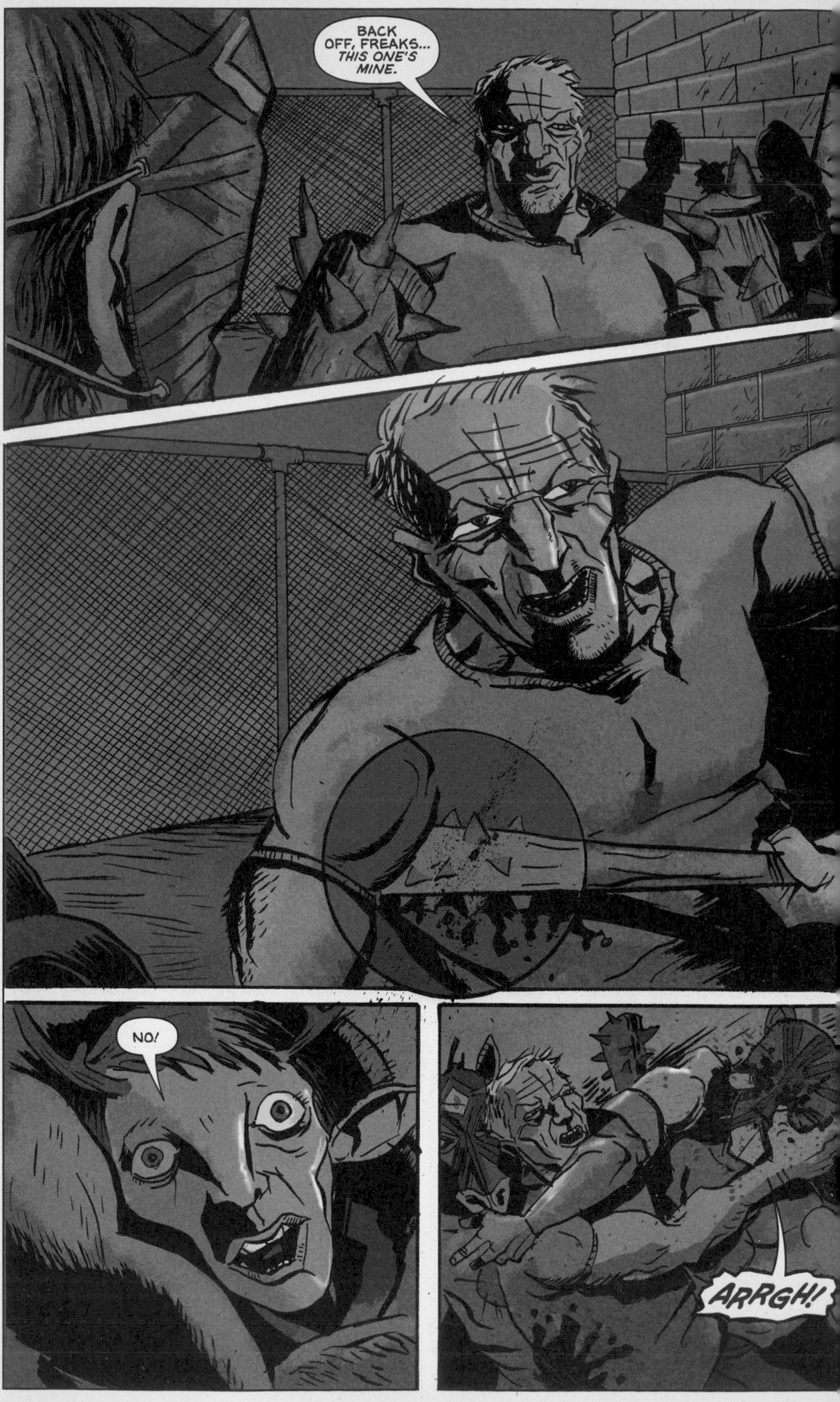
BACK OFF, FREAKS... THIS ONE'S MINE.
NO!
ARRGH!

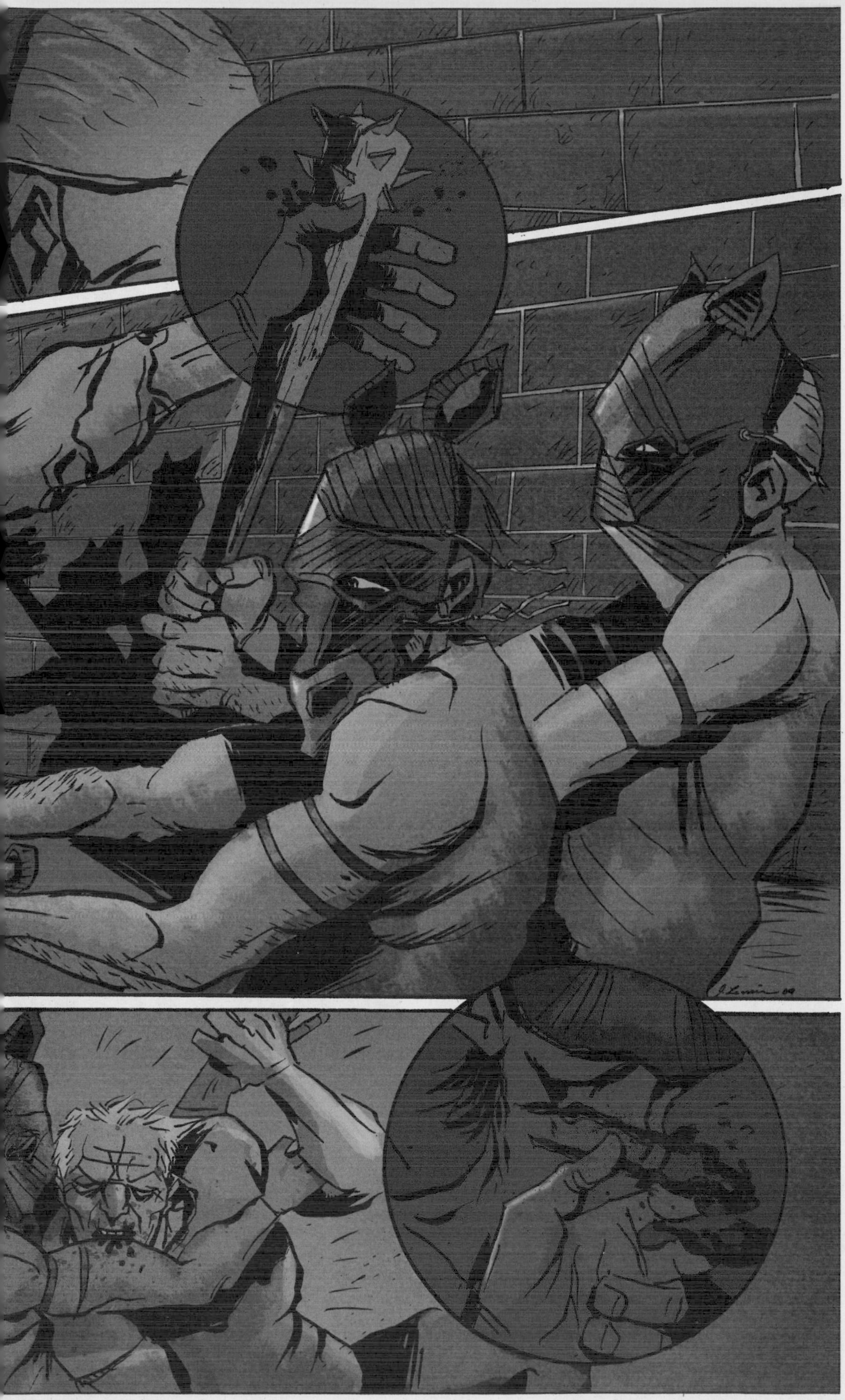

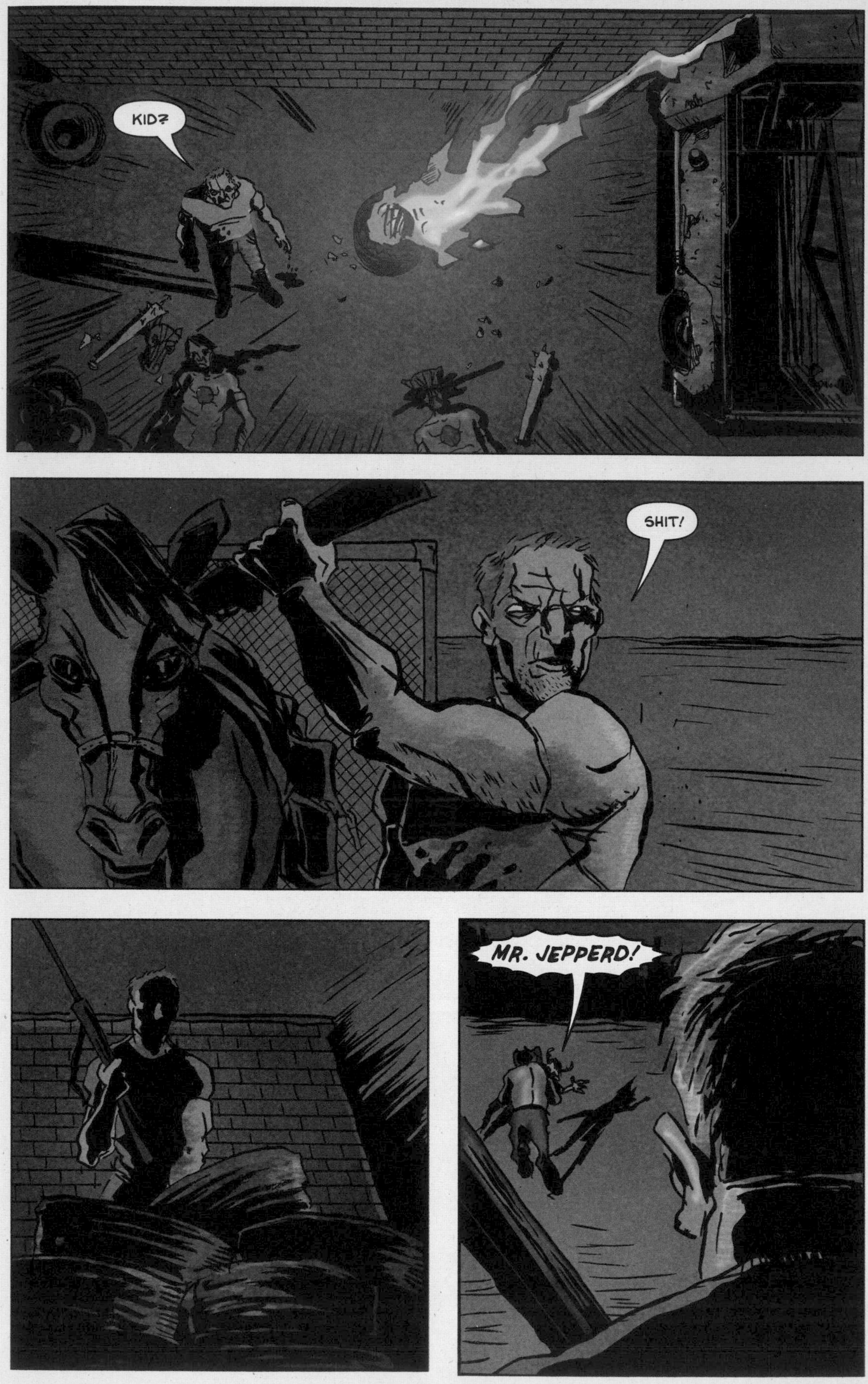
KID?
SHIT!
MR. JEPPERD!

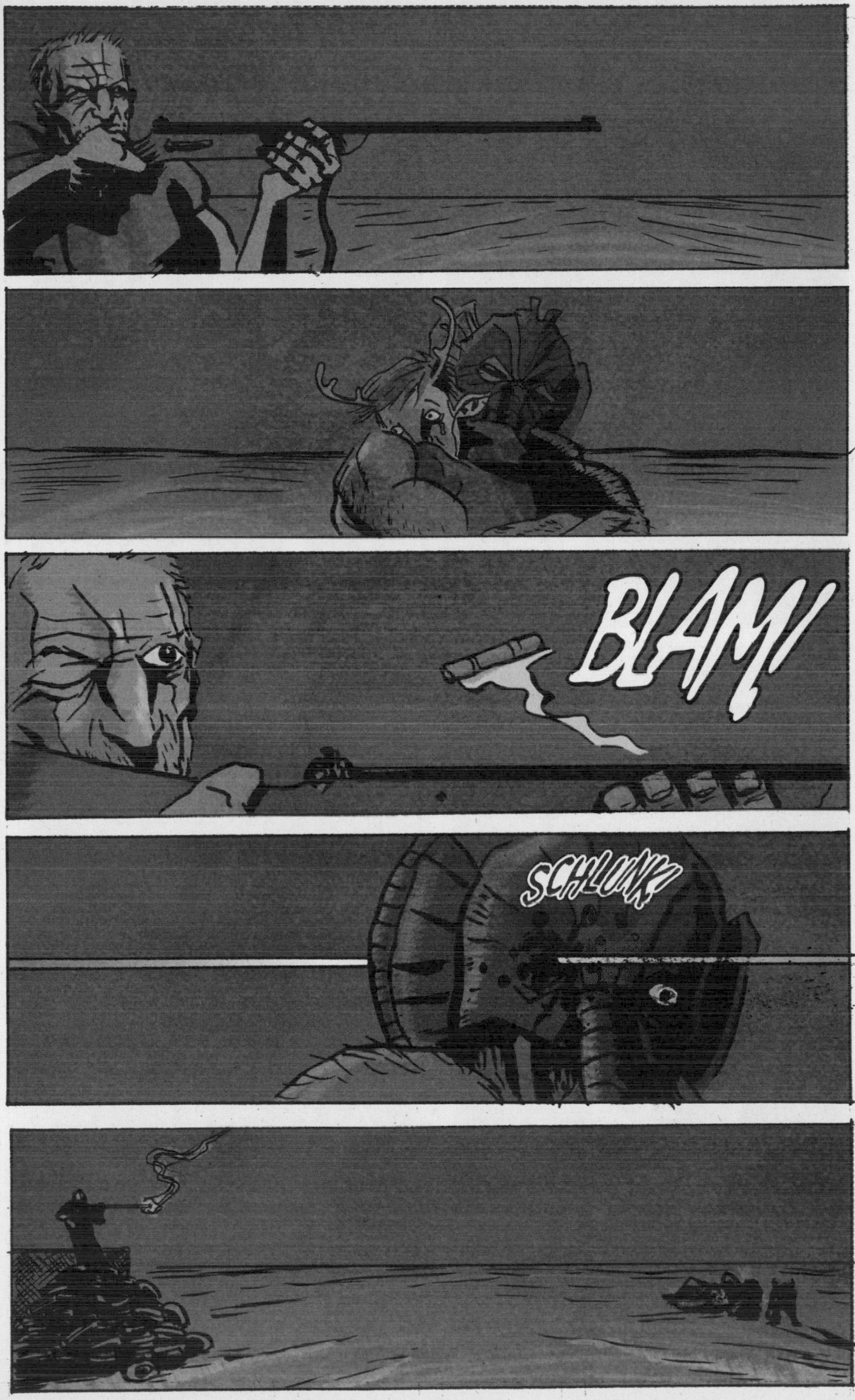
BLAM!
SCHLUNK!

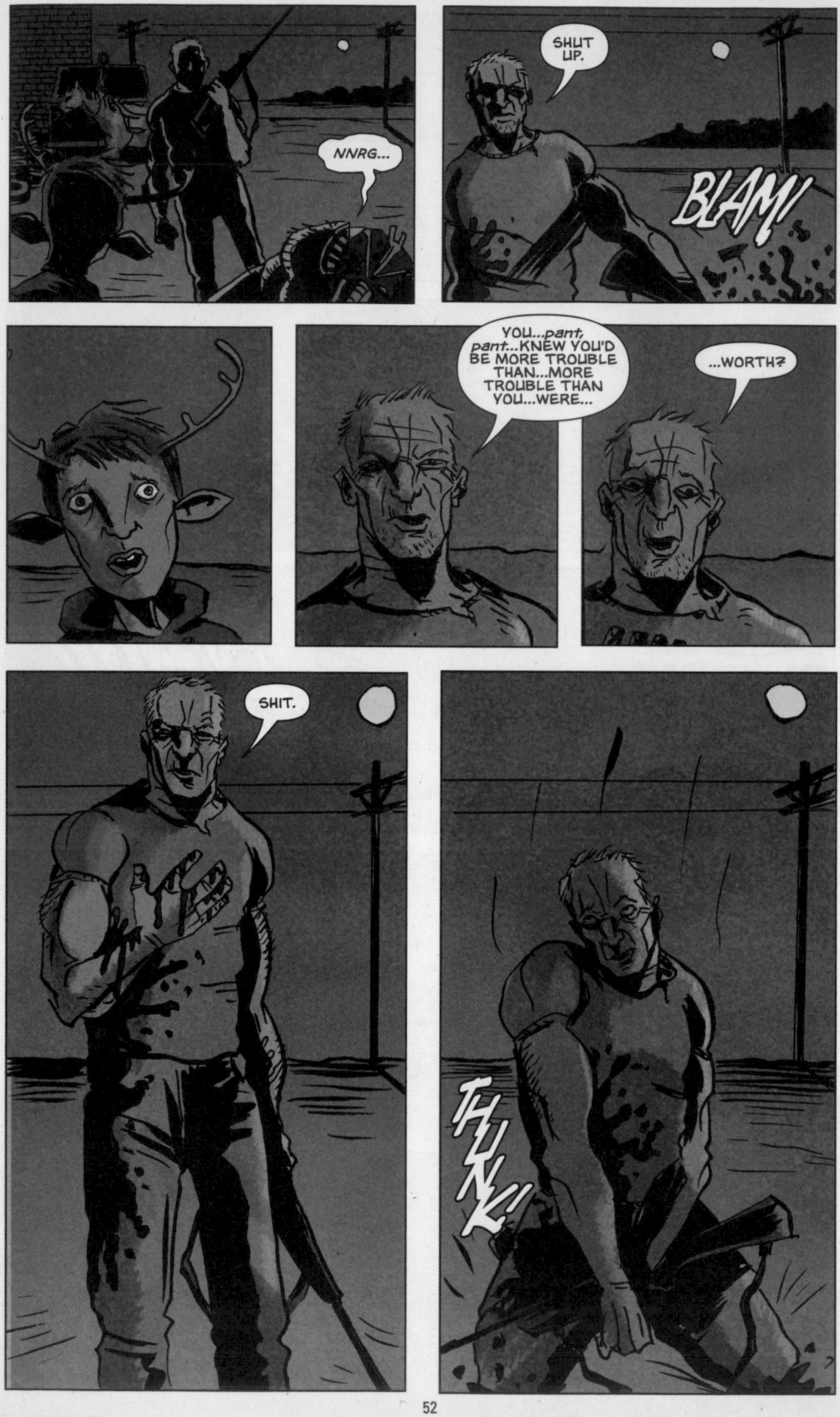
NNRG...
SHUT UP.
BLAM!
YOU...pant, pant...KNEW YOU'D BE MORE TROUBLE THAN...MORE TROUBLE THAN YOU...WERE...
...WORTH?
SHIT.
THUNK!

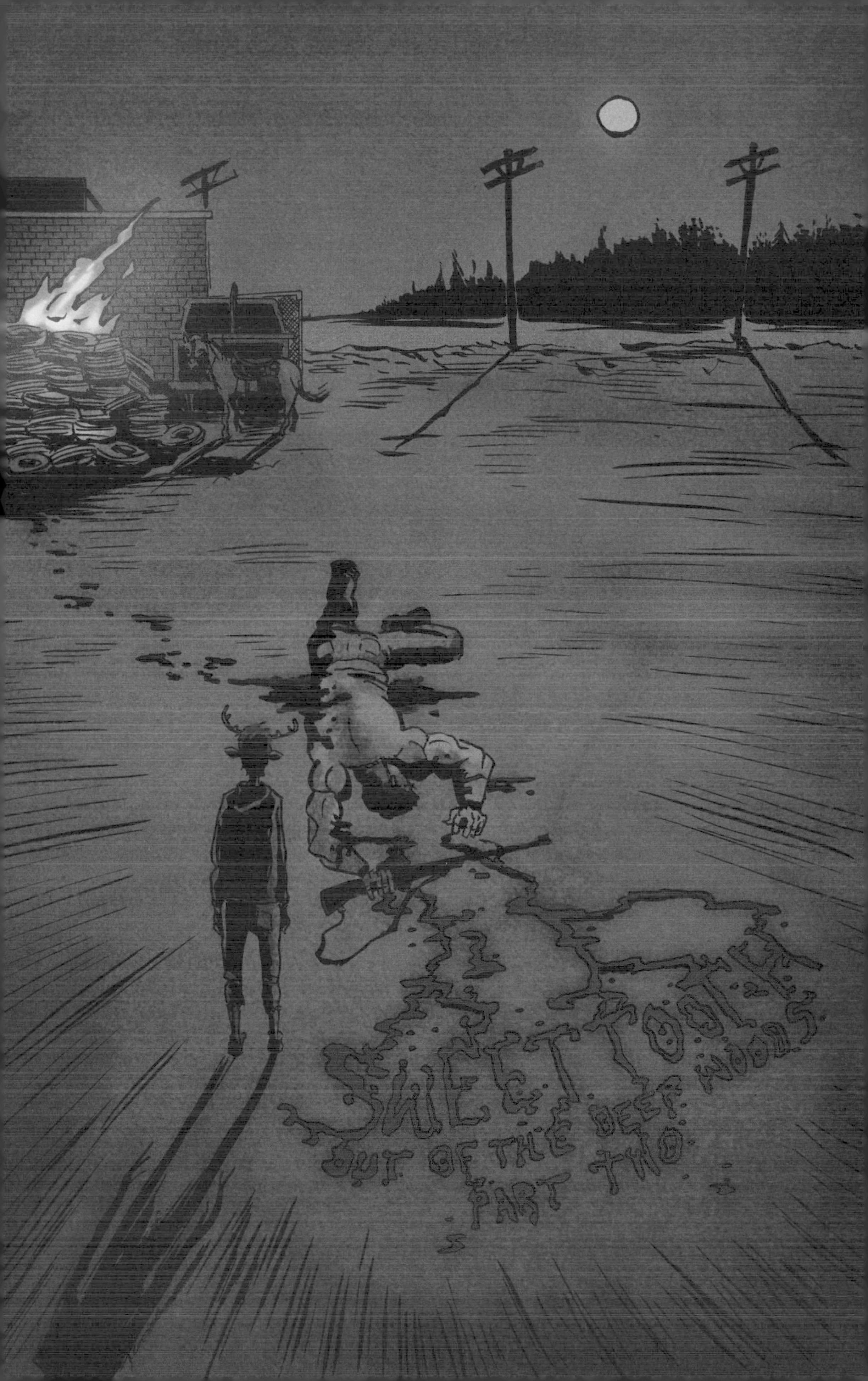
SWEET TOOTH
OUT OF THE DEEP WOODS
PART TWO

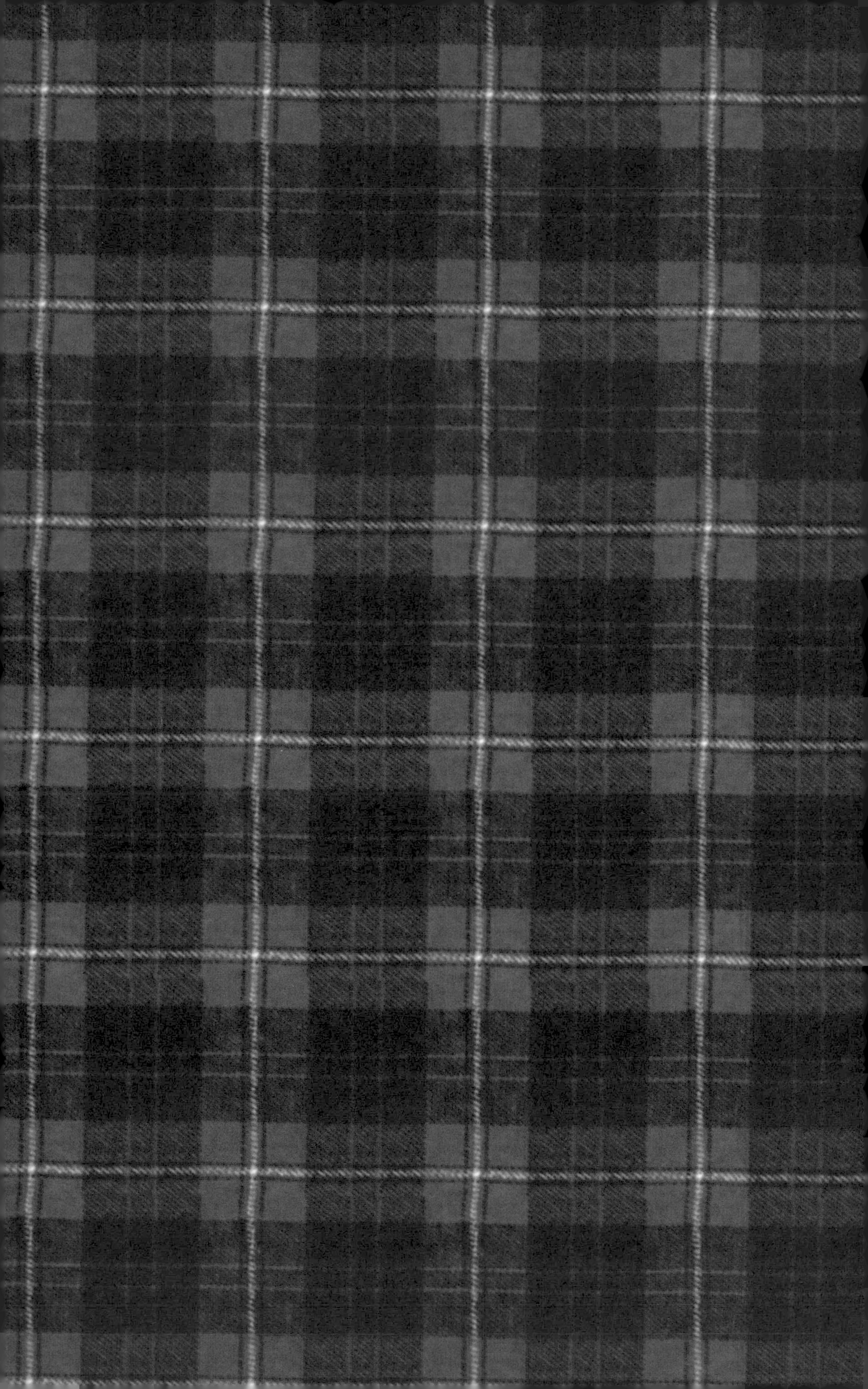

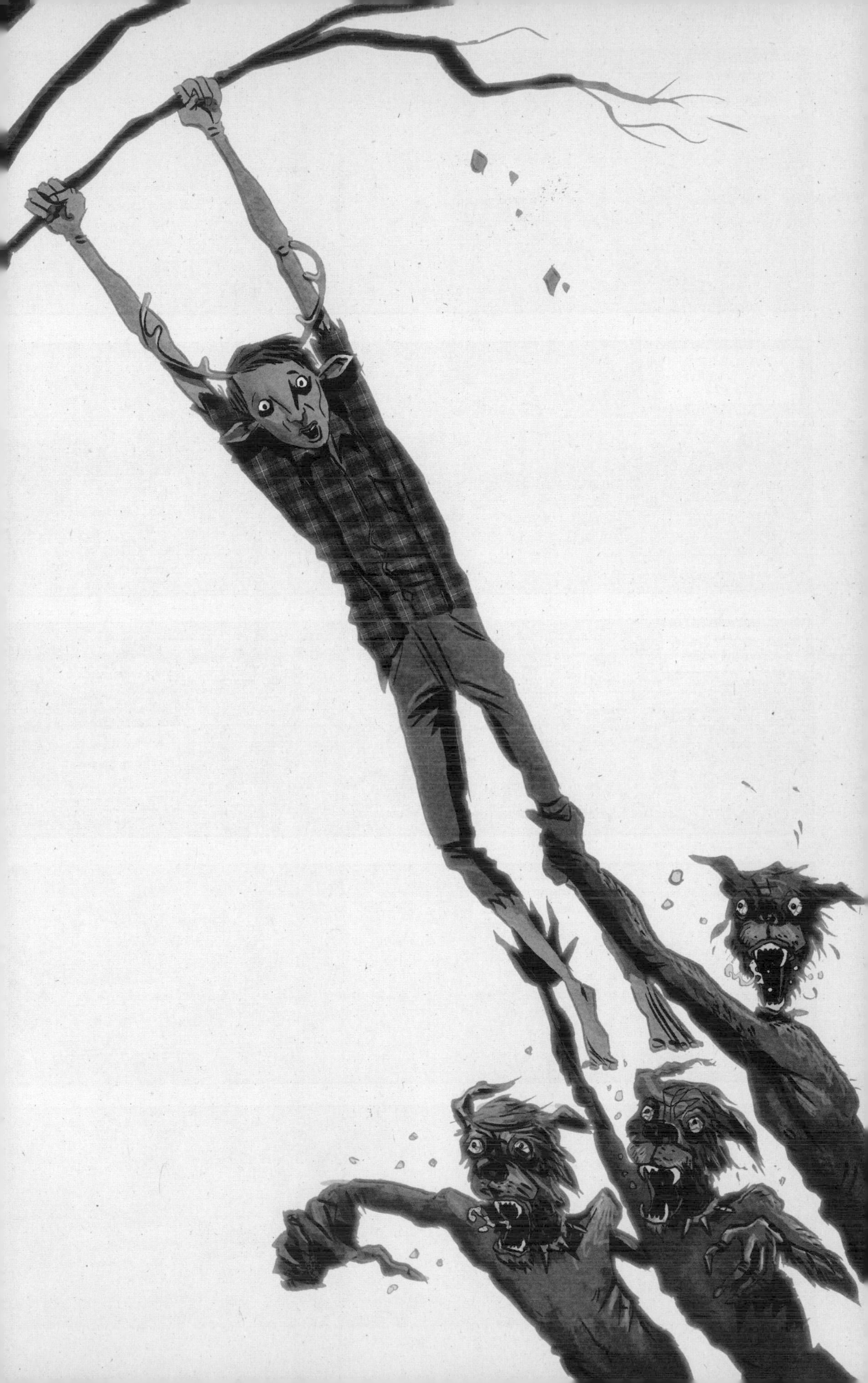

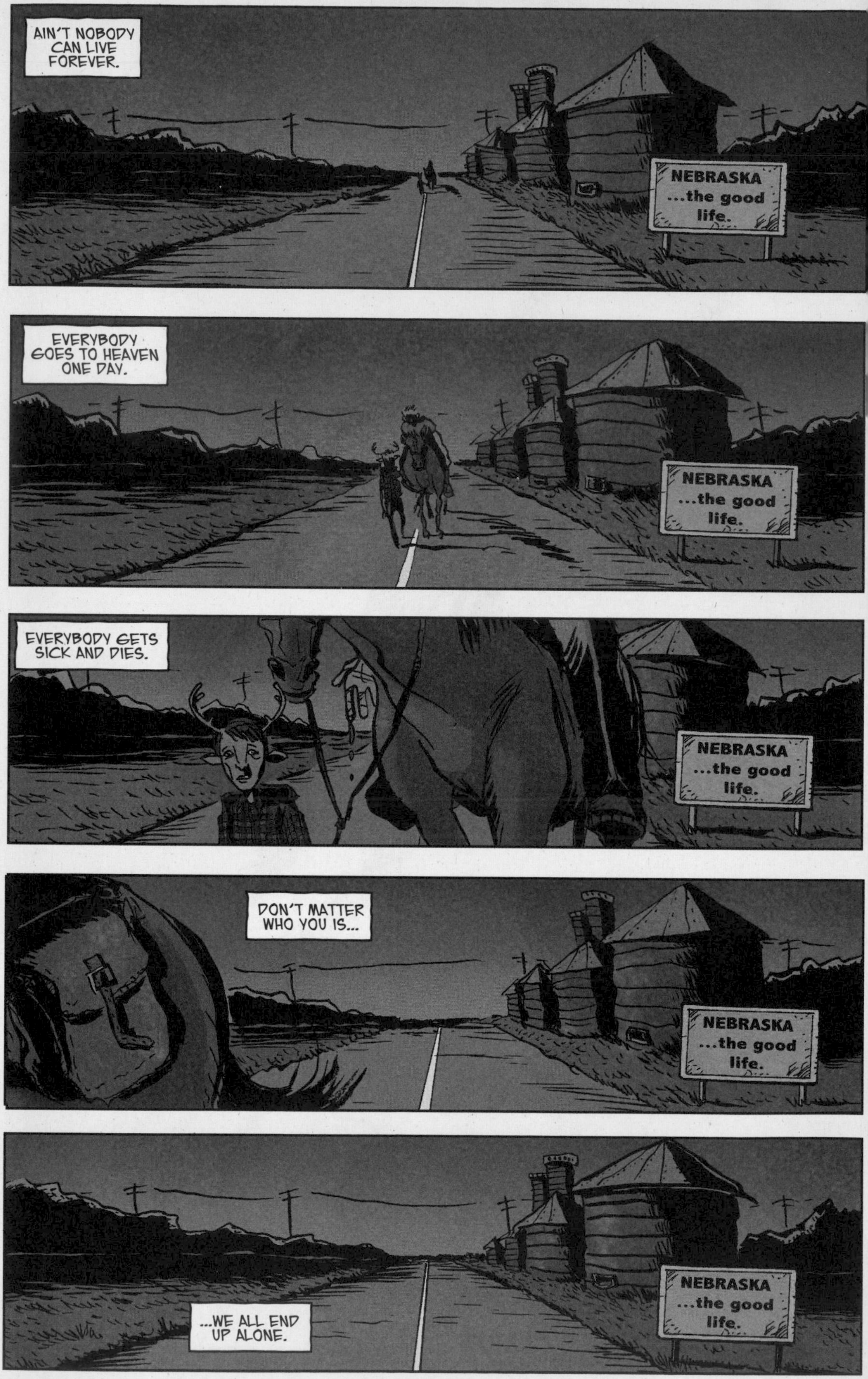
AIN'T NOBODY CAN LIVE FOREVER.
NEBRASKA ...the good life.
EVERYBODY GOES TO HEAVEN ONE DAY.
NEBRASKA ...the good life.
EVERYBODY GETS SICK AND DIES.
NEBRASKA ...the good life.
DON'T MATTER WHO YOU IS...
NEBRASKA ...the good life.
...WE ALL END UP ALONE.
NEBRASKA ...the good life.

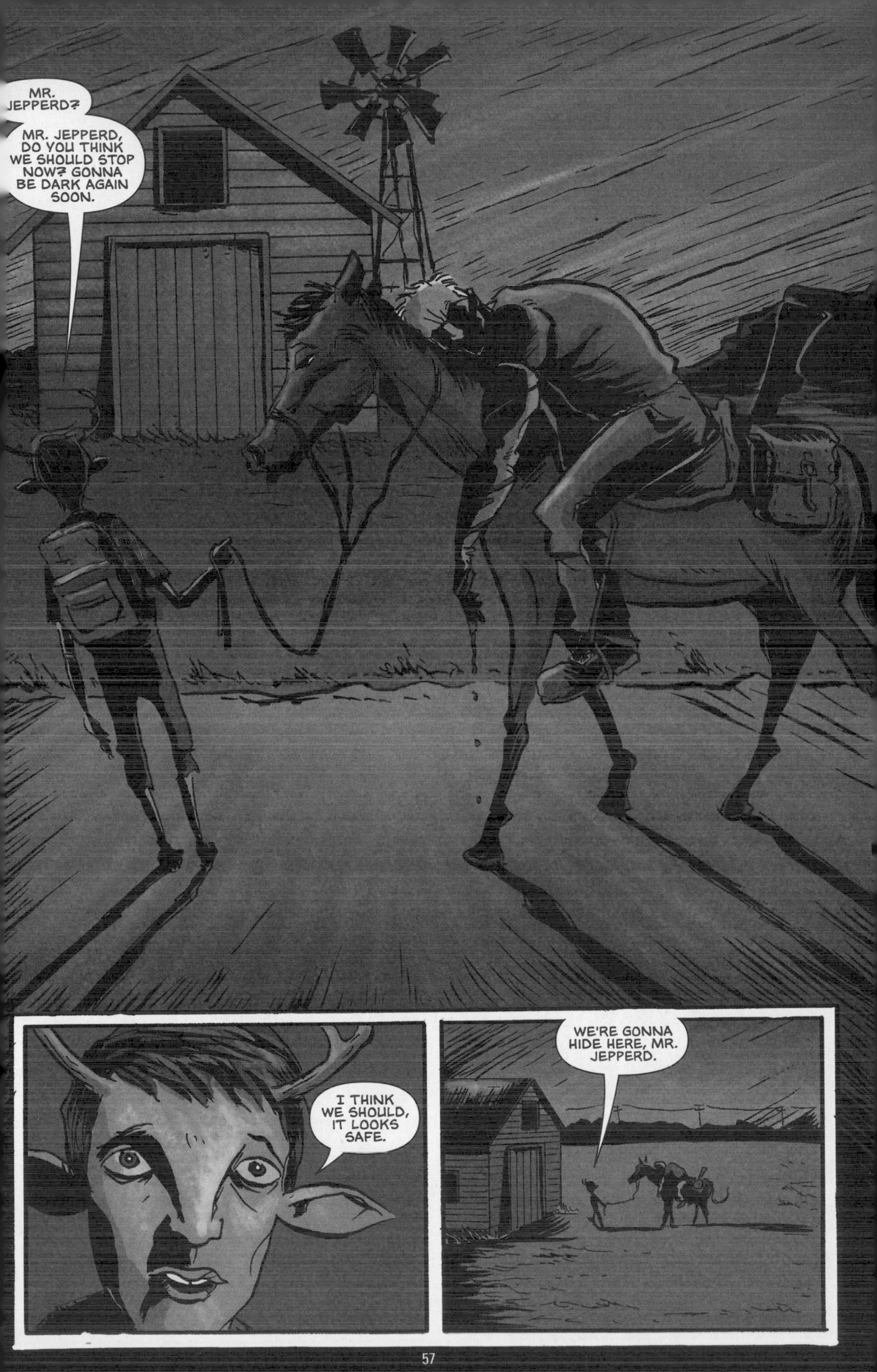
MR. JEPPERD?
MR. JEPPERD, DO YOU THINK WE SHOULD STOP NOW? GONNA BE DARK AGAIN SOON.
I THINK WE SHOULD, IT LOOKS SAFE.
WE'RE GONNA HIDE HERE, MR. JEPPERD.

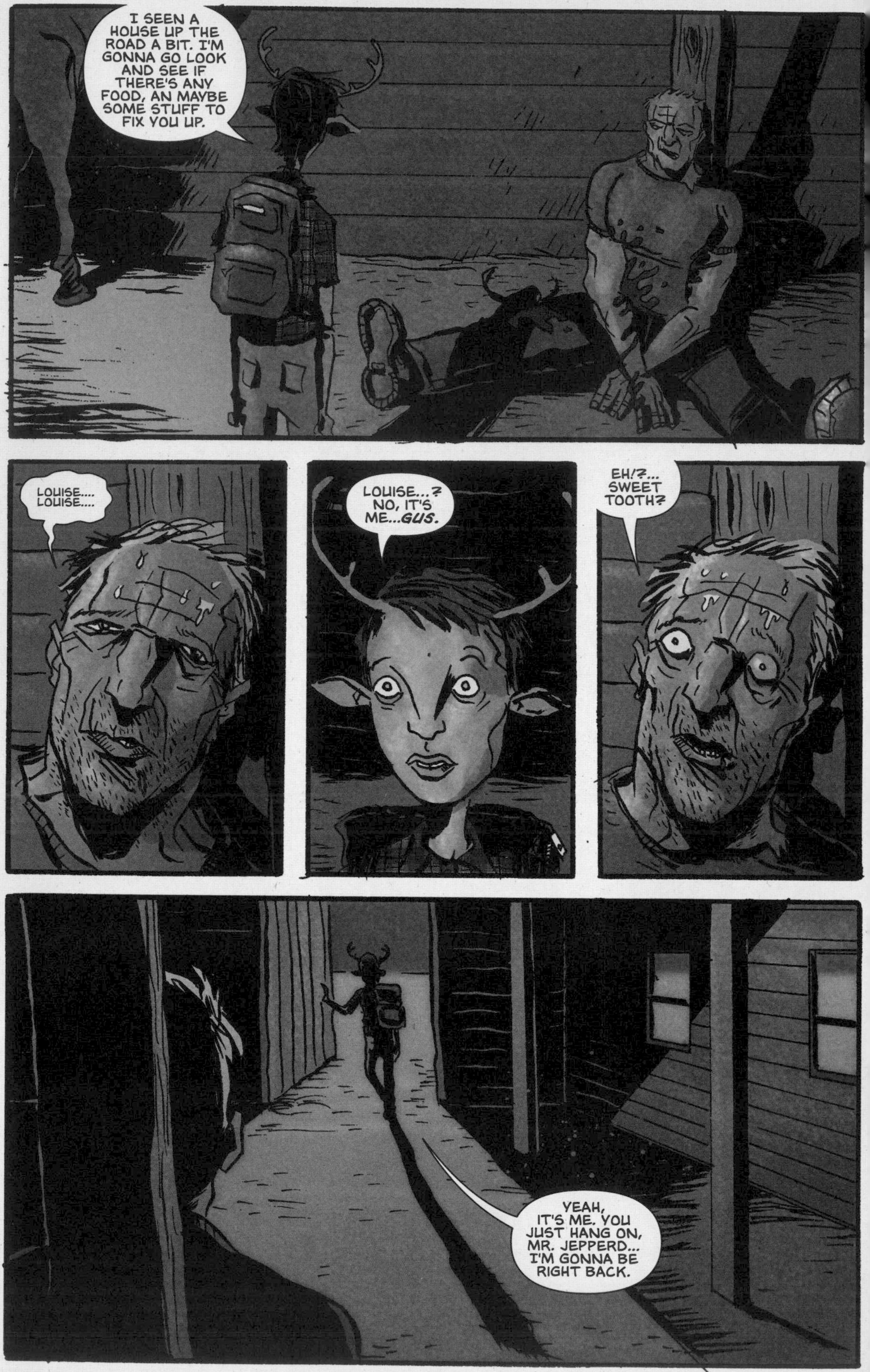
I SEEN A HOUSE UP THE ROAD A BIT. I'M GONNA GO LOOK AND SEE IF THERE'S ANY FOOD, AN MAYBE SOME STUFF TO FIX YOU UP.
LOUISE.... LOUISE....
LOUISE...? NO, IT'S ME...*GUS*.
EH!?... SWEET TOOTH?
YEAH, IT'S ME. YOU JUST HANG ON, MR. JEPPERD... I'M GONNA BE RIGHT BACK.

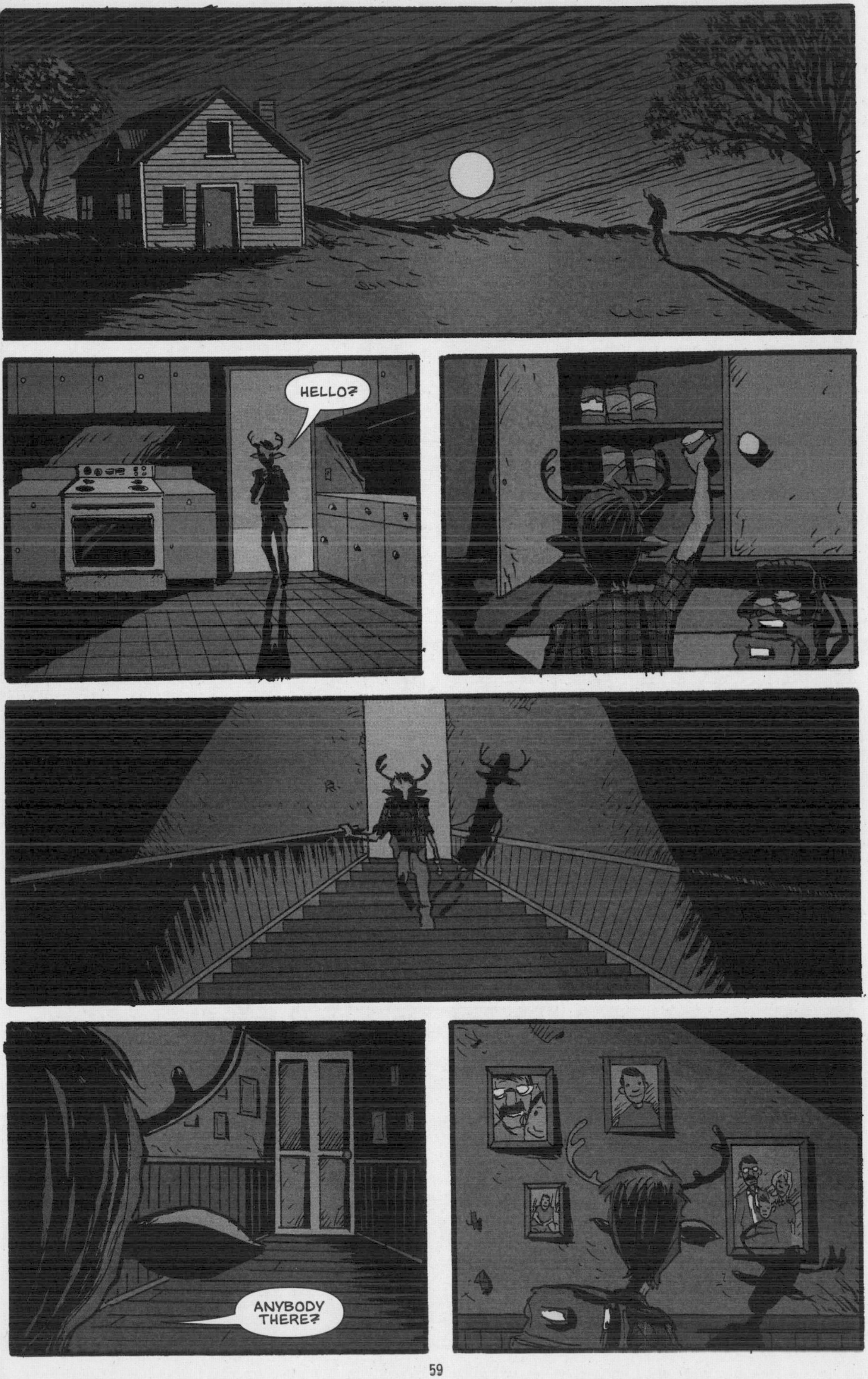
HELLO?
ANYBODY THERE?

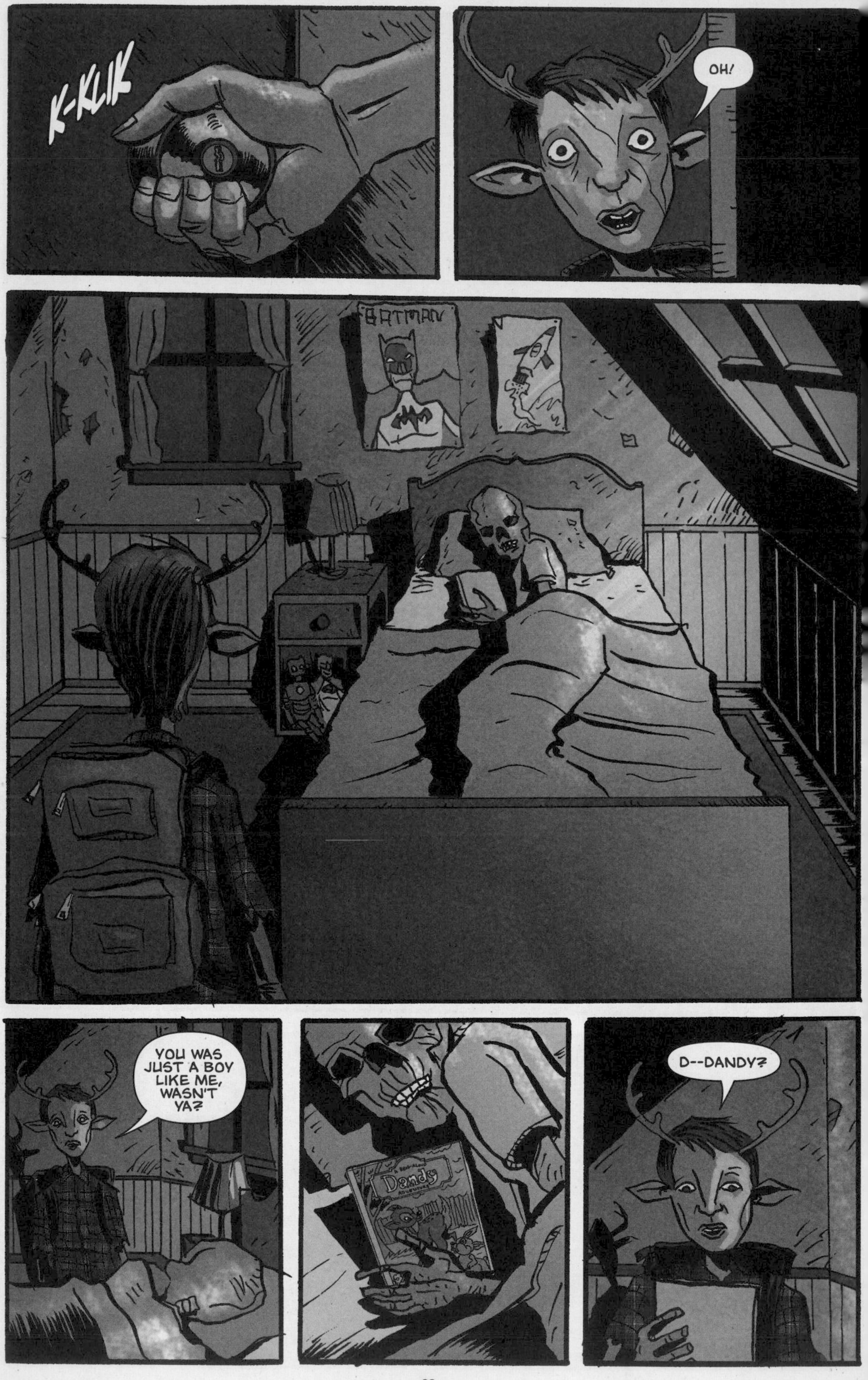
K-KLIK
OH!
BATMAN
YOU WAS JUST A BOY LIKE ME, WASN'T YA?
Dandy
D--DANDY?

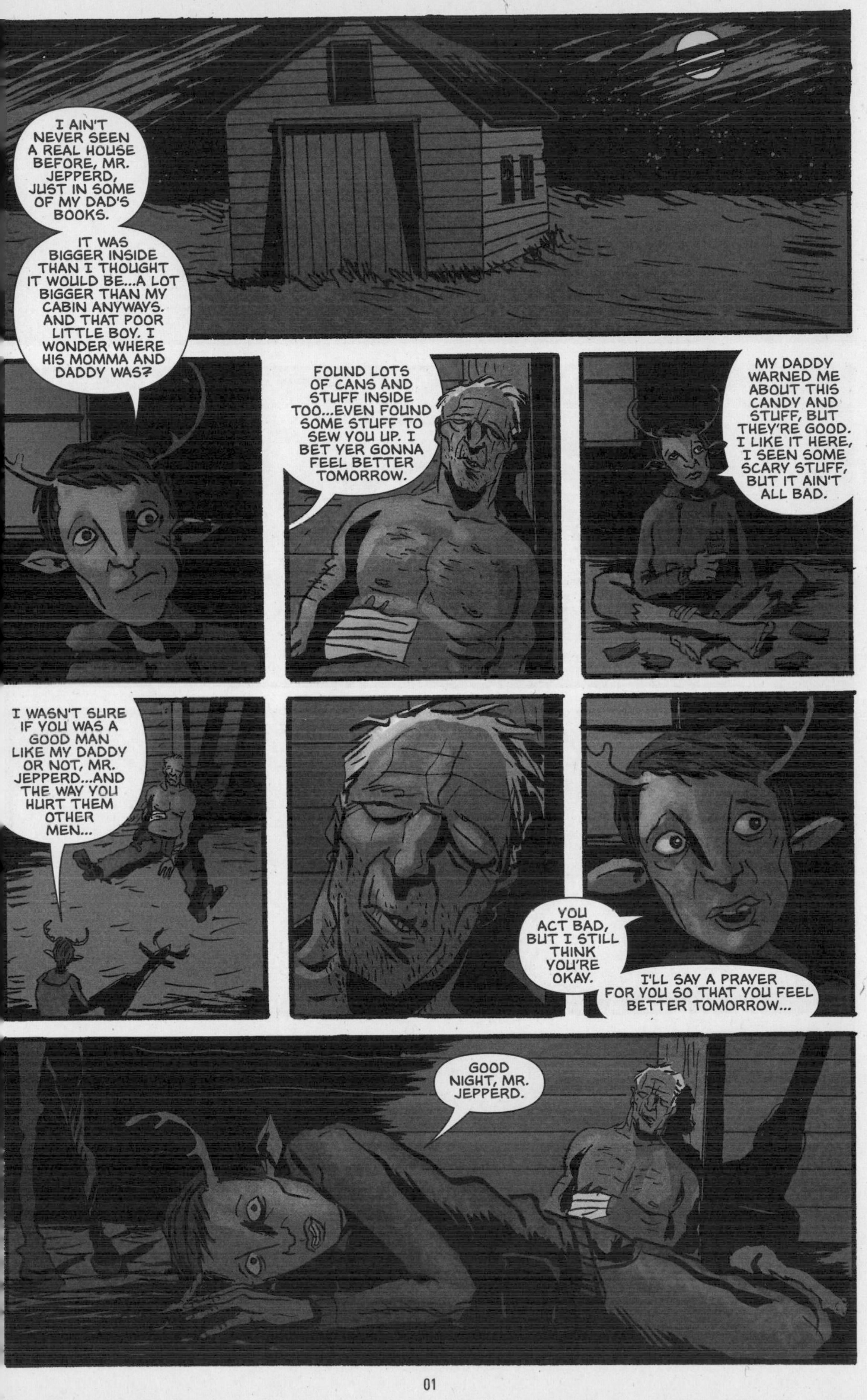
I AIN'T NEVER SEEN A REAL HOUSE BEFORE, MR. JEPPERD, JUST IN SOME OF MY DAD'S BOOKS.
IT WAS BIGGER INSIDE THAN I THOUGHT IT WOULD BE...A LOT BIGGER THAN MY CABIN ANYWAYS. AND THAT POOR LITTLE BOY. I WONDER WHERE HIS MOMMA AND DADDY WAS?
FOUND LOTS OF CANS AND STUFF INSIDE TOO...EVEN FOUND SOME STUFF TO SEW YOU UP. I BET YER GONNA FEEL BETTER TOMORROW.
MY DADDY WARNED ME ABOUT THIS CANDY AND STUFF, BUT THEY'RE GOOD. I LIKE IT HERE, I SEEN SOME SCARY STUFF, BUT IT AIN'T ALL BAD.
I WASN'T SURE IF YOU WAS A GOOD MAN LIKE MY DADDY OR NOT, MR. JEPPERD...AND THE WAY YOU HURT THEM OTHER MEN...
YOU ACT BAD, BUT I STILL THINK YOU'RE OKAY.
I'LL SAY A PRAYER FOR YOU SO THAT YOU FEEL BETTER TOMORROW...
GOOD NIGHT, MR. JEPPERD.

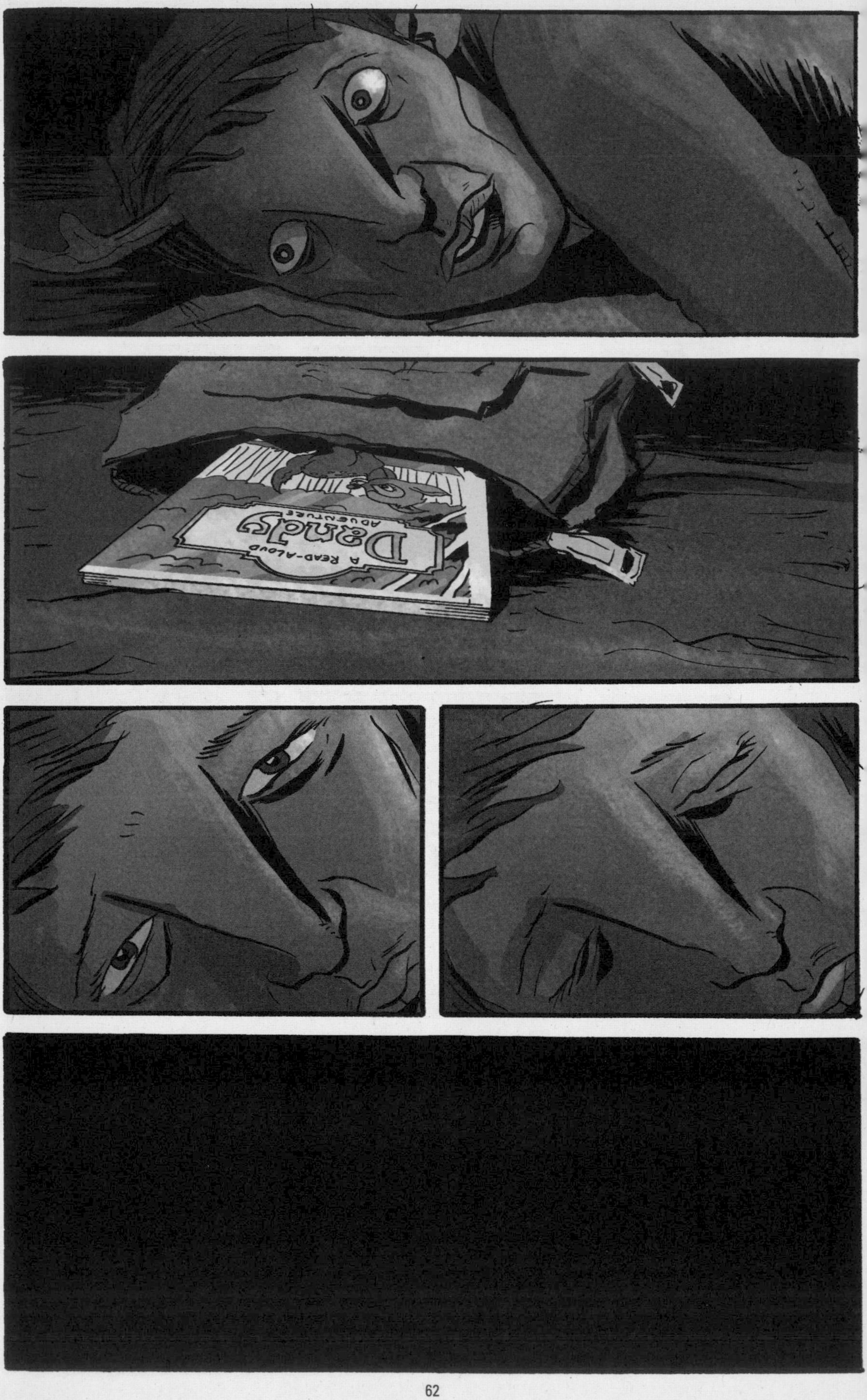
A READ-ALOUD
Dandy
ADVENTURE

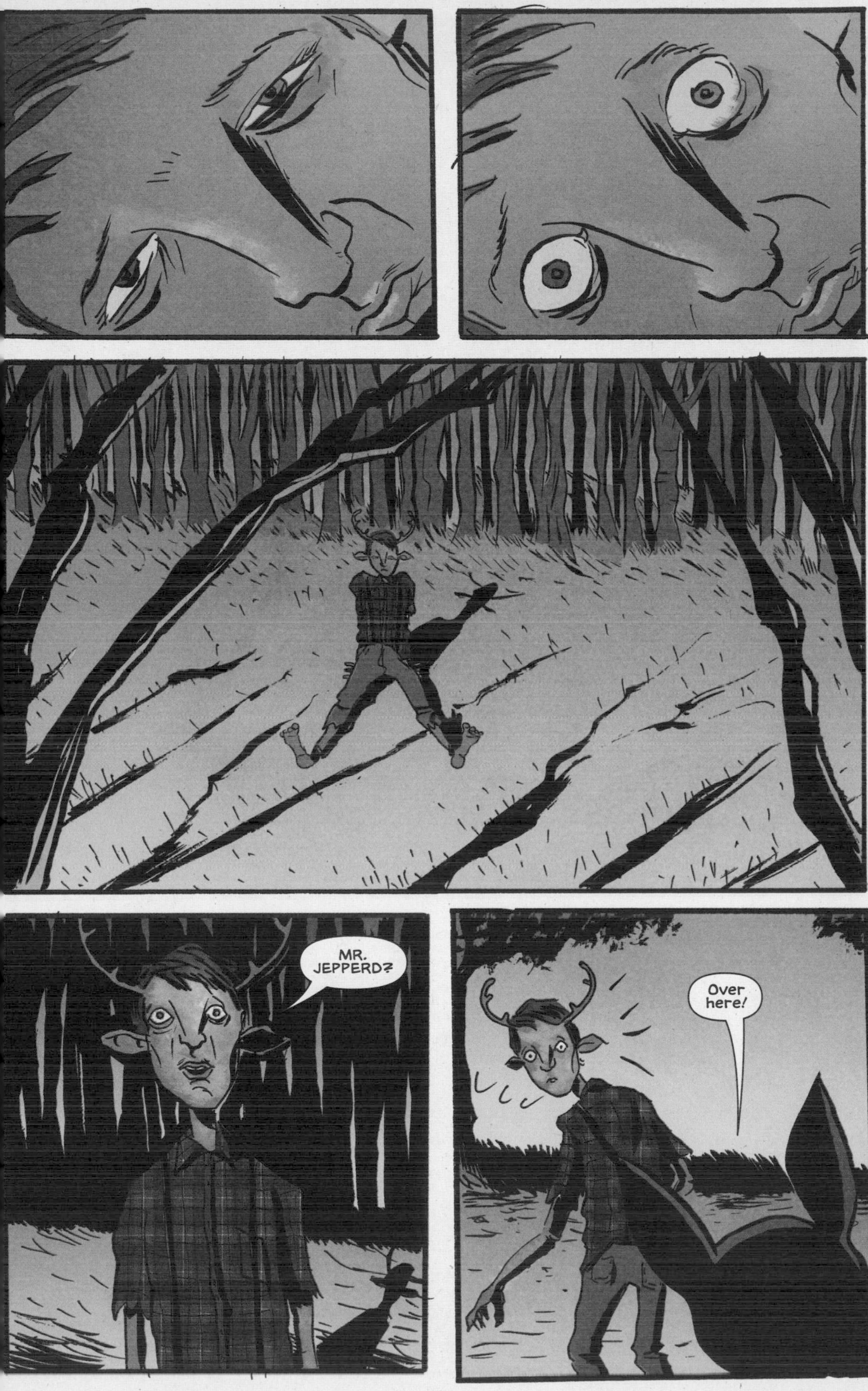

MR. JEPPERD?
Over here!

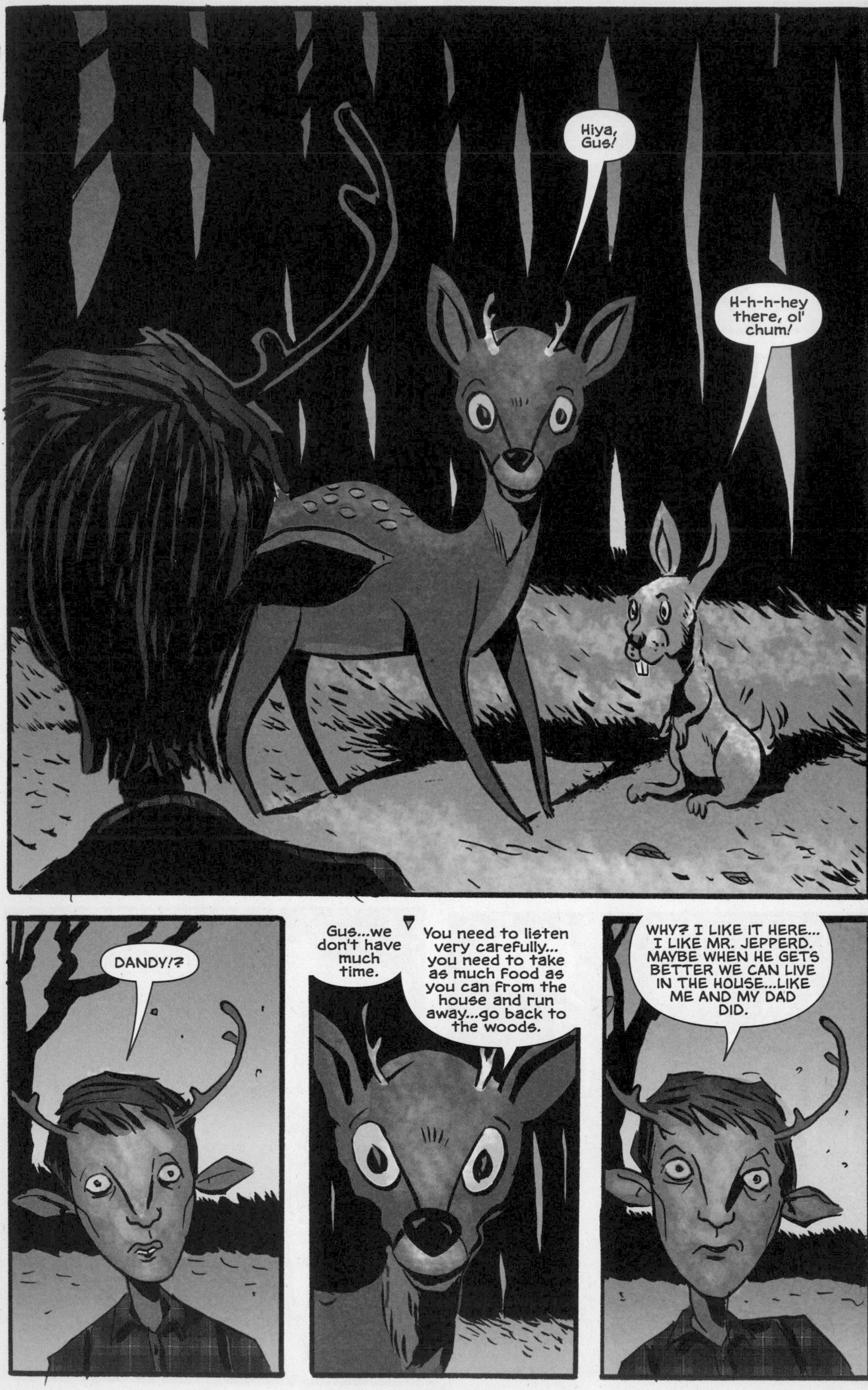
Hiya, Gus!
H-h-h-hey there, ol' chum!
DANDY!?
Gus...we don't have much time.
You need to listen very carefully... you need to take as much food as you can from the house and run away...go back to the woods.
WHY? I LIKE IT HERE... I LIKE MR. JEPPERD. MAYBE WHEN HE GETS BETTER WE CAN LIVE IN THE HOUSE...LIKE ME AND MY DAD DID.

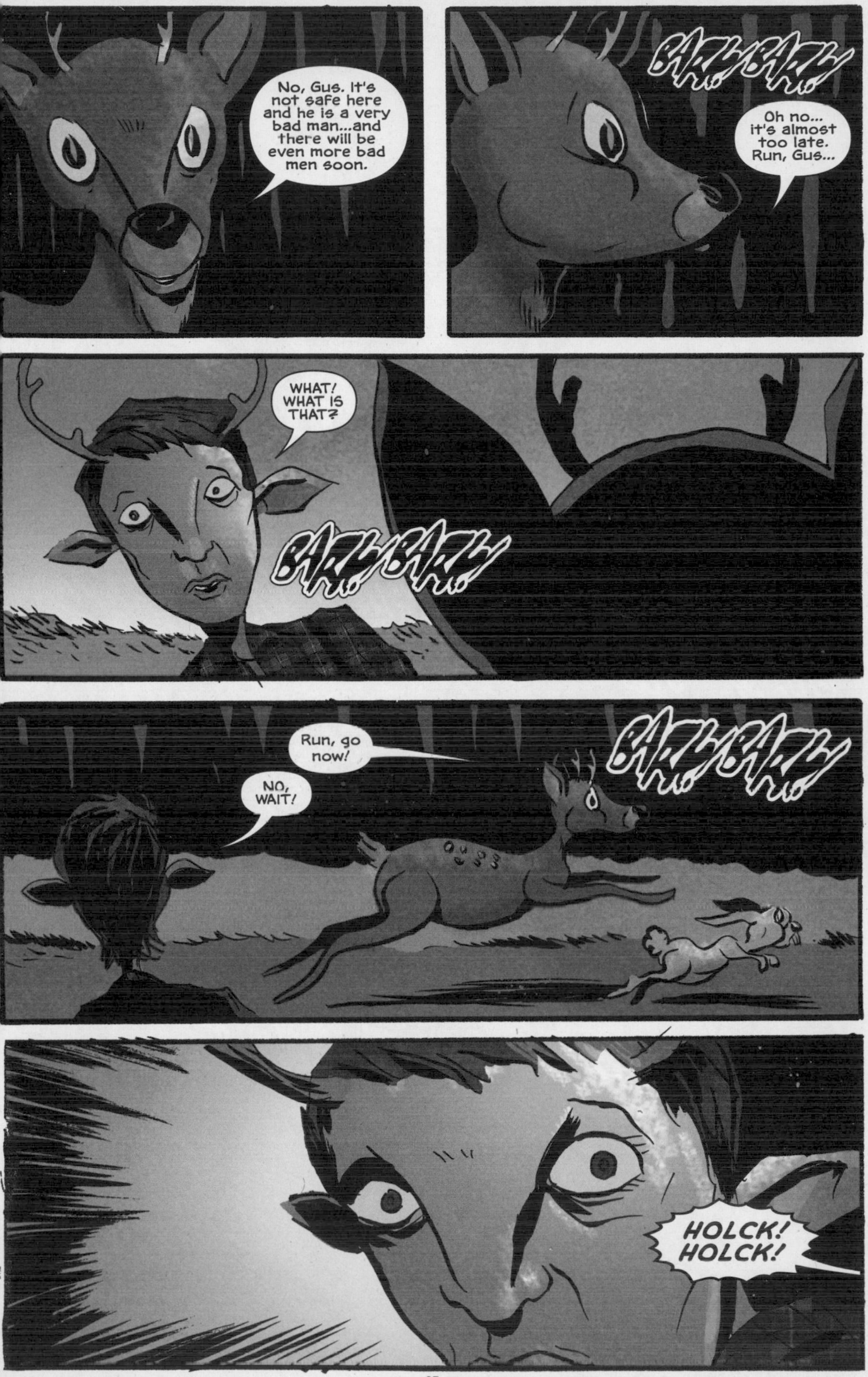
No, Gus. It's not safe here and he is a very bad man...and there will be even more bad men soon.
BARK BARK
Oh no... it's almost too late. Run, Gus...
WHAT! WHAT IS THAT?
BARK BARK
BARK BARK
Run, go now!
NO, WAIT!
HOLCK! HOLCK!

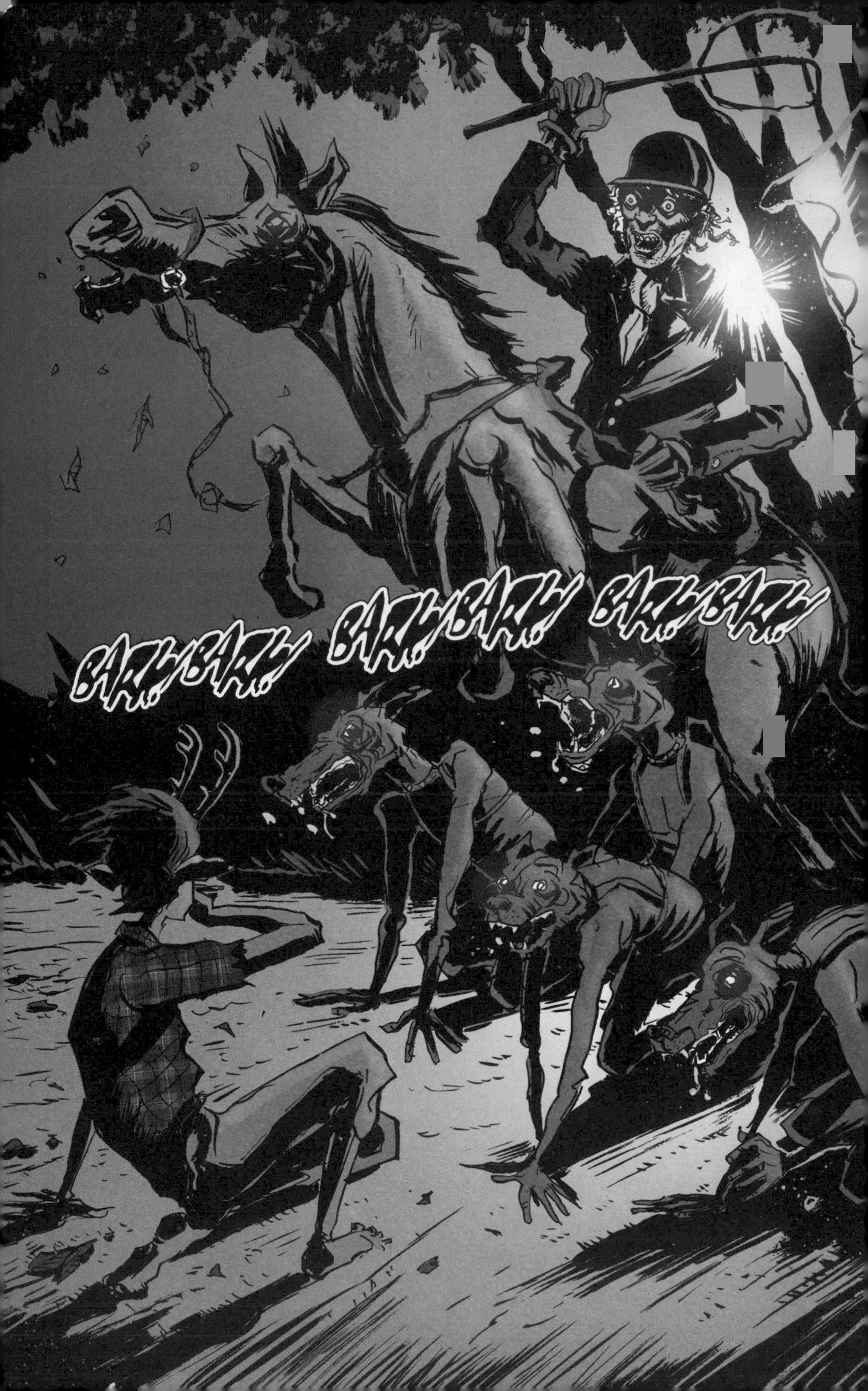
BARK BARK BARK BARK BARK BARK

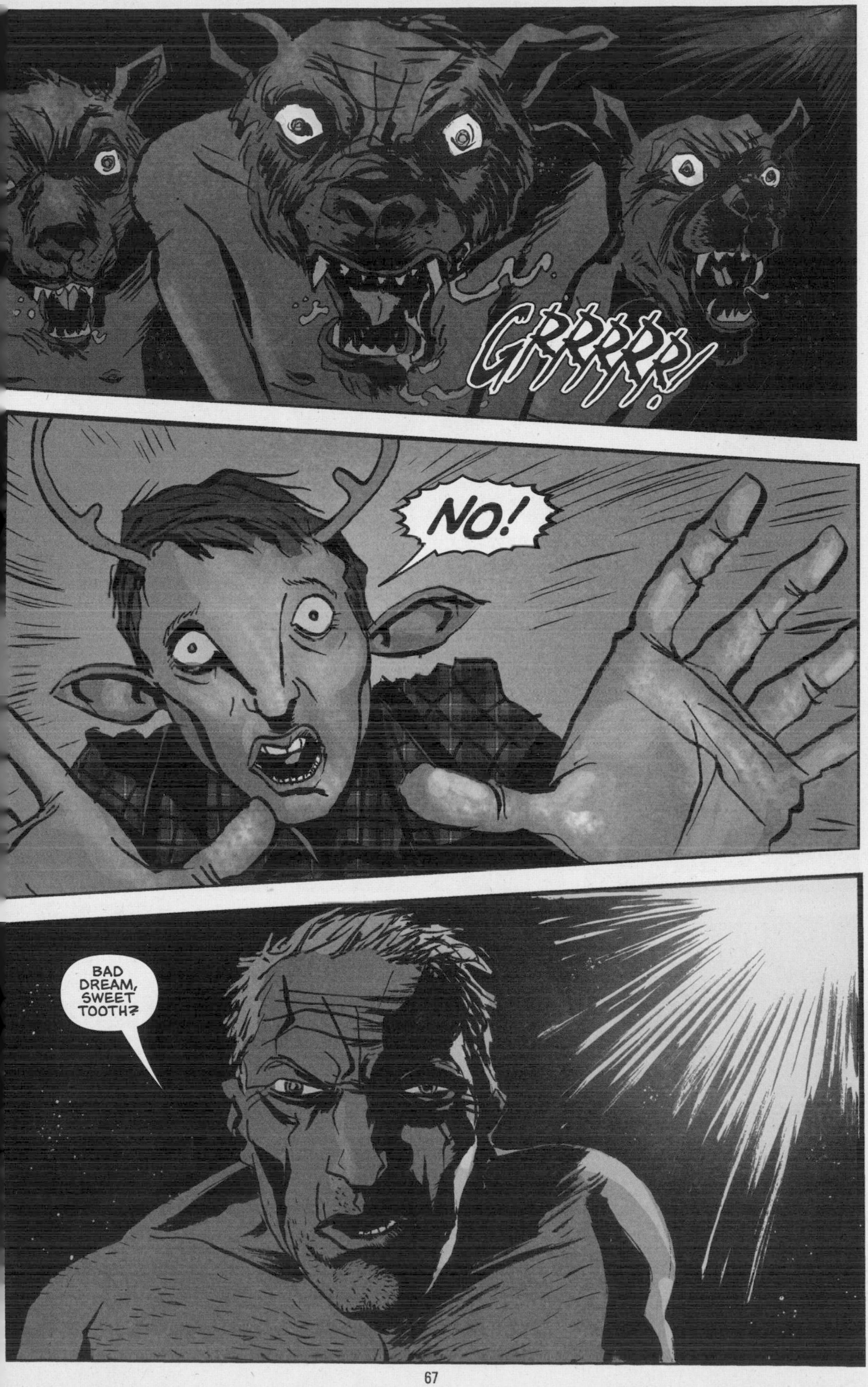
GRRRRR!
NO!
BAD DREAM, SWEET TOOTH?

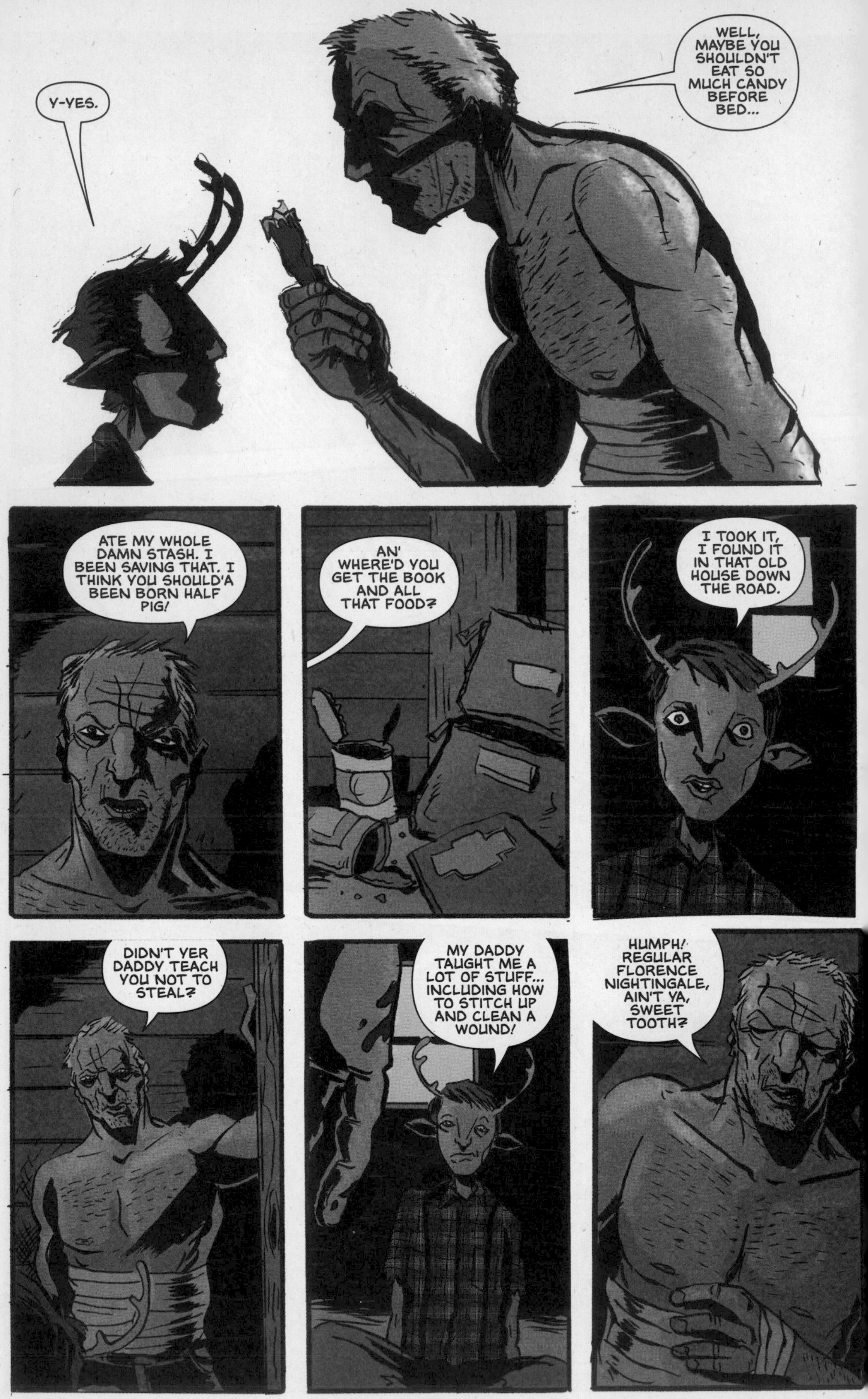
WELL, MAYBE YOU SHOULDN'T EAT SO MUCH CANDY BEFORE BED...
Y-YES.
ATE MY WHOLE DAMN STASH. I BEEN SAVING THAT. I THINK YOU SHOULD'A BEEN BORN HALF PIG!
AN' WHERE'D YOU GET THE BOOK AND ALL THAT FOOD?
I TOOK IT, I FOUND IT IN THAT OLD HOUSE DOWN THE ROAD.
DIDN'T YER DADDY TEACH YOU NOT TO STEAL?
MY DADDY TAUGHT ME A LOT OF STUFF... INCLUDING HOW TO STITCH UP AND CLEAN A WOUND!
HUMPH! REGULAR FLORENCE NIGHTINGALE, AIN'T YA, SWEET TOOTH?

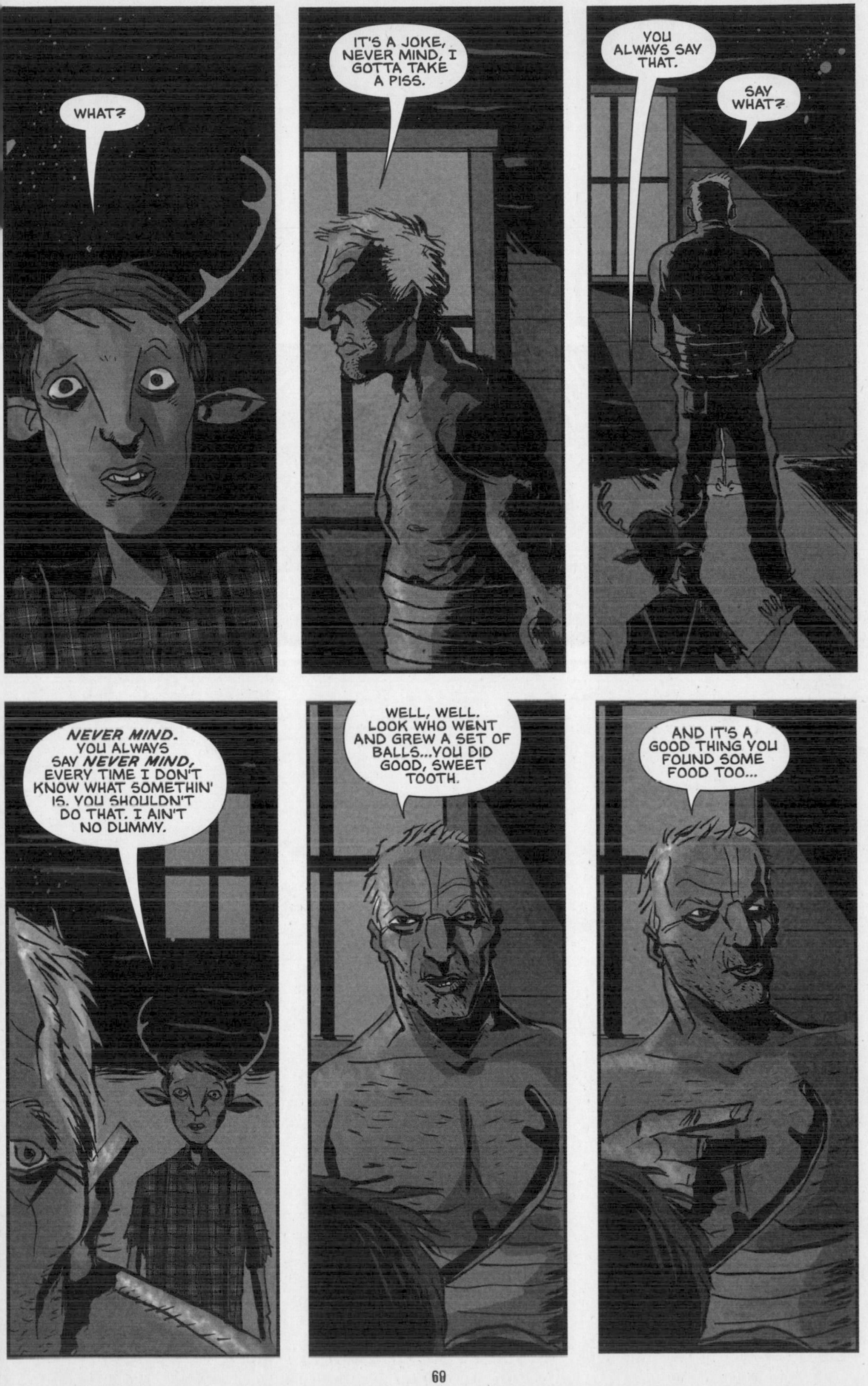
WHAT?
IT'S A JOKE, NEVER MIND, I GOTTA TAKE A PISS.
YOU ALWAYS SAY THAT.
SAY WHAT?
NEVER MIND. YOU ALWAYS SAY NEVER MIND, EVERY TIME I DON'T KNOW WHAT SOMETHIN' IS. YOU SHOULDN'T DO THAT. I AIN'T NO DUMMY.
WELL, WELL. LOOK WHO WENT AND GREW A SET OF BALLS...YOU DID GOOD, SWEET TOOTH.
AND IT'S A GOOD THING YOU FOUND SOME FOOD TOO...

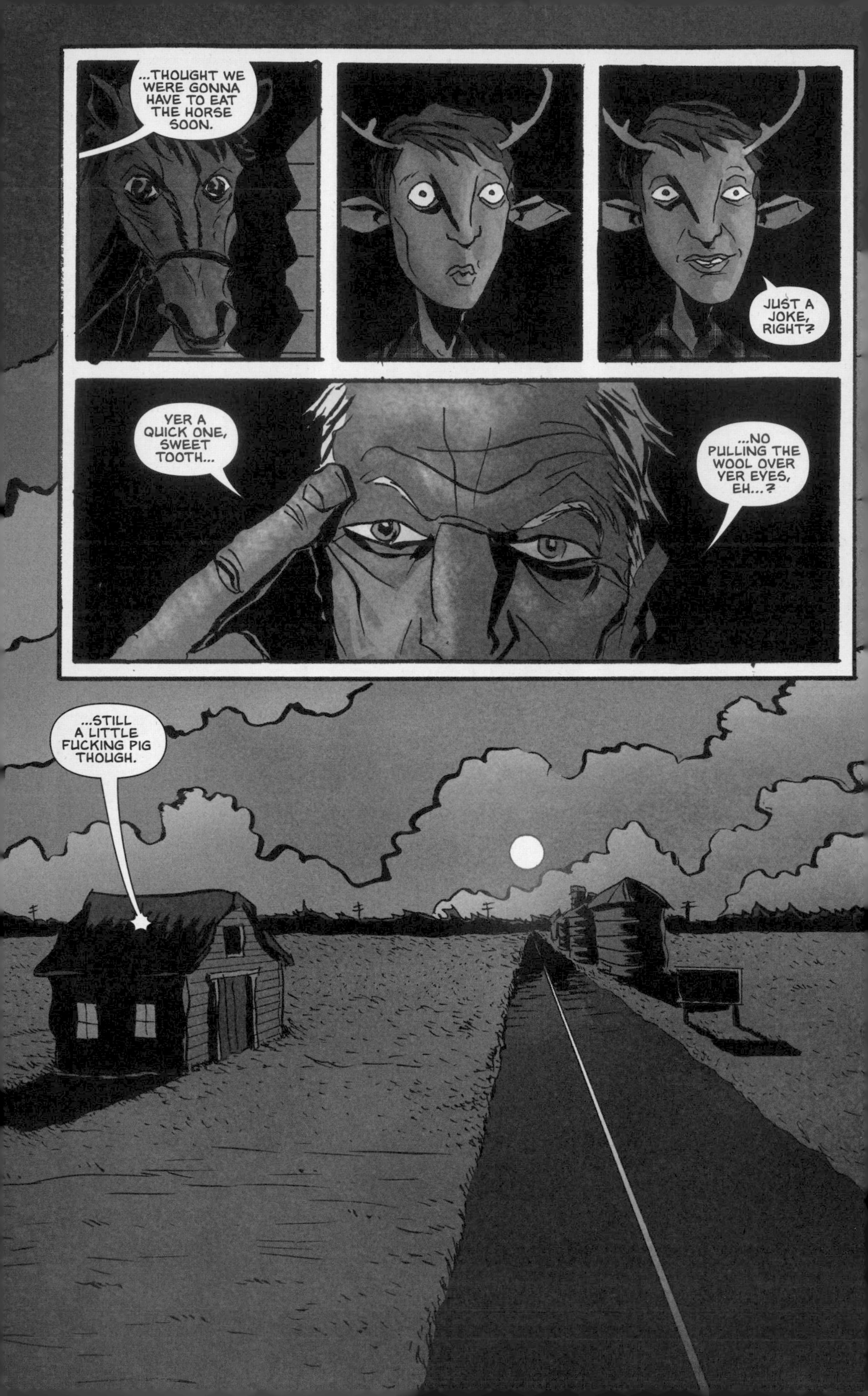
...THOUGHT WE WERE GONNA HAVE TO EAT THE HORSE SOON.
JUST A JOKE, RIGHT?
YER A QUICK ONE, SWEET TOOTH...
...NO PULLING THE WOOL OVER YER EYES, EH...?
...STILL A LITTLE FUCKING PIG THOUGH.

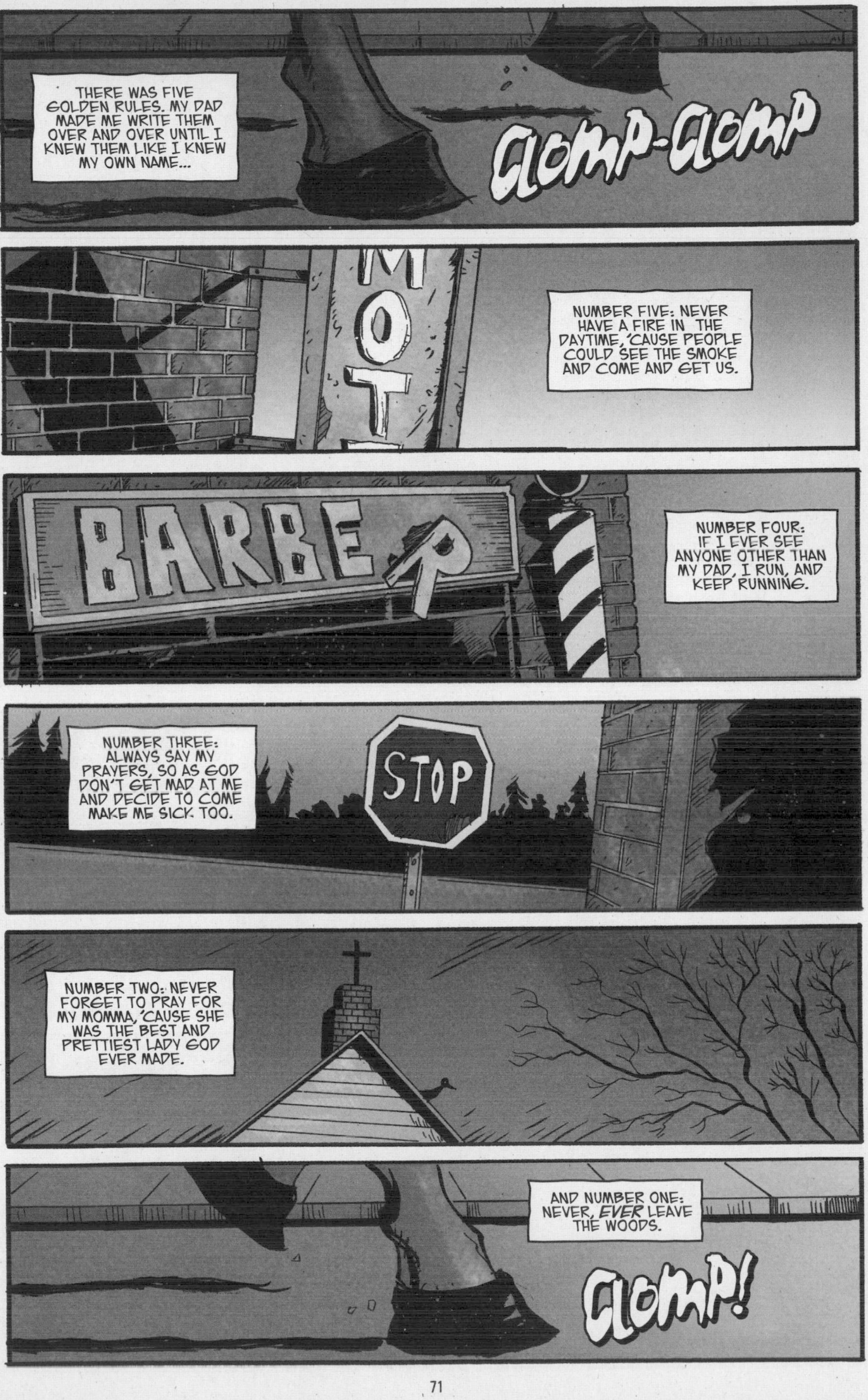
THERE WAS FIVE GOLDEN RULES. MY DAD MADE ME WRITE THEM OVER AND OVER UNTIL I KNEW THEM LIKE I KNEW MY OWN NAME...
CLOMP-CLOMP
MOT
NUMBER FIVE: NEVER HAVE A FIRE IN THE DAYTIME, 'CAUSE PEOPLE COULD SEE THE SMOKE AND COME AND GET US.
BARBER
NUMBER FOUR: IF I EVER SEE ANYONE OTHER THAN MY DAD, I RUN, AND KEEP RUNNING.
NUMBER THREE: ALWAYS SAY MY PRAYERS, SO AS GOD DON'T GET MAD AT ME AND DECIDE TO COME MAKE ME SICK TOO.
STOP
NUMBER TWO: NEVER FORGET TO PRAY FOR MY MOMMA, 'CAUSE SHE WAS THE BEST AND PRETTIEST LADY GOD EVER MADE.
AND NUMBER ONE: NEVER, *EVER* LEAVE THE WOODS.
CLOMP!

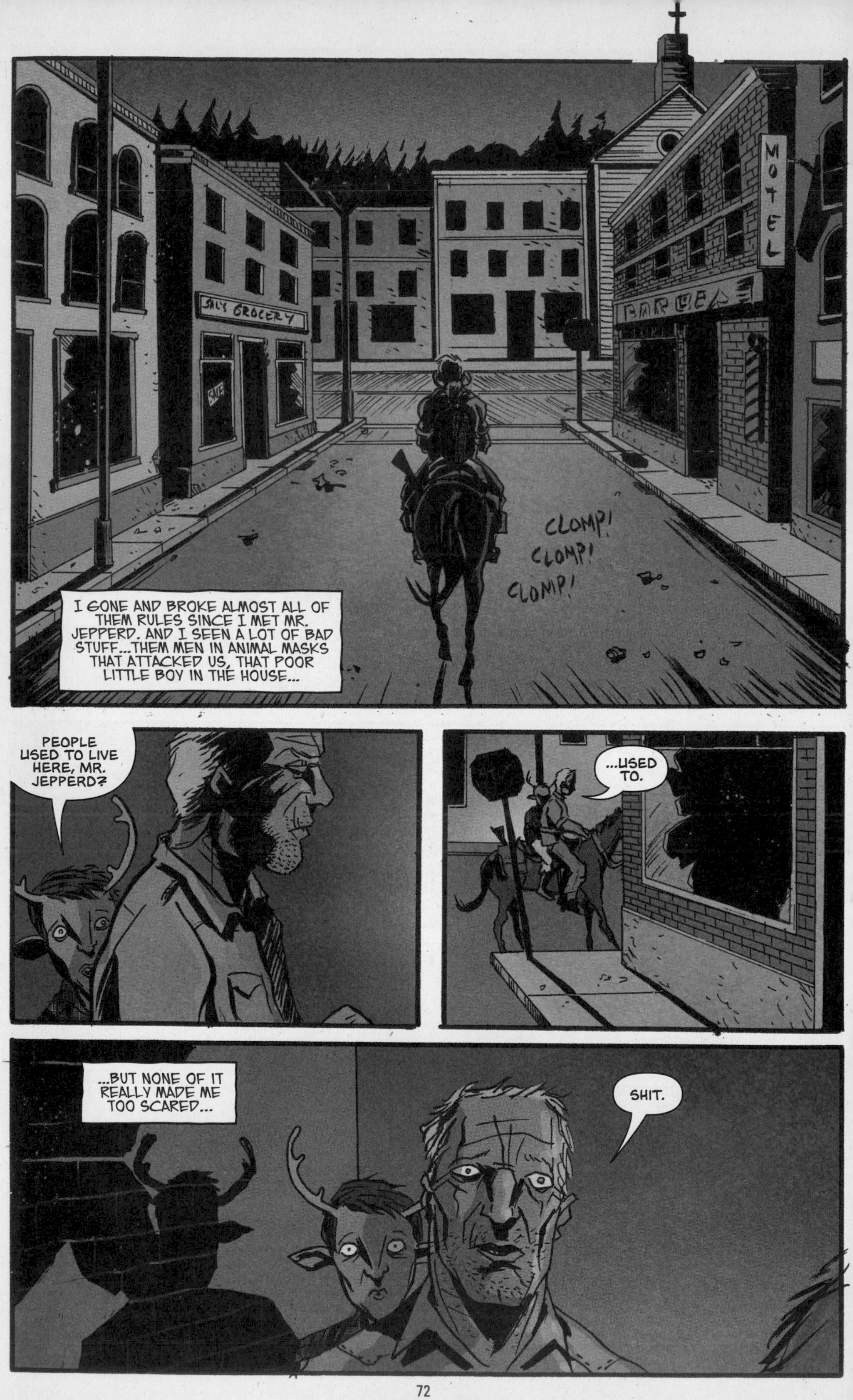
SAL'S GROCERY
SALE
MOTEL
CLOMP! CLOMP! CLOMP!
I GONE AND BROKE ALMOST ALL OF THEM RULES SINCE I MET MR. JEPPERD. AND I SEEN A LOT OF BAD STUFF...THEM MEN IN ANIMAL MASKS THAT ATTACKED US, THAT POOR LITTLE BOY IN THE HOUSE...
PEOPLE USED TO LIVE HERE, MR. JEPPERD?
...USED TO.
...BUT NONE OF IT REALLY MADE ME TOO SCARED...
SHIT.

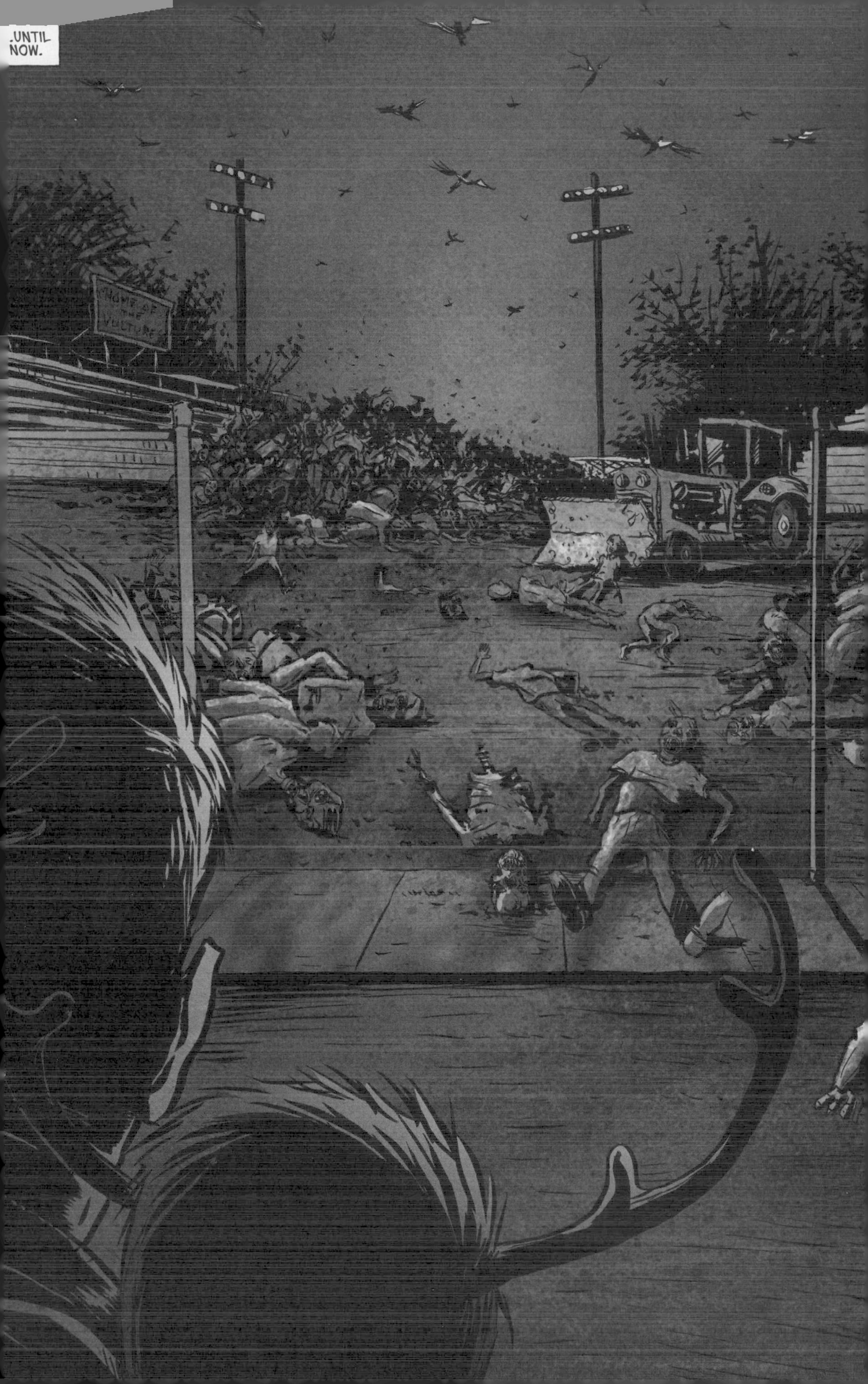
.UNTIL NOW.
HOME OF THE VULTURES

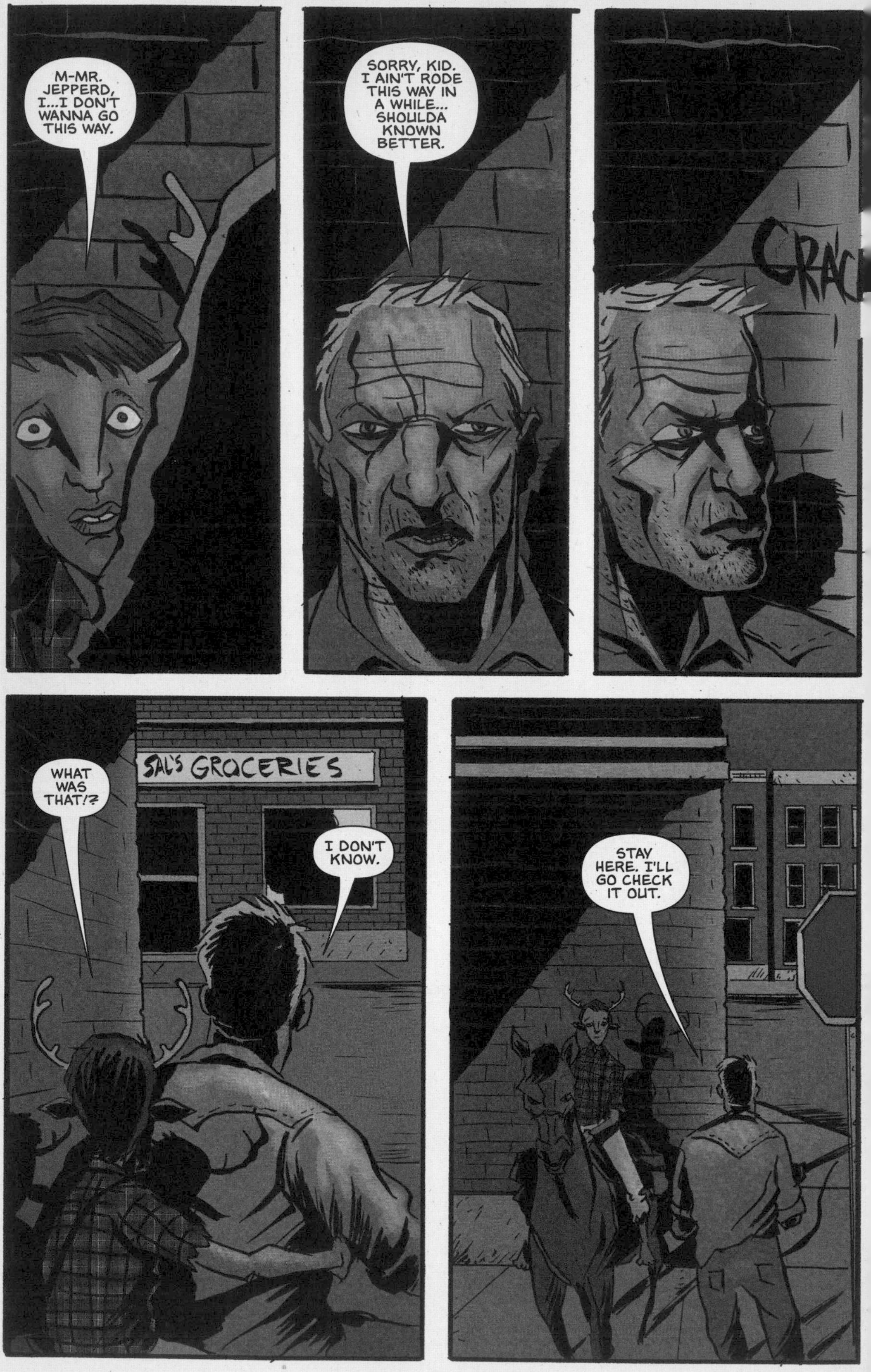
M-MR. JEPPERD, I...I DON'T WANNA GO THIS WAY.
SORRY, KID. I AIN'T RODE THIS WAY IN A WHILE... SHOULDA KNOWN BETTER.
CRACK
SAL'S GROCERIES
WHAT WAS THAT!?
I DON'T KNOW.
STAY HERE. I'LL GO CHECK IT OUT.

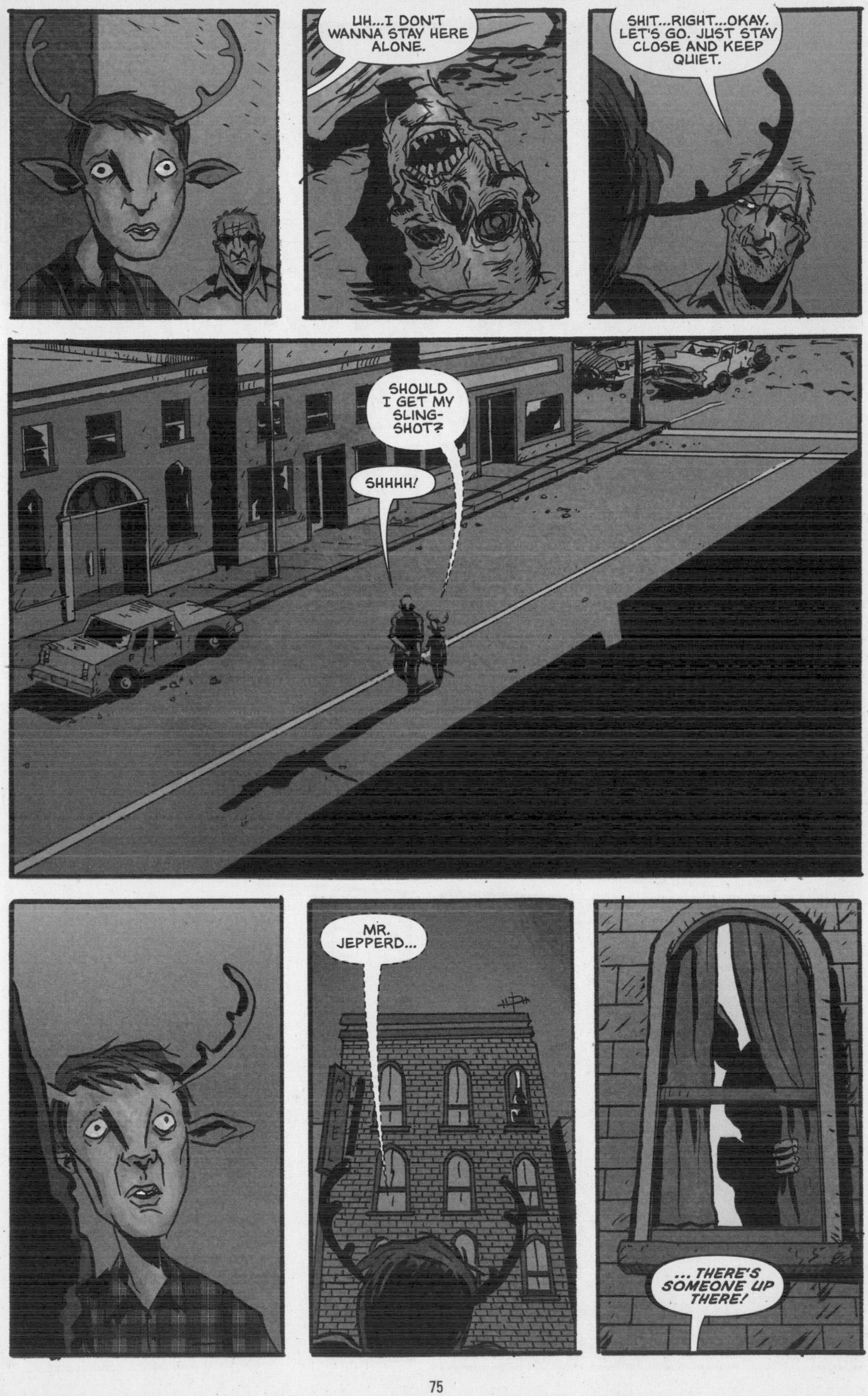
UH...I DON'T WANNA STAY HERE ALONE.
SHIT...RIGHT...OKAY. LET'S GO. JUST STAY CLOSE AND KEEP QUIET.
SHOULD I GET MY SLING-SHOT?
SHHHH!
MR. JEPPERD...
... THERE'S SOMEONE UP THERE!

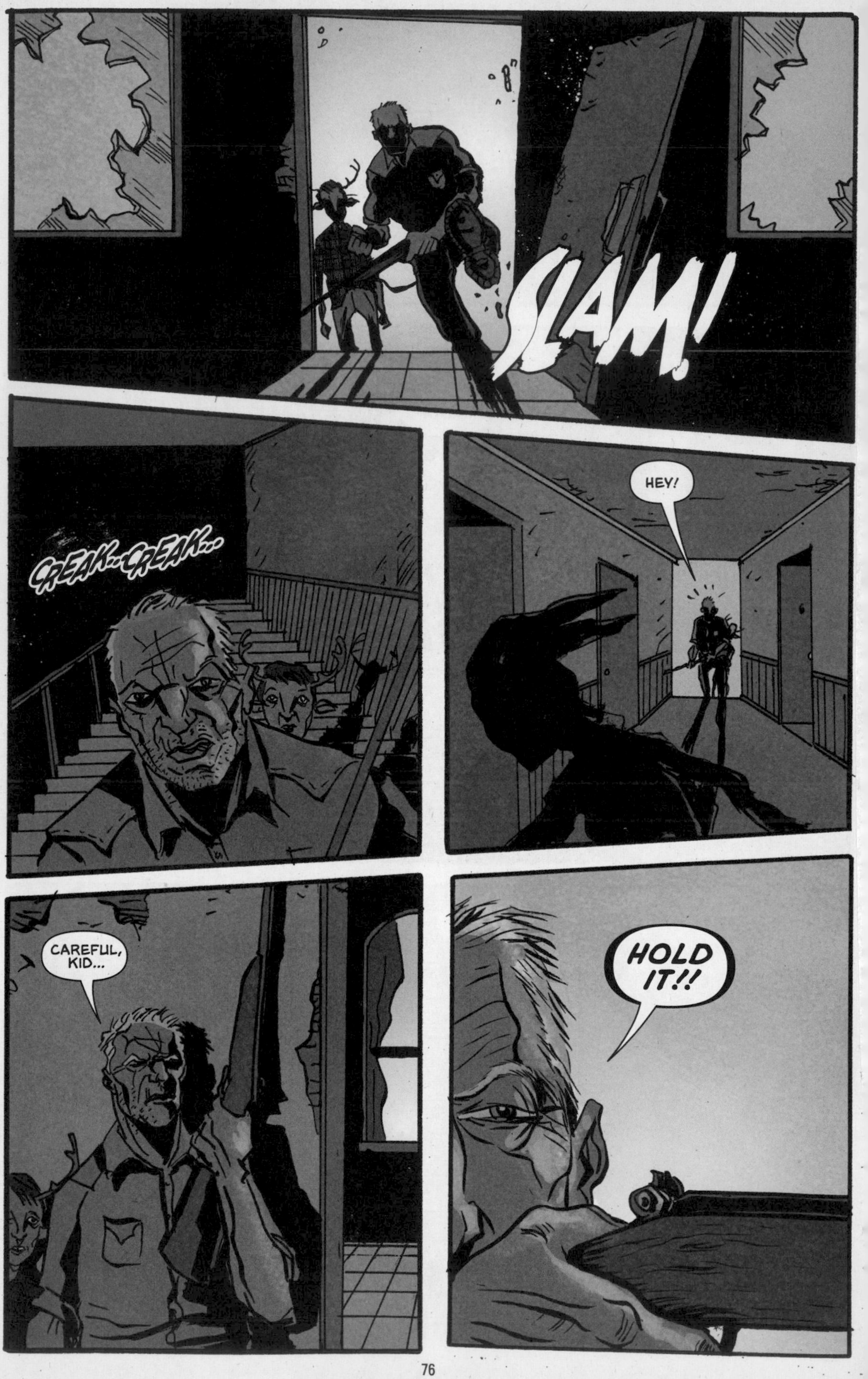
SLAM!
CREAK..CREAK..
HEY!
CAREFUL, KID...
HOLD IT!!

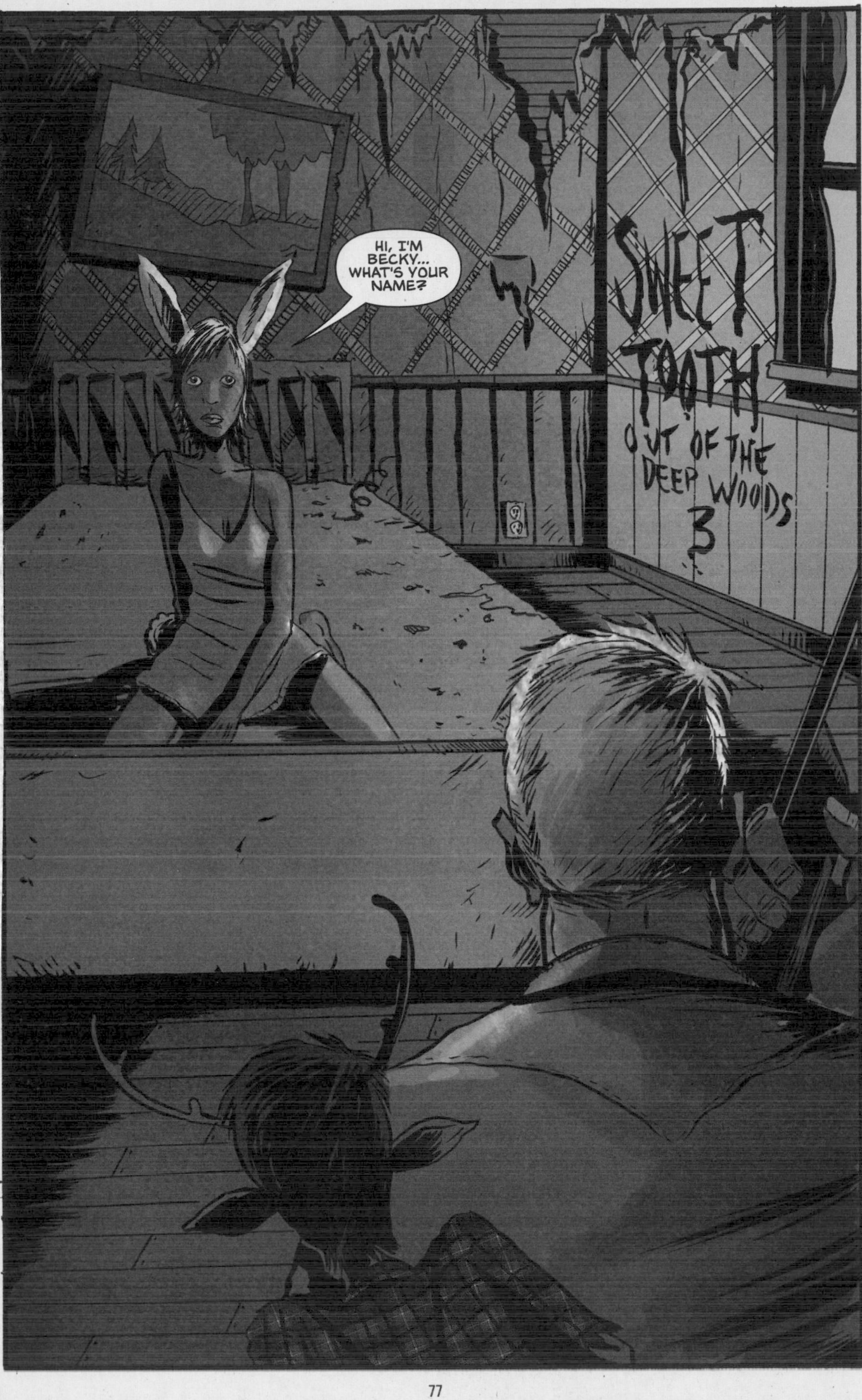
HI, I'M BECKY... WHAT'S YOUR NAME?
SWEET TOOTH
OUT OF THE DEEP WOODS
3

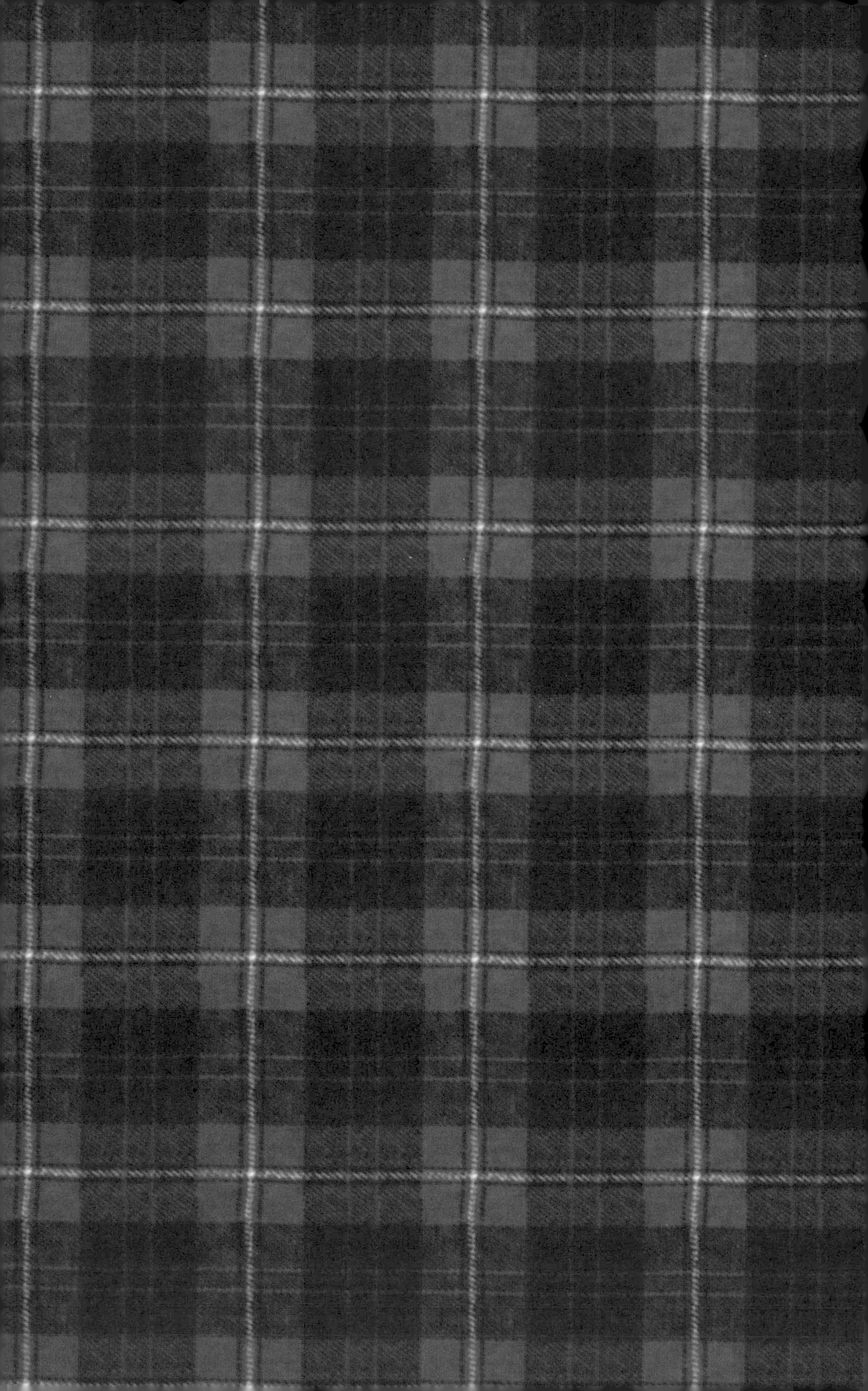

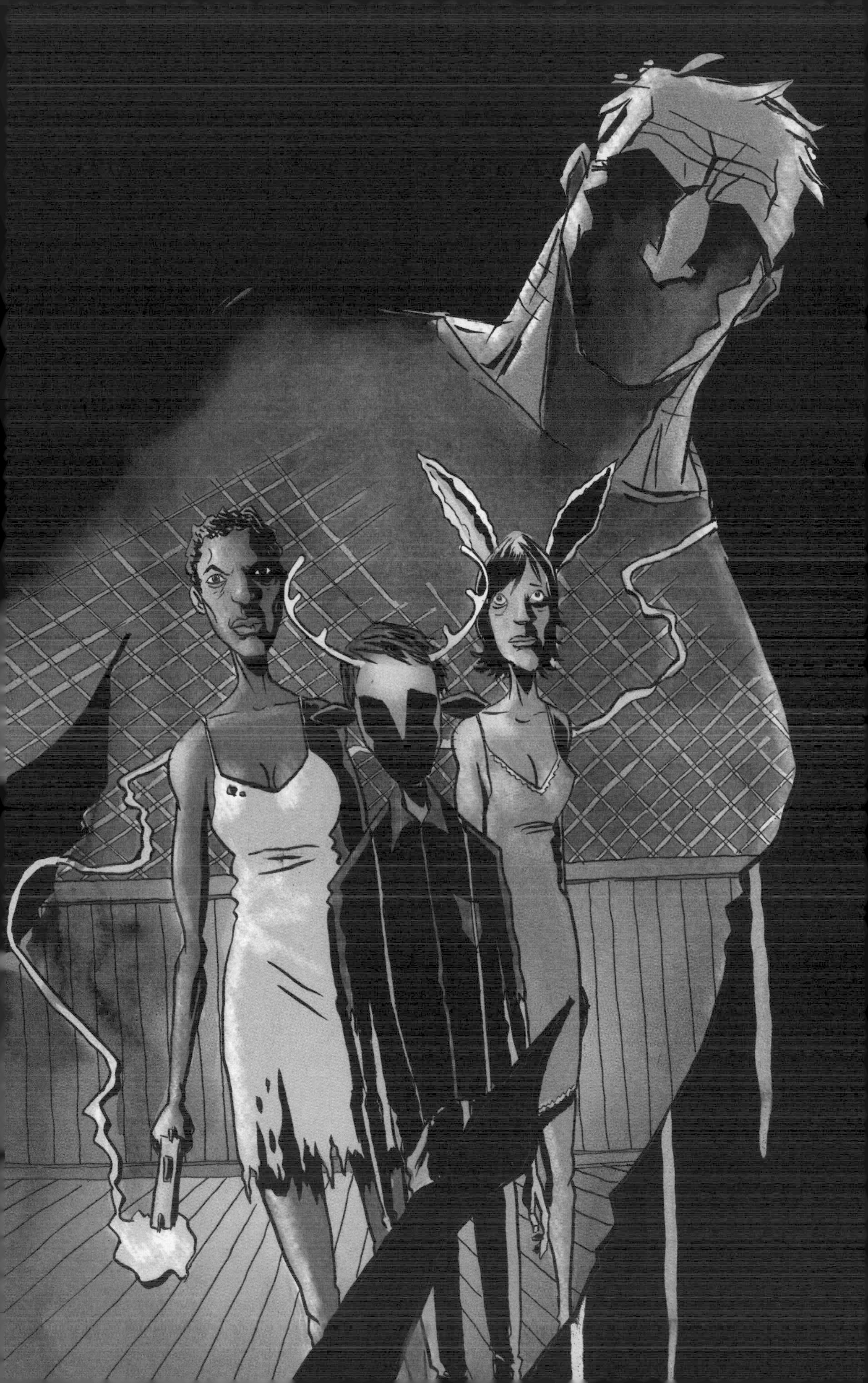

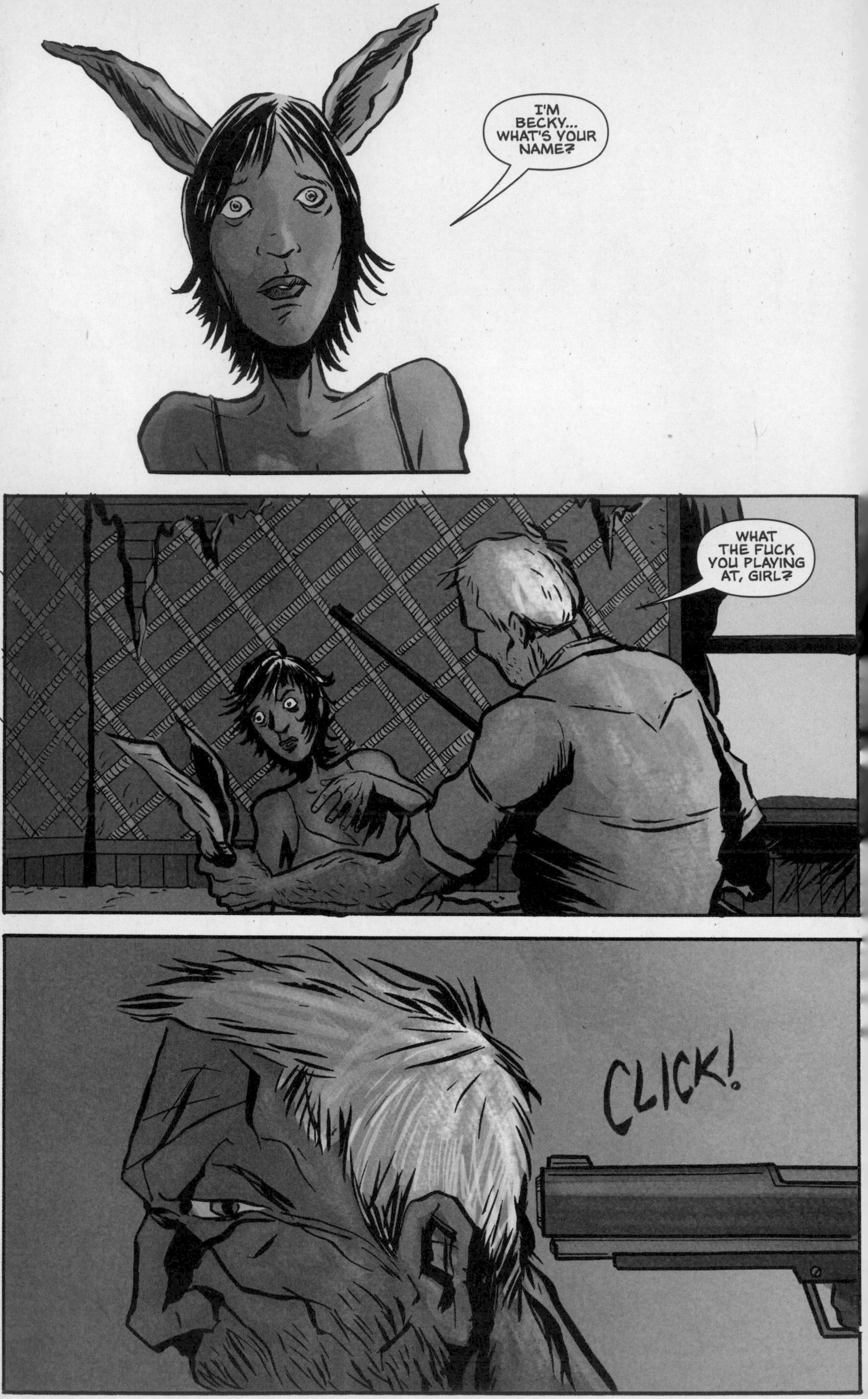
I'M BECKY... WHAT'S YOUR NAME?
WHAT THE FUCK YOU PLAYING AT, GIRL?
CLICK!

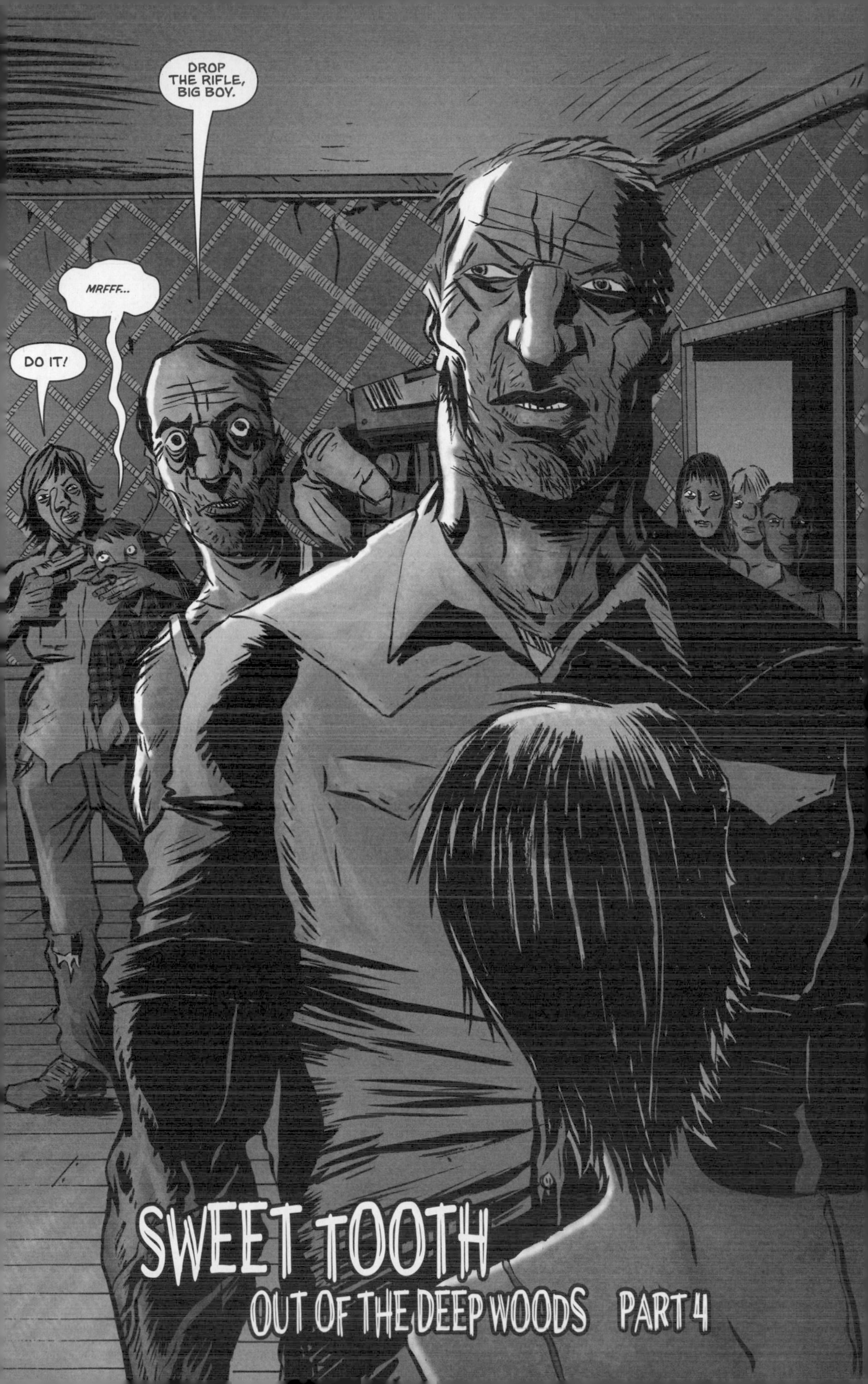
DO IT!
MRFFF...
DROP THE RIFLE, BIG BOY.
SWEET TOOTH
OUT OF THE DEEP WOODS PART 4

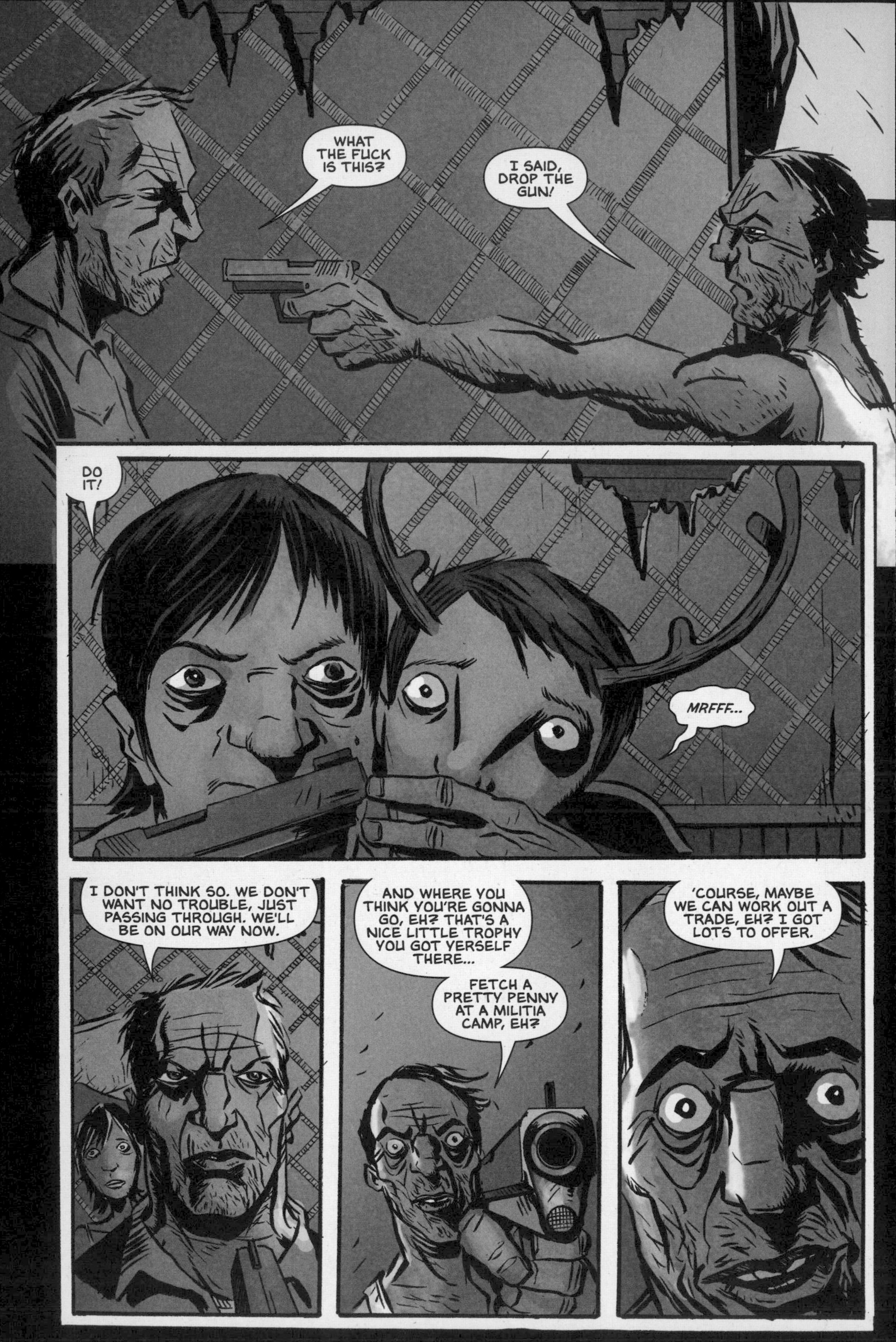
WHAT THE FUCK IS THIS?
I SAID, DROP THE GUN!
DO IT!
MRFFF...
I DON'T THINK SO. WE DON'T WANT NO TROUBLE, JUST PASSING THROUGH. WE'LL BE ON OUR WAY NOW.
AND WHERE YOU THINK YOU'RE GONNA GO, EH? THAT'S A NICE LITTLE TROPHY YOU GOT YERSELF THERE...
FETCH A PRETTY PENNY AT A MILITIA CAMP, EH?
'COURSE, MAYBE WE CAN WORK OUT A TRADE, EH? I GOT LOTS TO OFFER.

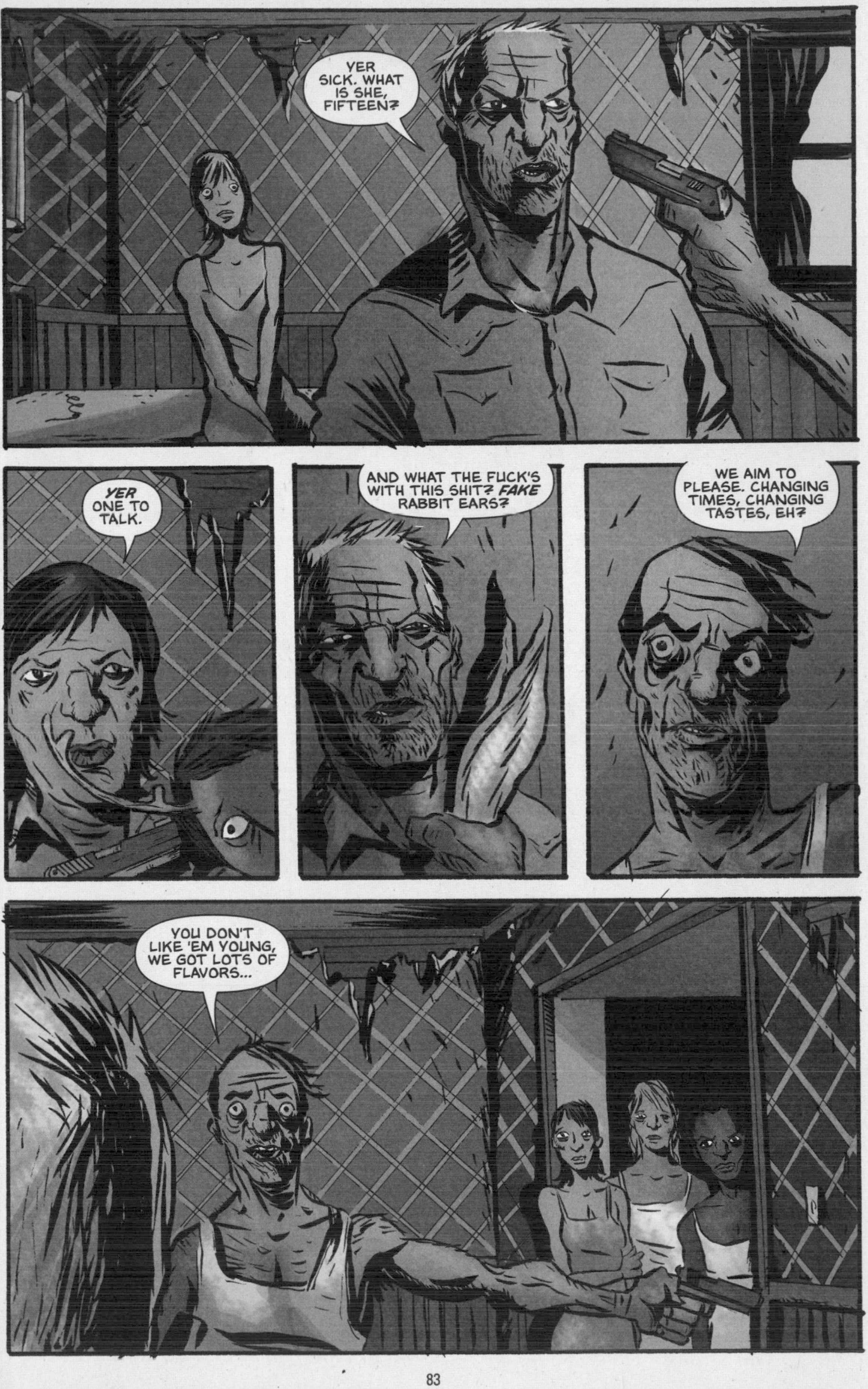
YER SICK. WHAT IS SHE, FIFTEEN?
YER ONE TO TALK.
AND WHAT THE FUCK'S WITH THIS SHIT? *FAKE* RABBIT EARS?
WE AIM TO PLEASE. CHANGING TIMES, CHANGING TASTES, EH?
YOU DON'T LIKE 'EM YOUNG, WE GOT LOTS OF FLAVORS...

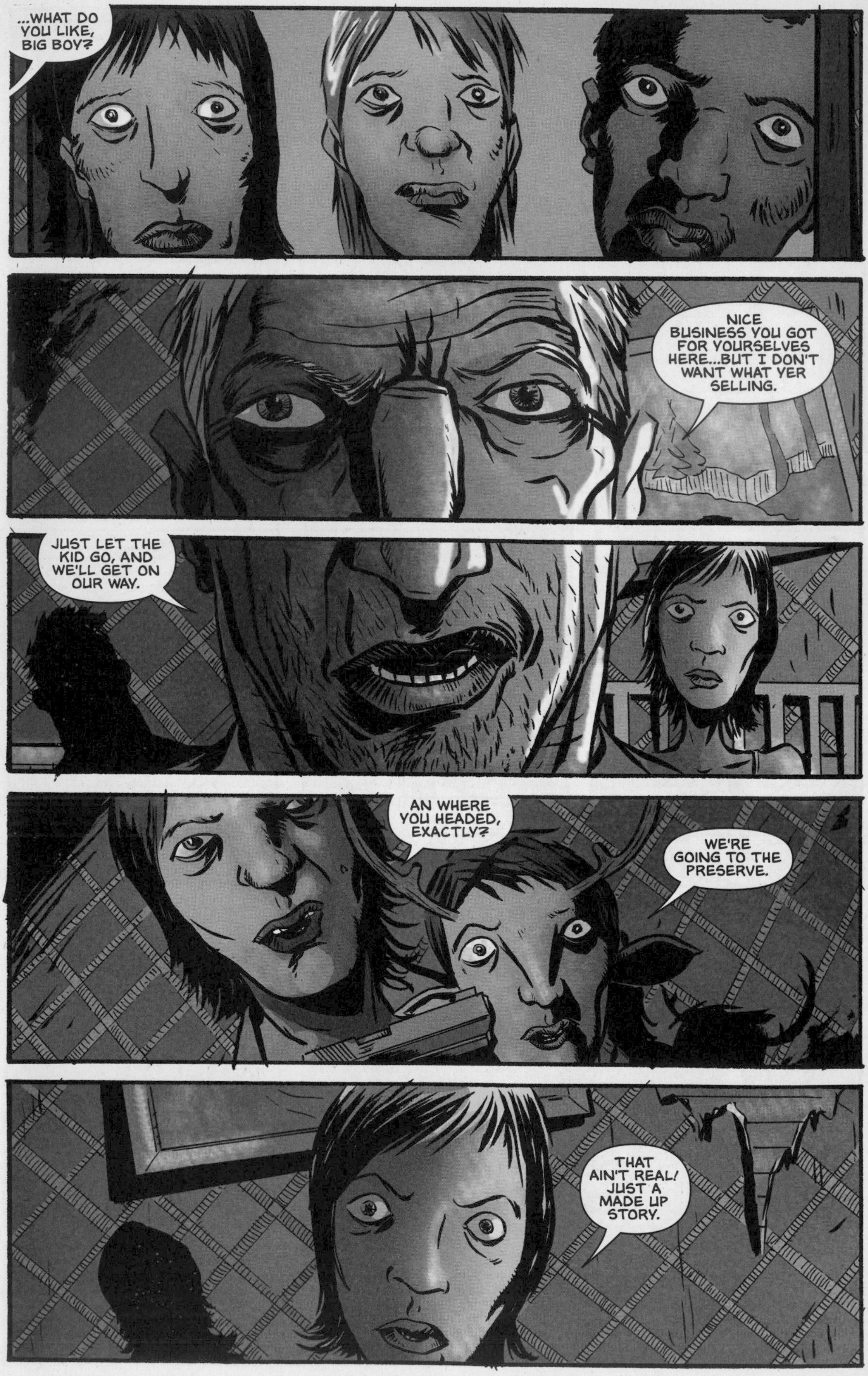
...WHAT DO YOU LIKE, BIG BOY?
NICE BUSINESS YOU GOT FOR YOURSELVES HERE...BUT I DON'T WANT WHAT YER SELLING.
JUST LET THE KID GO, AND WE'LL GET ON OUR WAY.
AN WHERE YOU HEADED, EXACTLY?
WE'RE GOING TO THE PRESERVE.
THAT AIN'T REAL! JUST A MADE UP STORY.

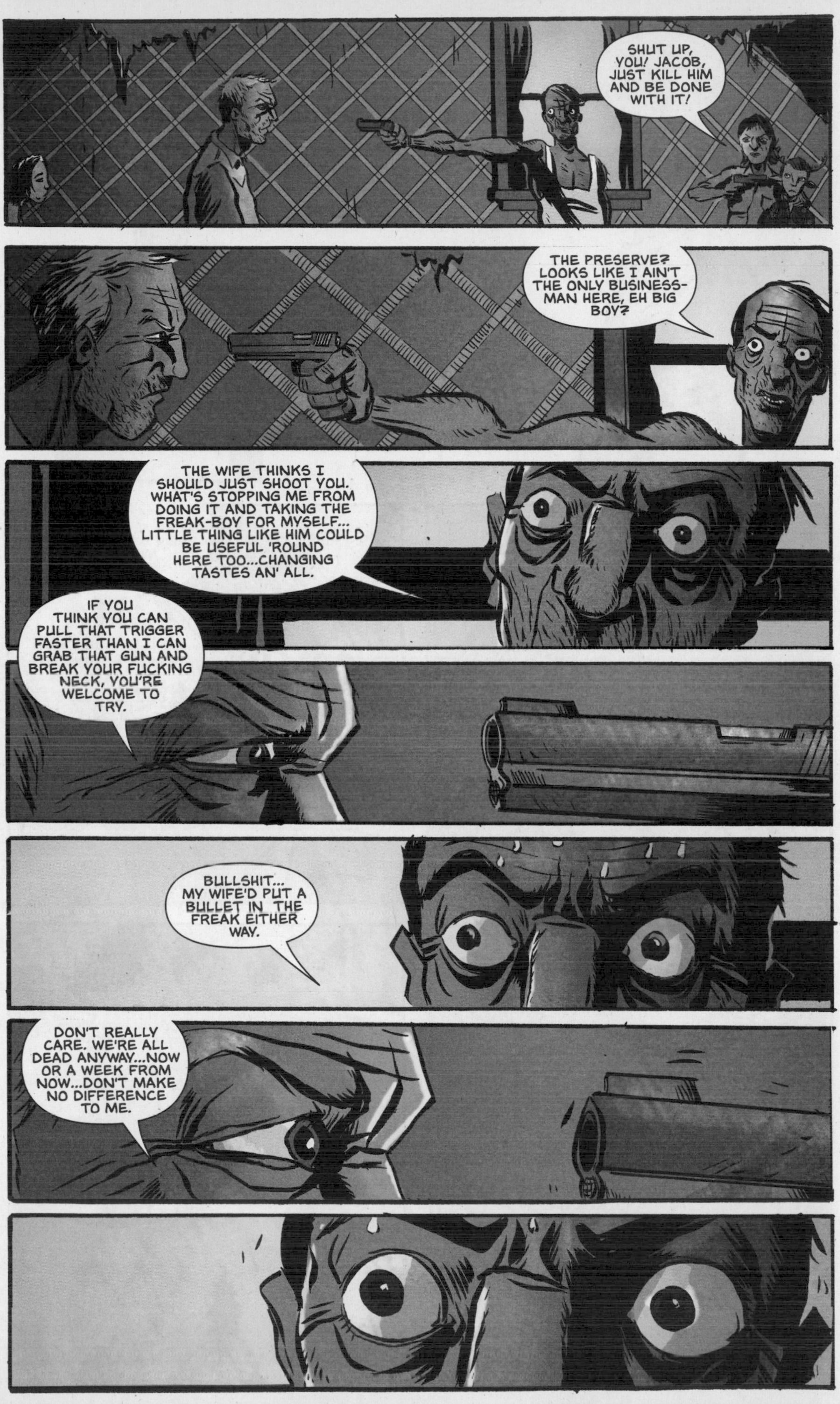
SHUT UP, YOU! JACOB, JUST KILL HIM AND BE DONE WITH IT!
THE PRESERVE? LOOKS LIKE I AIN'T THE ONLY BUSINESS-MAN HERE, EH BIG BOY?
THE WIFE THINKS I SHOULD JUST SHOOT YOU. WHAT'S STOPPING ME FROM DOING IT AND TAKING THE FREAK-BOY FOR MYSELF... LITTLE THING LIKE HIM COULD BE USEFUL 'ROUND HERE TOO...CHANGING TASTES AN' ALL.
IF YOU THINK YOU CAN PULL THAT TRIGGER FASTER THAN I CAN GRAB THAT GUN AND BREAK YOUR FUCKING NECK, YOU'RE WELCOME TO TRY.
BULLSHIT... MY WIFE'D PUT A BULLET IN THE FREAK EITHER WAY.
DON'T REALLY CARE. WE'RE ALL DEAD ANYWAY...NOW OR A WEEK FROM NOW...DON'T MAKE NO DIFFERENCE TO ME.

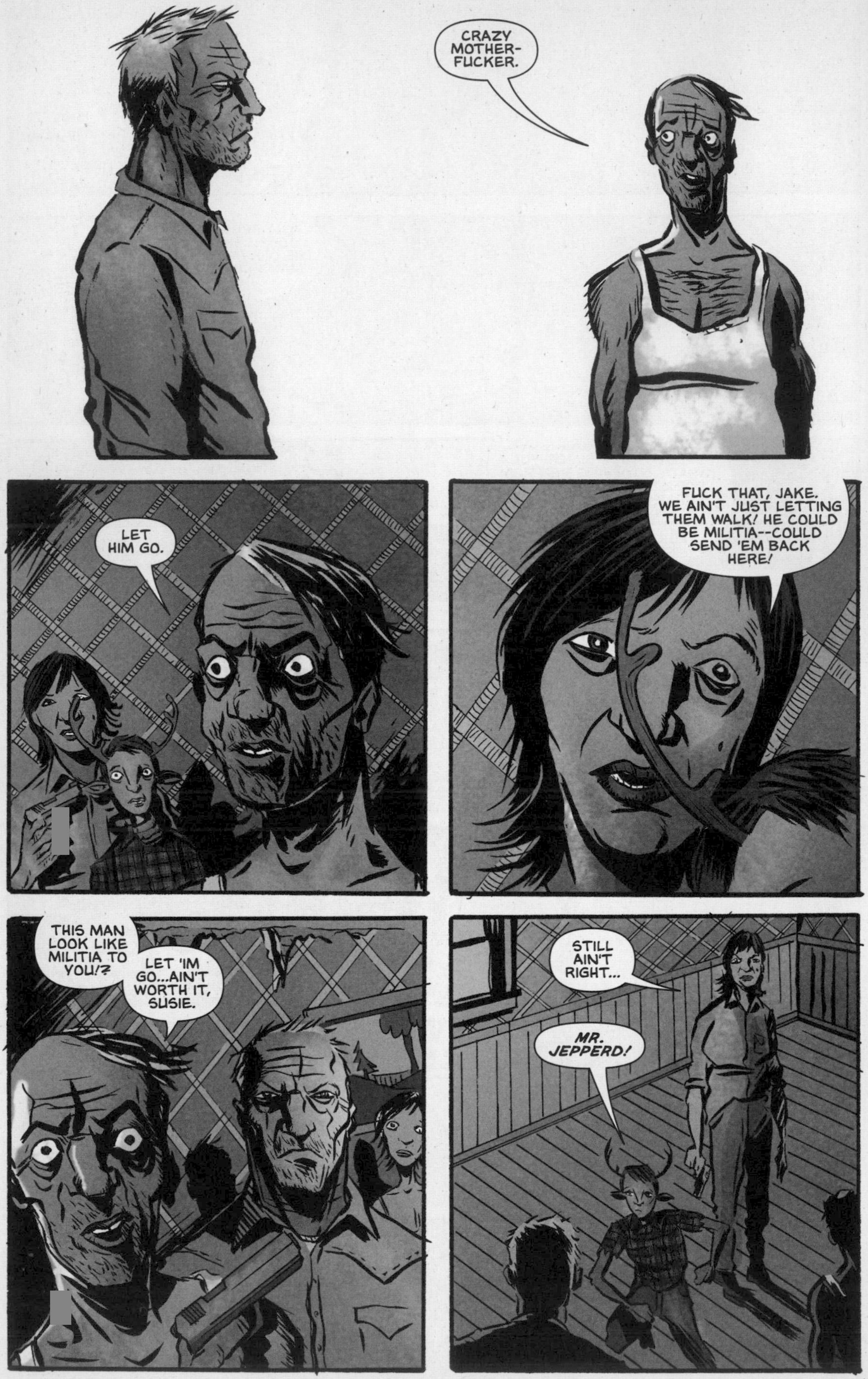
CRAZY MOTHER-FUCKER.
LET HIM GO.
FUCK THAT, JAKE. WE AIN'T JUST LETTING THEM WALK! HE COULD BE MILITIA--COULD SEND 'EM BACK HERE!
THIS MAN LOOK LIKE MILITIA TO YOU!?
LET 'IM GO...AIN'T WORTH IT, SUSIE.
STILL AIN'T RIGHT...
MR. JEPPERD!

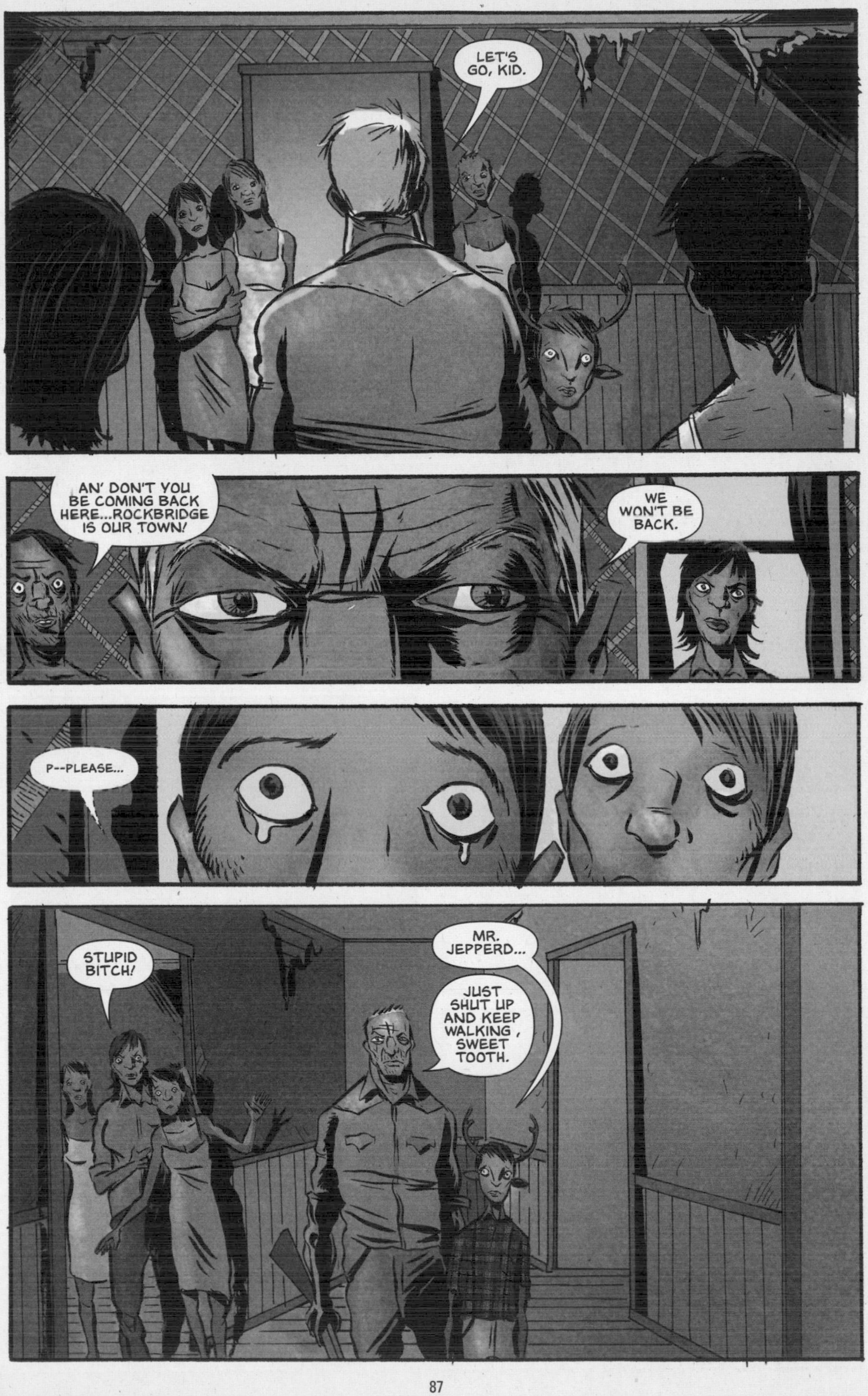
LET'S GO, KID.
AN' DON'T YOU BE COMING BACK HERE...ROCKBRIDGE IS OUR TOWN!
WE WON'T BE BACK.
P--PLEASE...
STUPID BITCH!
MR. JEPPERD...
JUST SHUT UP AND KEEP WALKING, SWEET TOOTH.

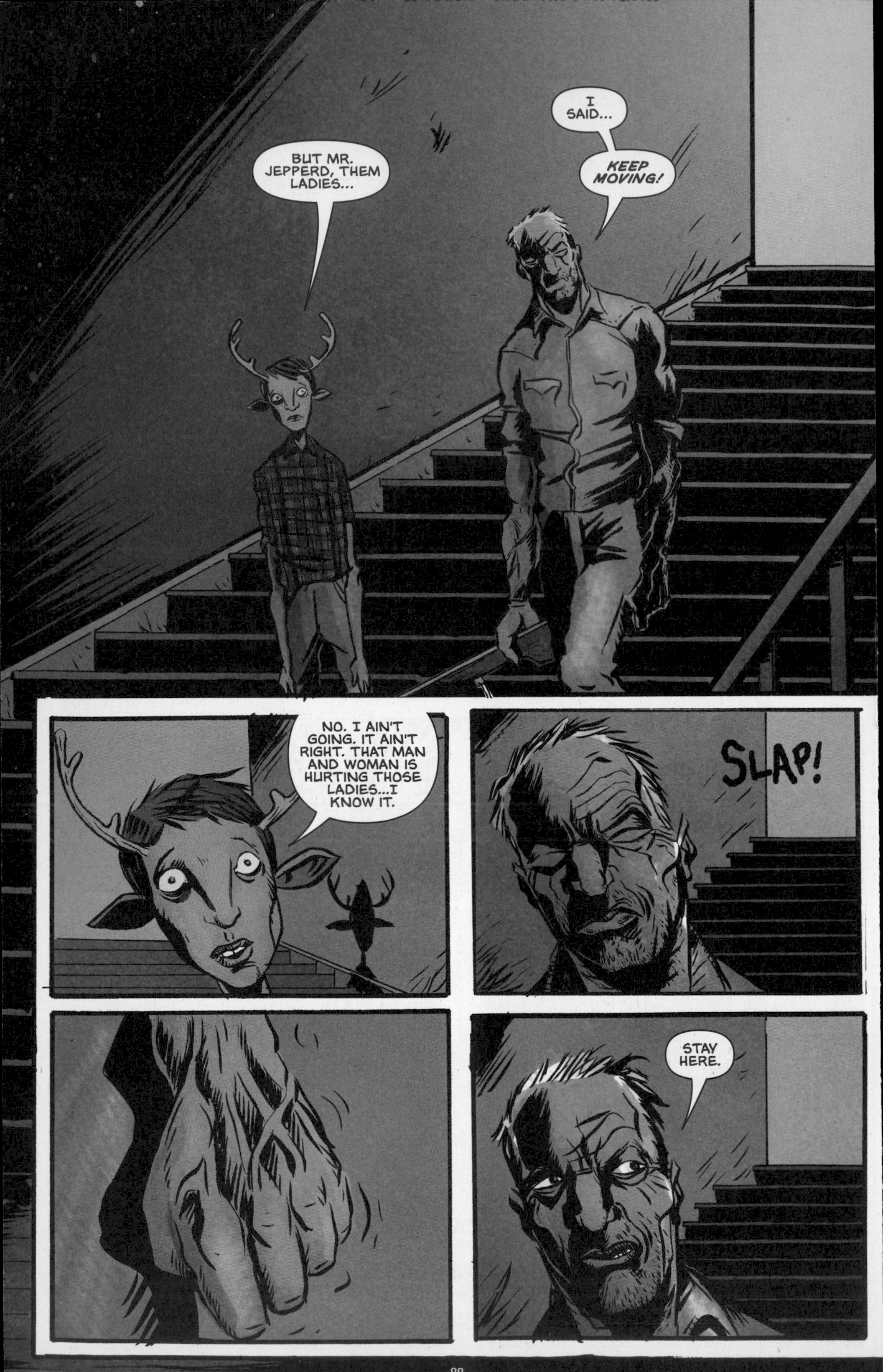
BUT MR. JEPPERD, THEM LADIES...
I SAID...
KEEP MOVING!
NO. I AIN'T GOING. IT AIN'T RIGHT. THAT MAN AND WOMAN IS HURTING THOSE LADIES...I KNOW IT.
SLAP!
STAY HERE.

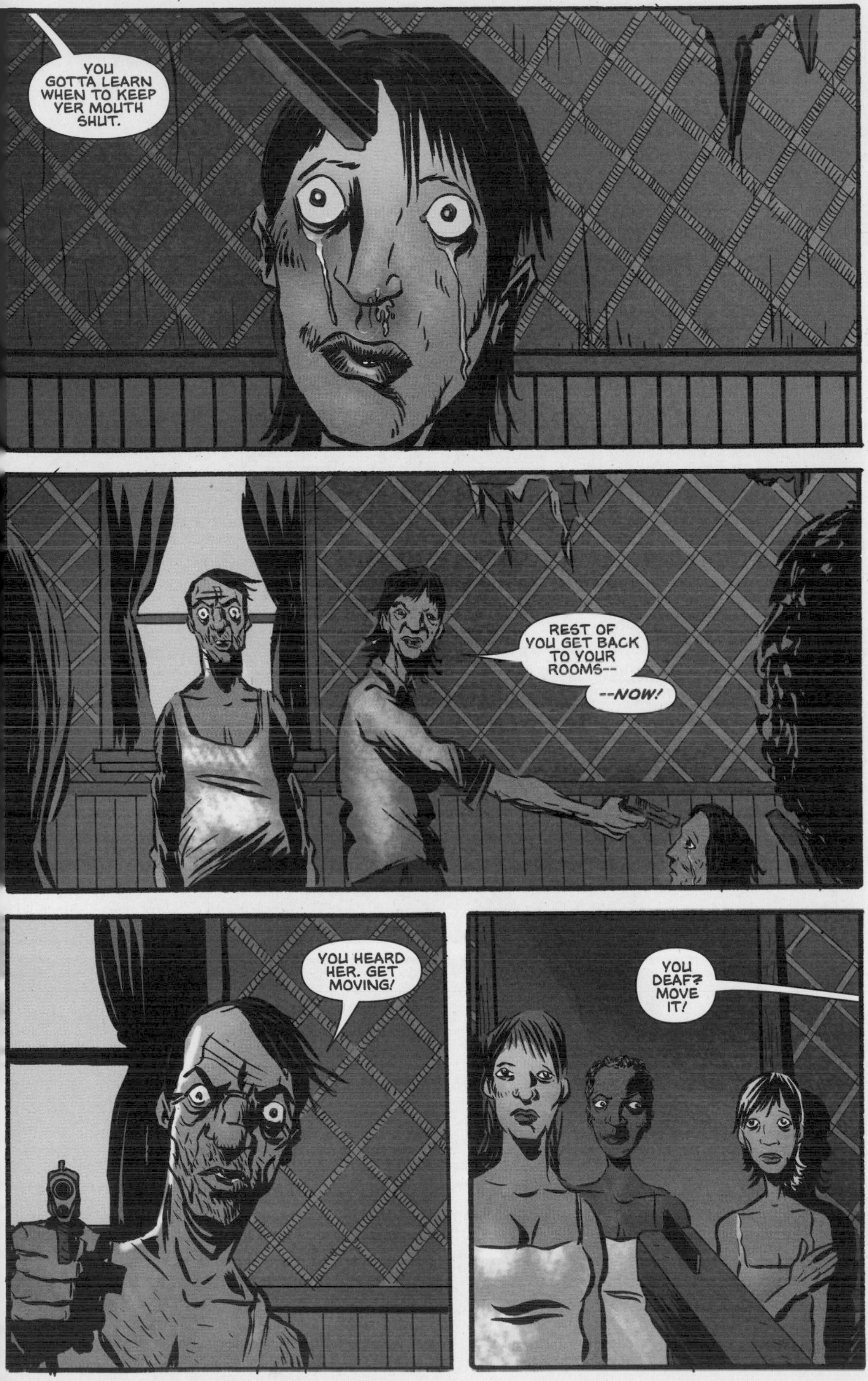
YOU GOTTA LEARN WHEN TO KEEP YER MOUTH SHUT.
REST OF YOU GET BACK TO YOUR ROOMS--
--NOW!
YOU HEARD HER. GET MOVING!
YOU DEAF? MOVE IT!

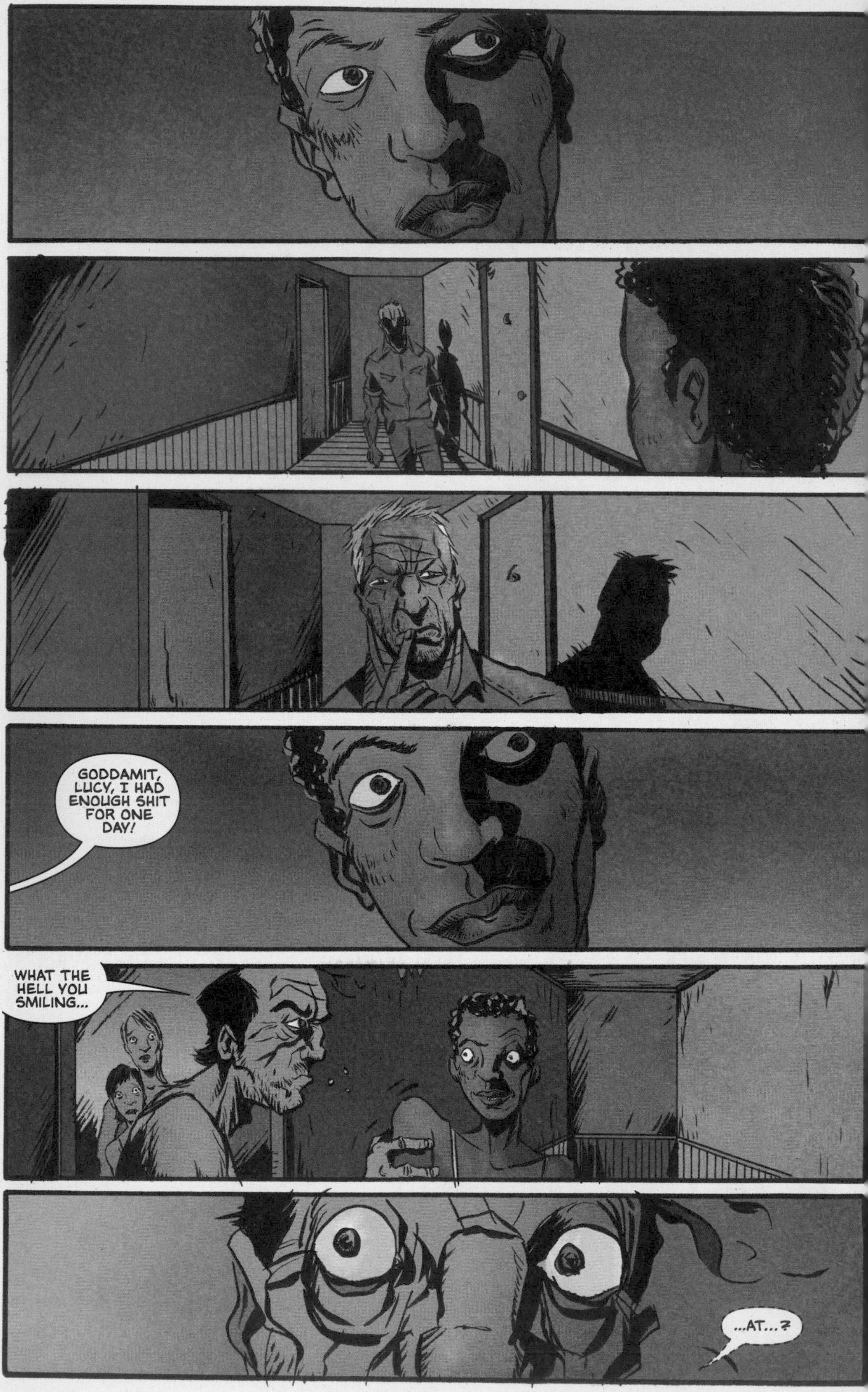
GODDAMIT, LUCY, I HAD ENOUGH SHIT FOR ONE DAY!
WHAT THE HELL YOU SMILING...
...AT...?

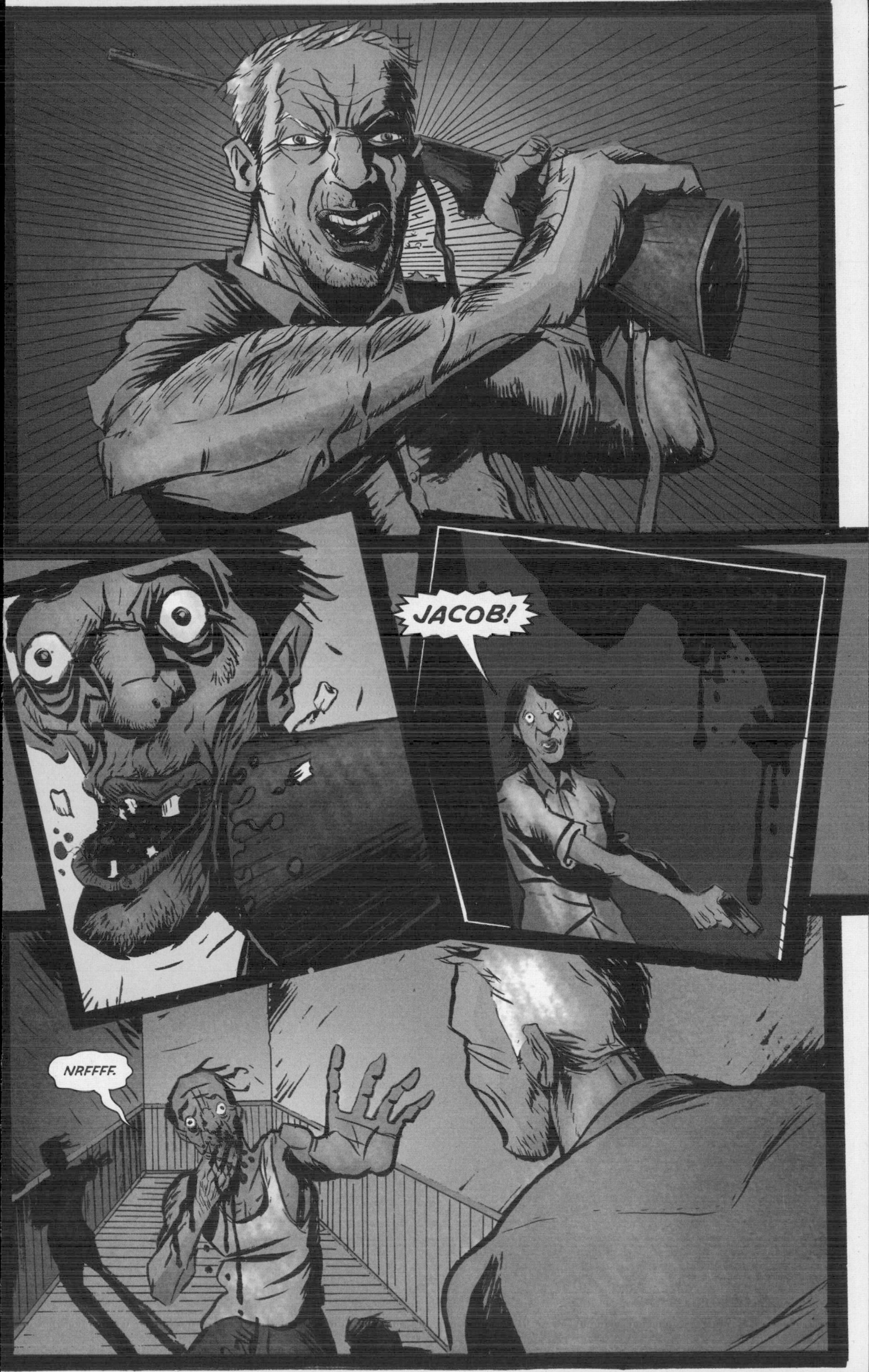
JACOB!
NRFFFF.

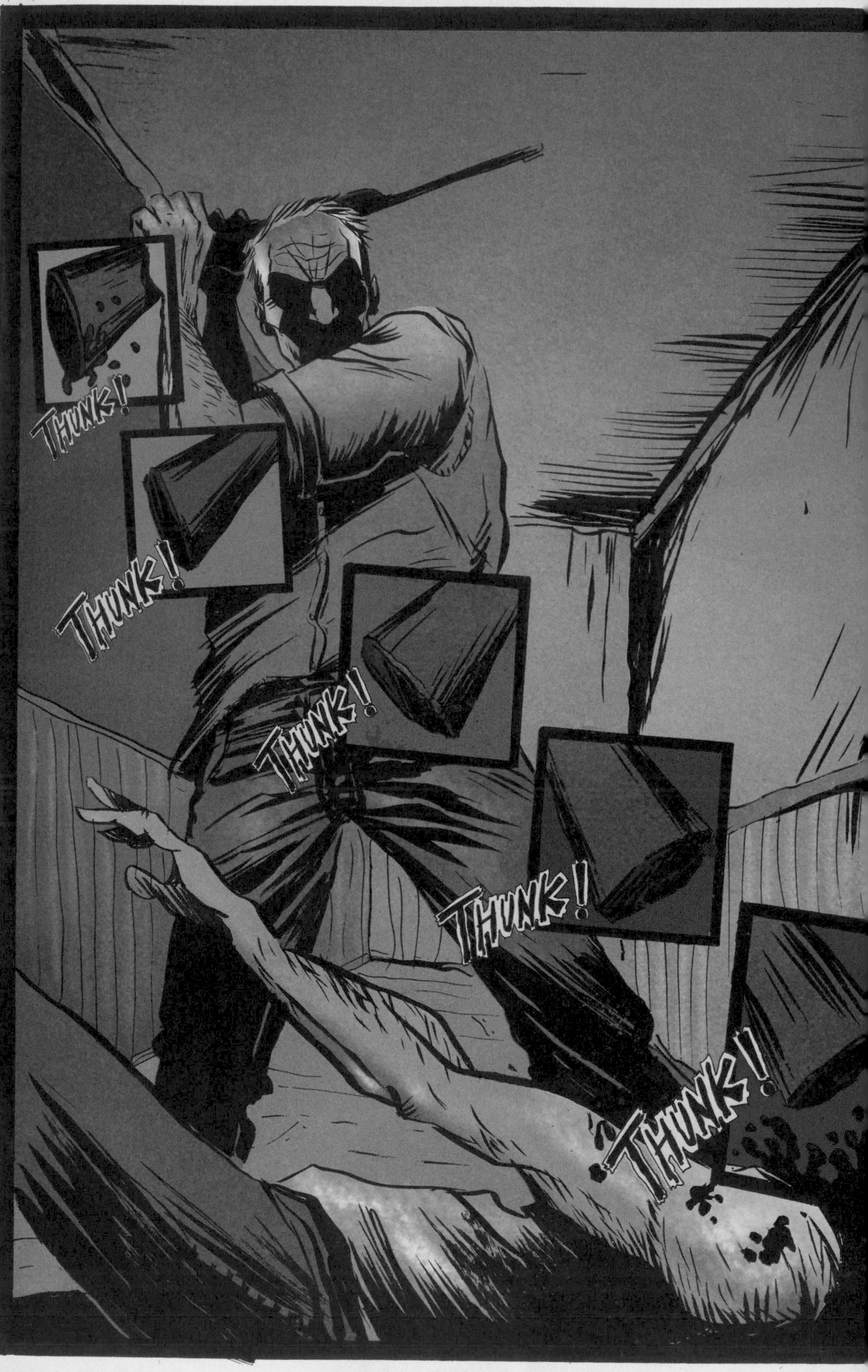
THUNK!
THUNK!
THUNK!
THUNK!
THUNK!

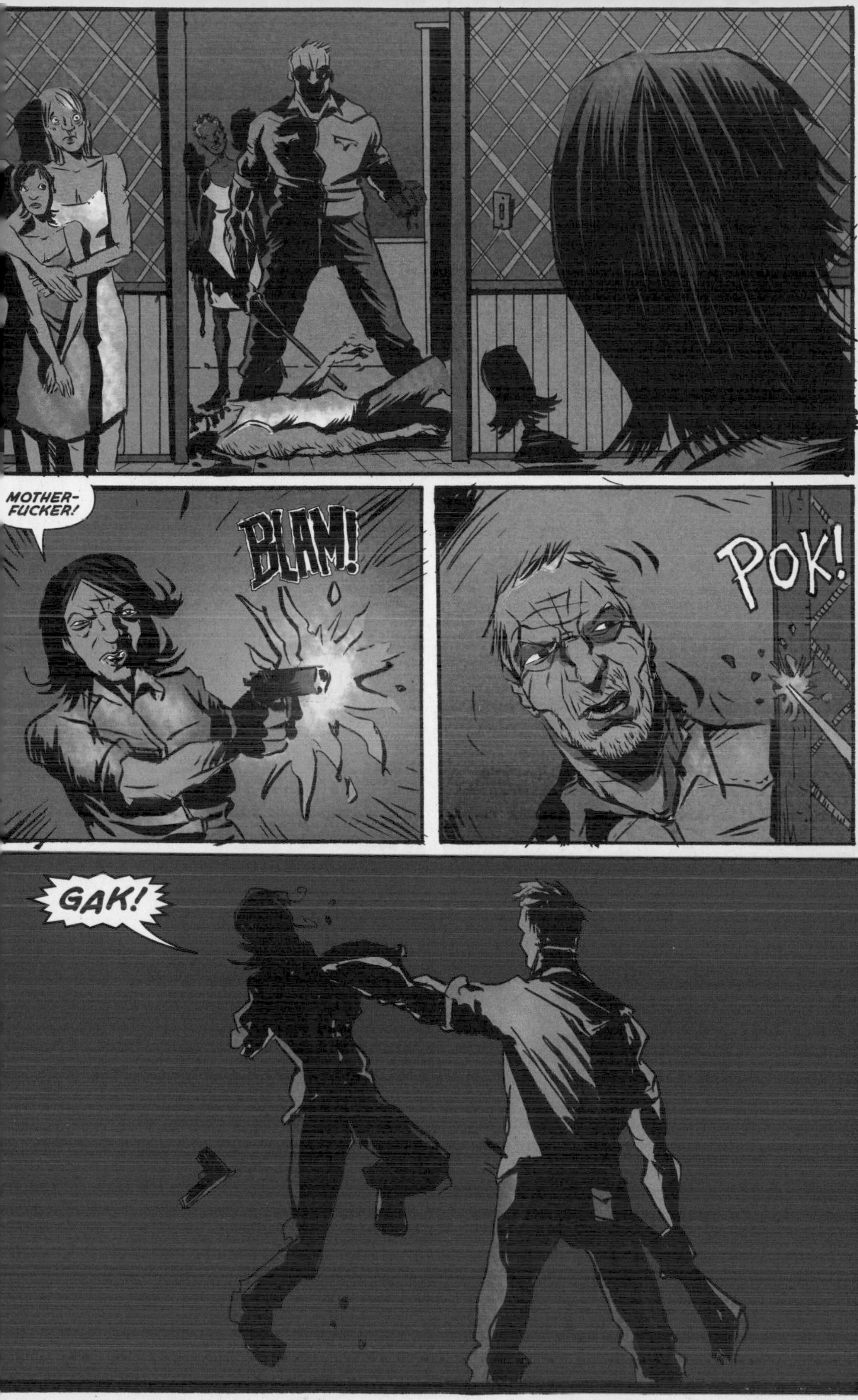
MOTHER-FUCKER!
BLAM!
POK!
GAK!

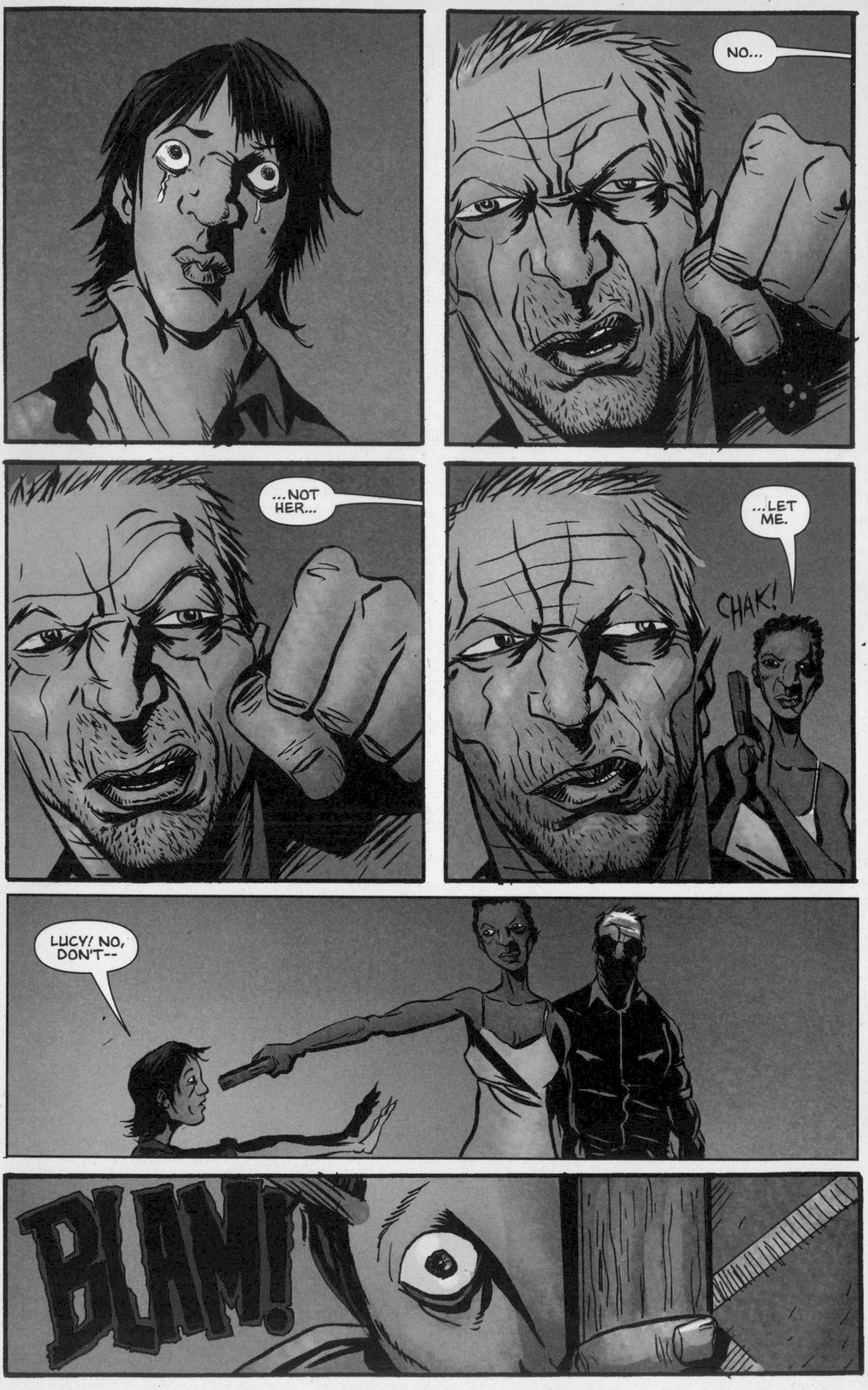
NO...
...NOT HER...
...LET ME.
CHAK!
LUCY! NO, DON'T--
BLAM!

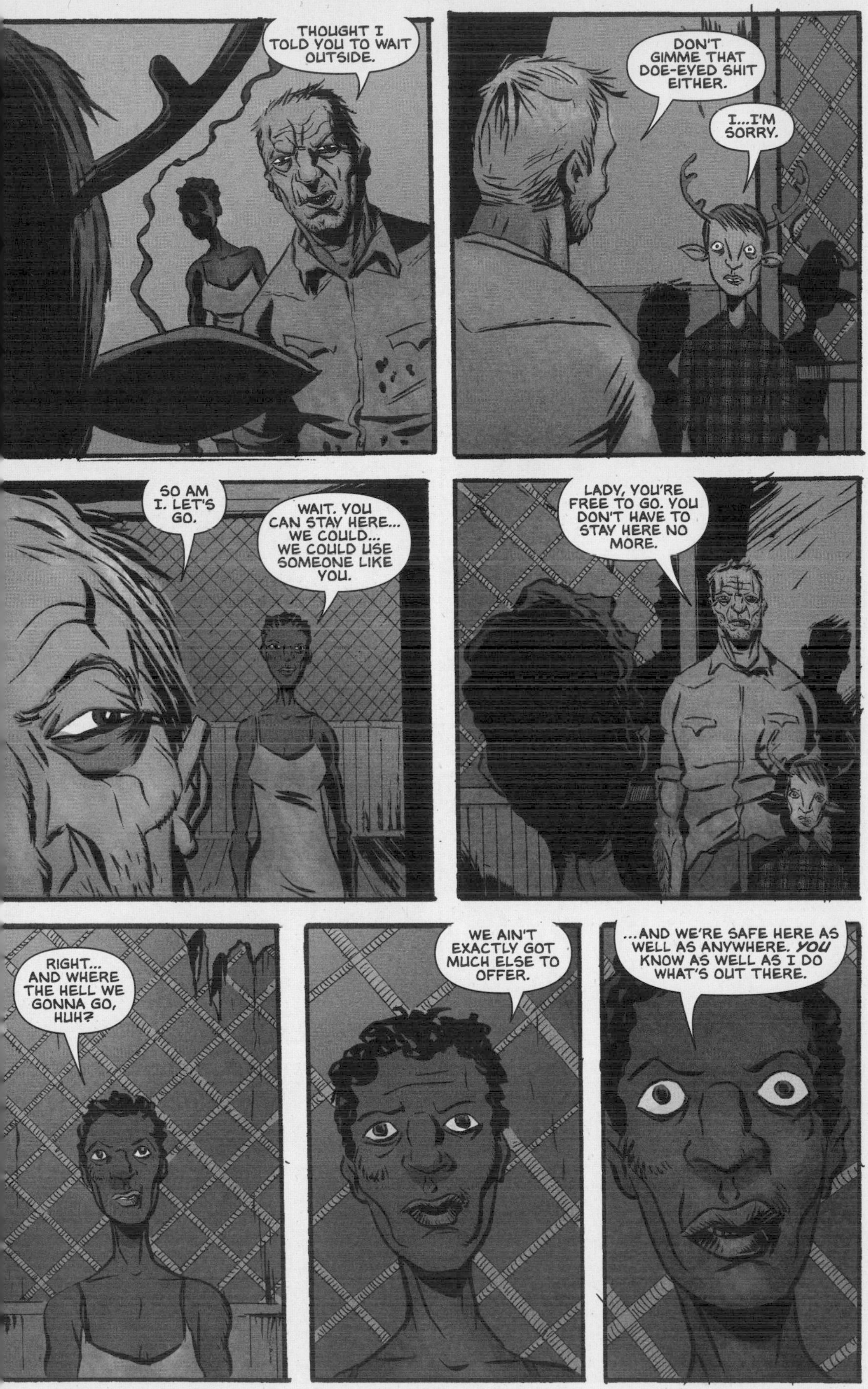
THOUGHT I TOLD YOU TO WAIT OUTSIDE.
DON'T GIMME THAT DOE-EYED SHIT EITHER.
I...I'M SORRY.
SO AM I. LET'S GO.
WAIT. YOU CAN STAY HERE... WE COULD... WE COULD USE SOMEONE LIKE YOU.
LADY, YOU'RE FREE TO GO. YOU DON'T HAVE TO STAY HERE NO MORE.
RIGHT... AND WHERE THE HELL WE GONNA GO, HUH?
WE AIN'T EXACTLY GOT MUCH ELSE TO OFFER.
...AND WE'RE SAFE HERE AS WELL AS ANYWHERE. *YOU* KNOW AS WELL AS I DO WHAT'S OUT THERE.

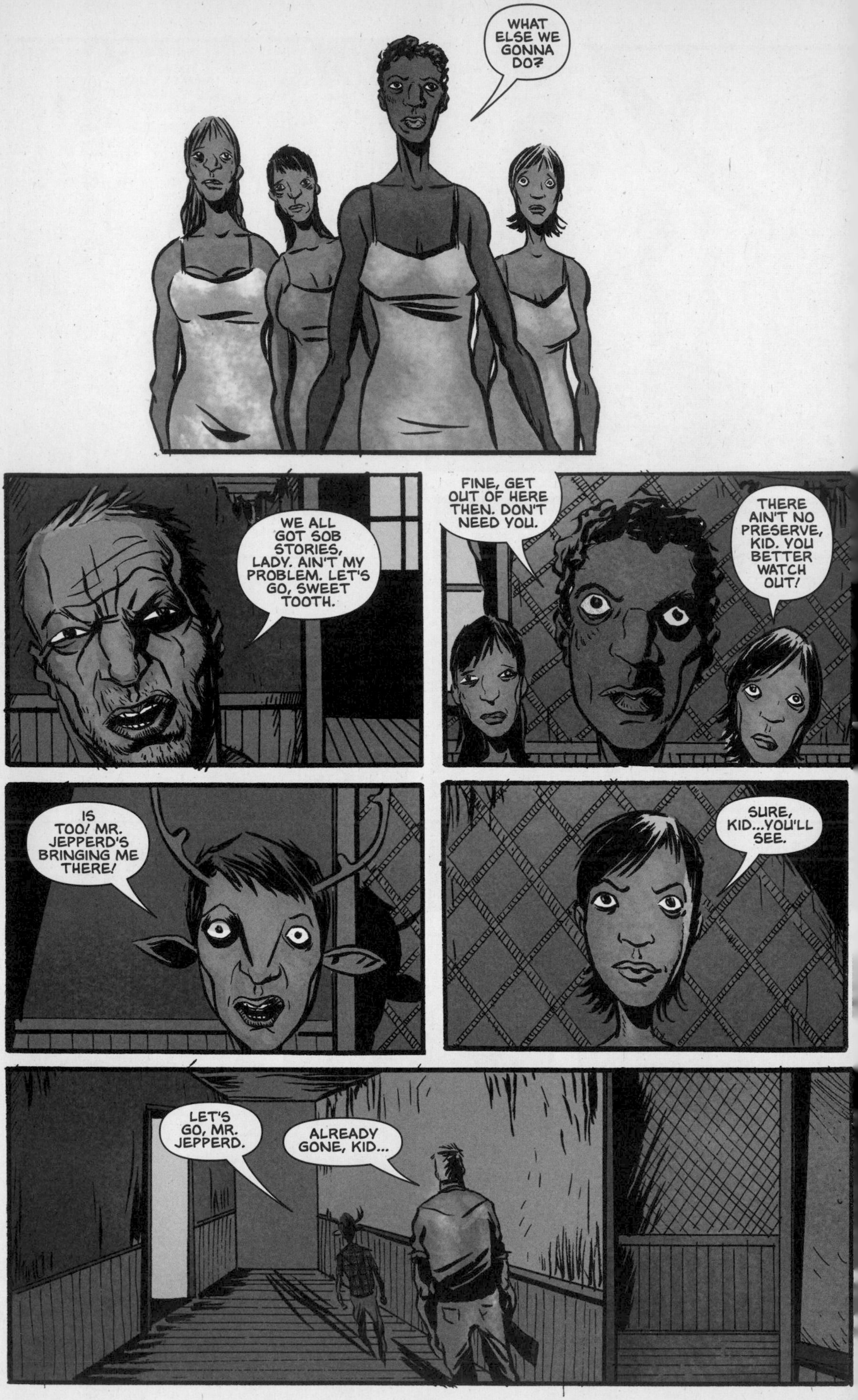
WHAT ELSE WE GONNA DO?
WE ALL GOT SOB STORIES, LADY. AIN'T MY PROBLEM. LET'S GO, SWEET TOOTH.
FINE, GET OUT OF HERE THEN. DON'T NEED YOU.
THERE AIN'T NO PRESERVE, KID. YOU BETTER WATCH OUT!
IS TOO! MR. JEPPERD'S BRINGING ME THERE!
SURE, KID...YOU'LL SEE.
LET'S GO, MR. JEPPERD.
ALREADY GONE, KID...

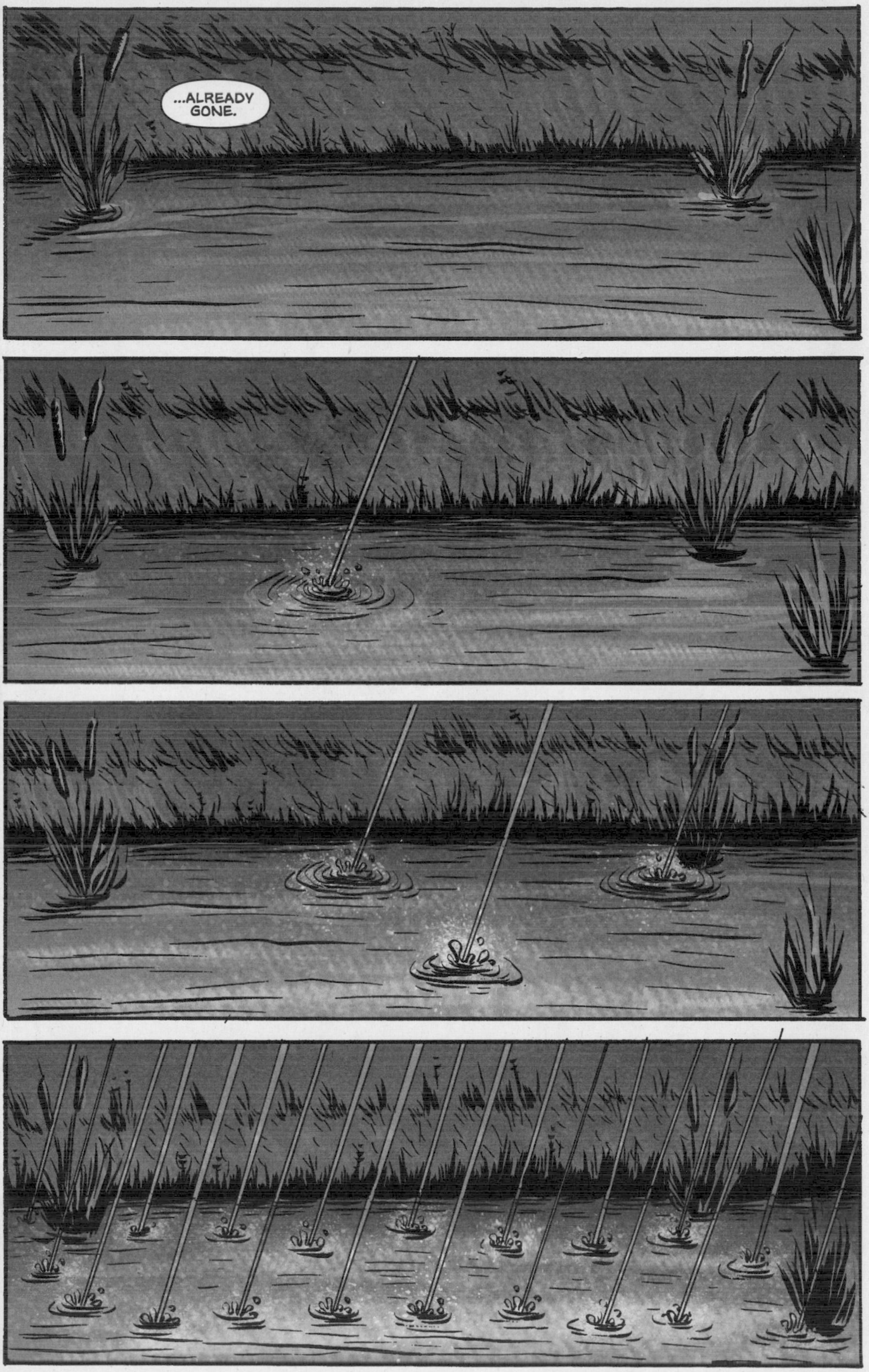
...ALREADY GONE.

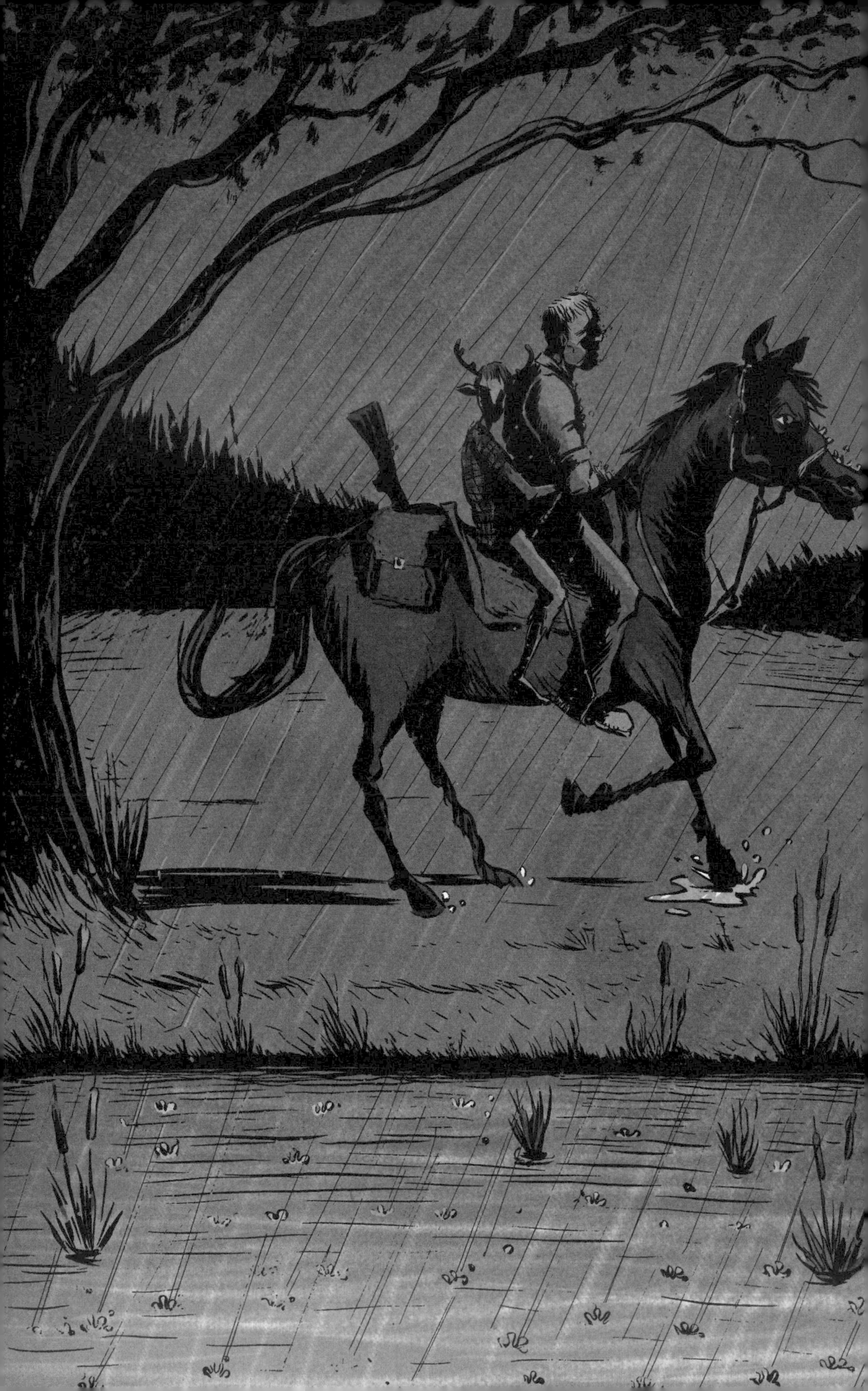

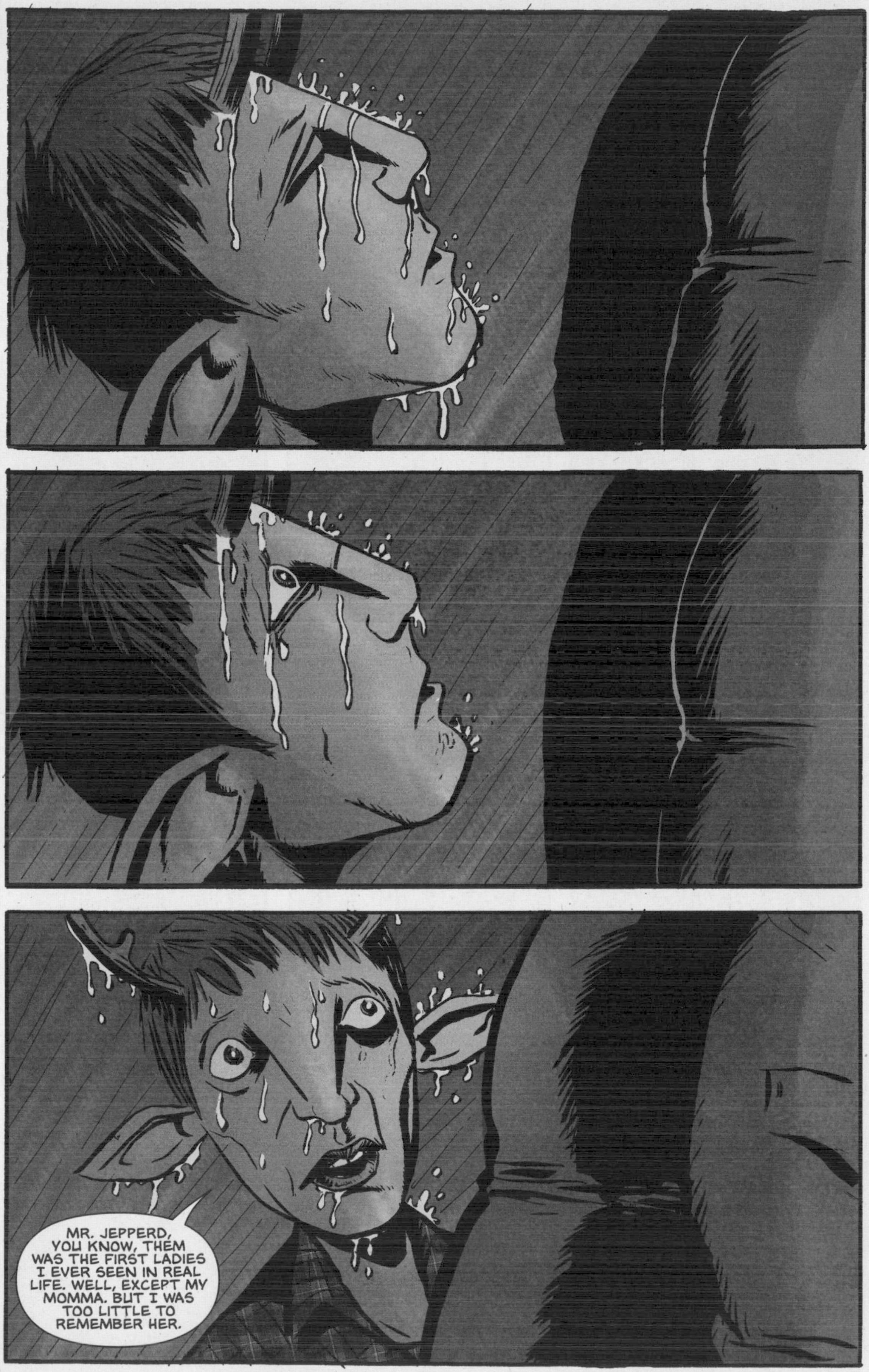
MR. JEPPERD, YOU KNOW, THEM WAS THE FIRST LADIES I EVER SEEN IN REAL LIFE. WELL, EXCEPT MY MOMMA. BUT I WAS TOO LITTLE TO REMEMBER HER.

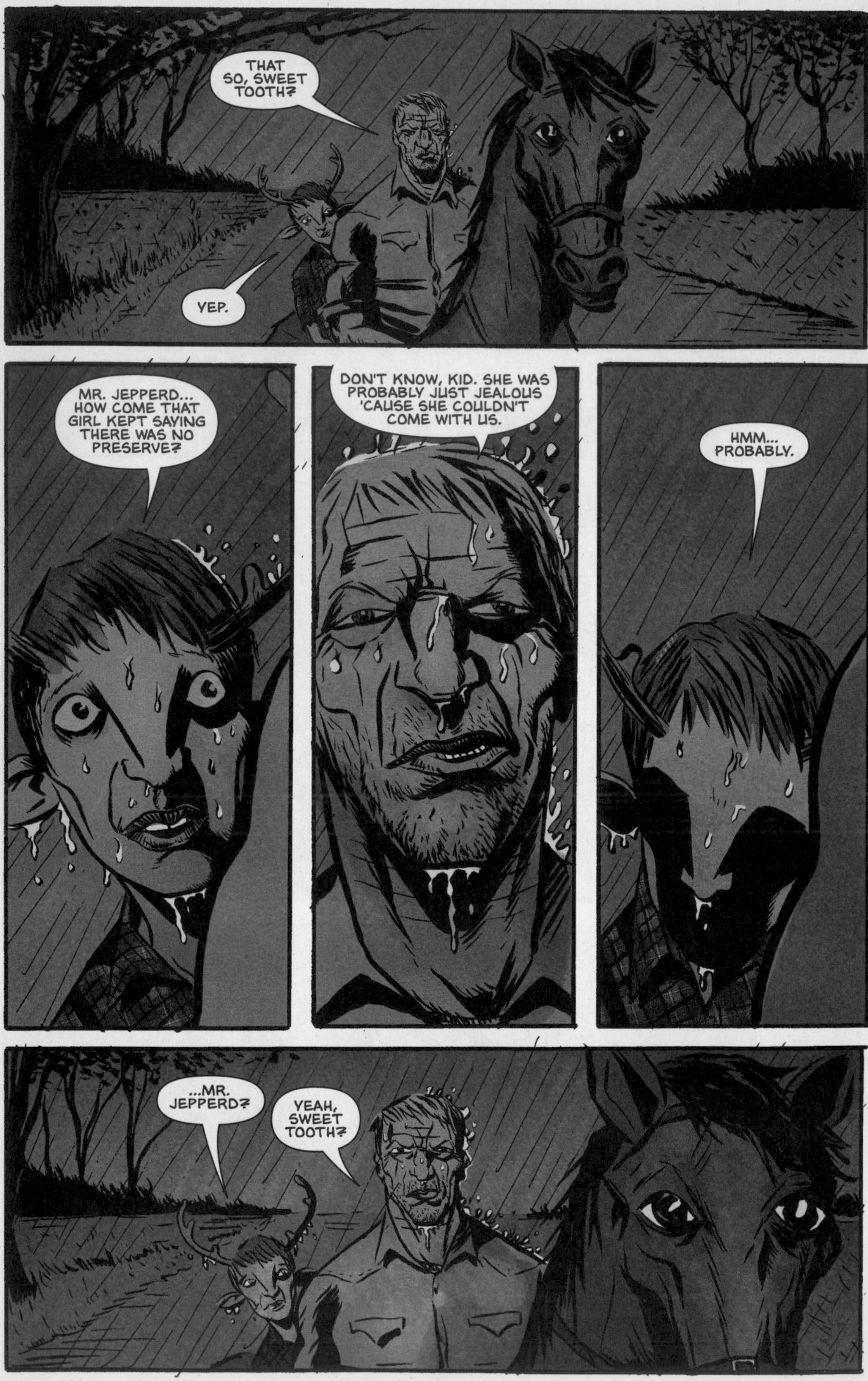
THAT SO, SWEET TOOTH?
YEP.
MR. JEPPERD... HOW COME THAT GIRL KEPT SAYING THERE WAS NO PRESERVE?
DON'T KNOW, KID. SHE WAS PROBABLY JUST JEALOUS 'CAUSE SHE COULDN'T COME WITH US.
HMM... PROBABLY.
...MR. JEPPERD?
YEAH, SWEET TOOTH?

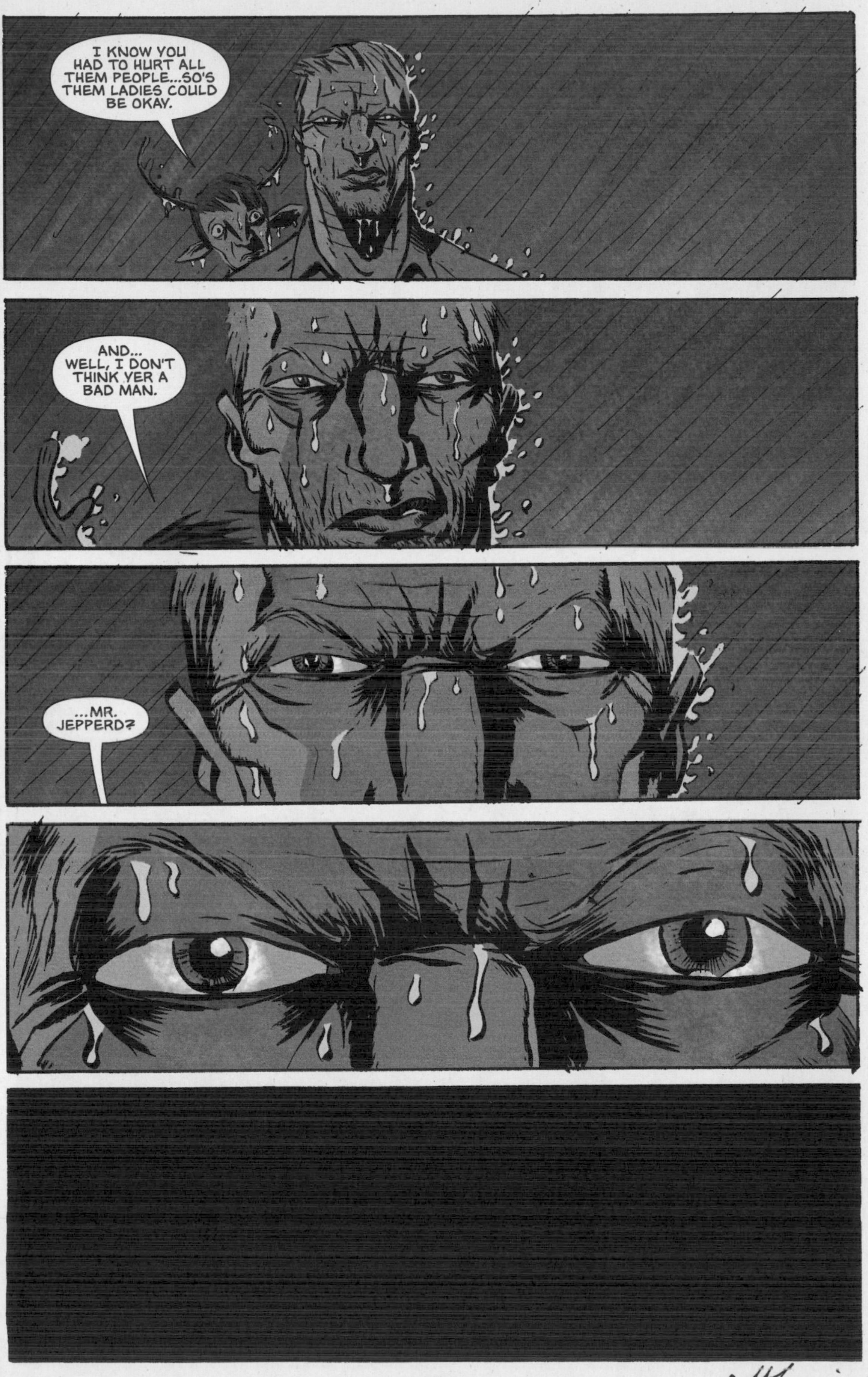
I KNOW YOU HAD TO HURT ALL THEM PEOPLE...SO'S THEM LADIES COULD BE OKAY.
AND... WELL, I DON'T THINK YER A BAD MAN.
...MR. JEPPERD?

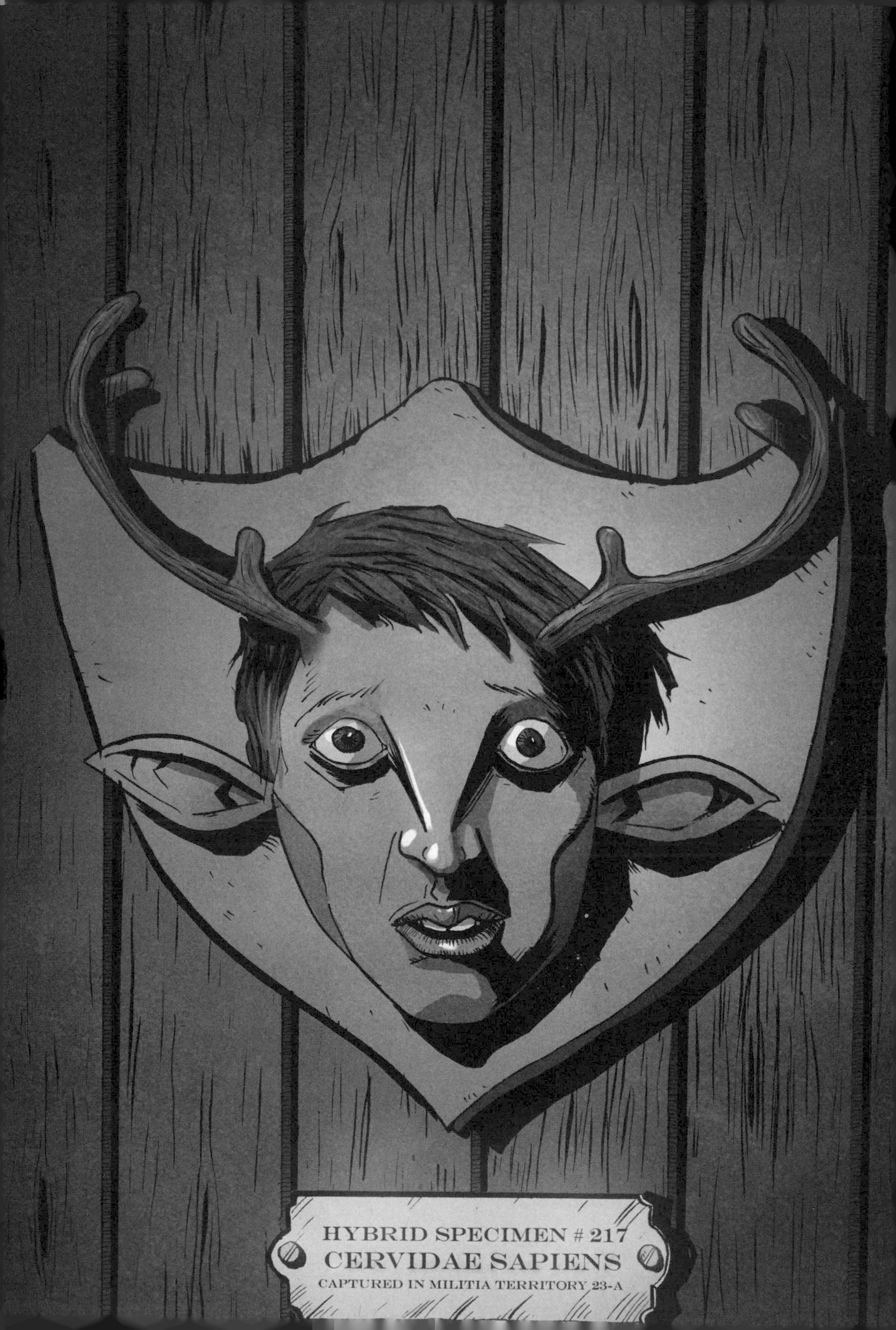
HYBRID SPECIMEN # 217
CERVIDAE SAPIENS
CAPTURED IN MILITIA TERRITORY 23-A

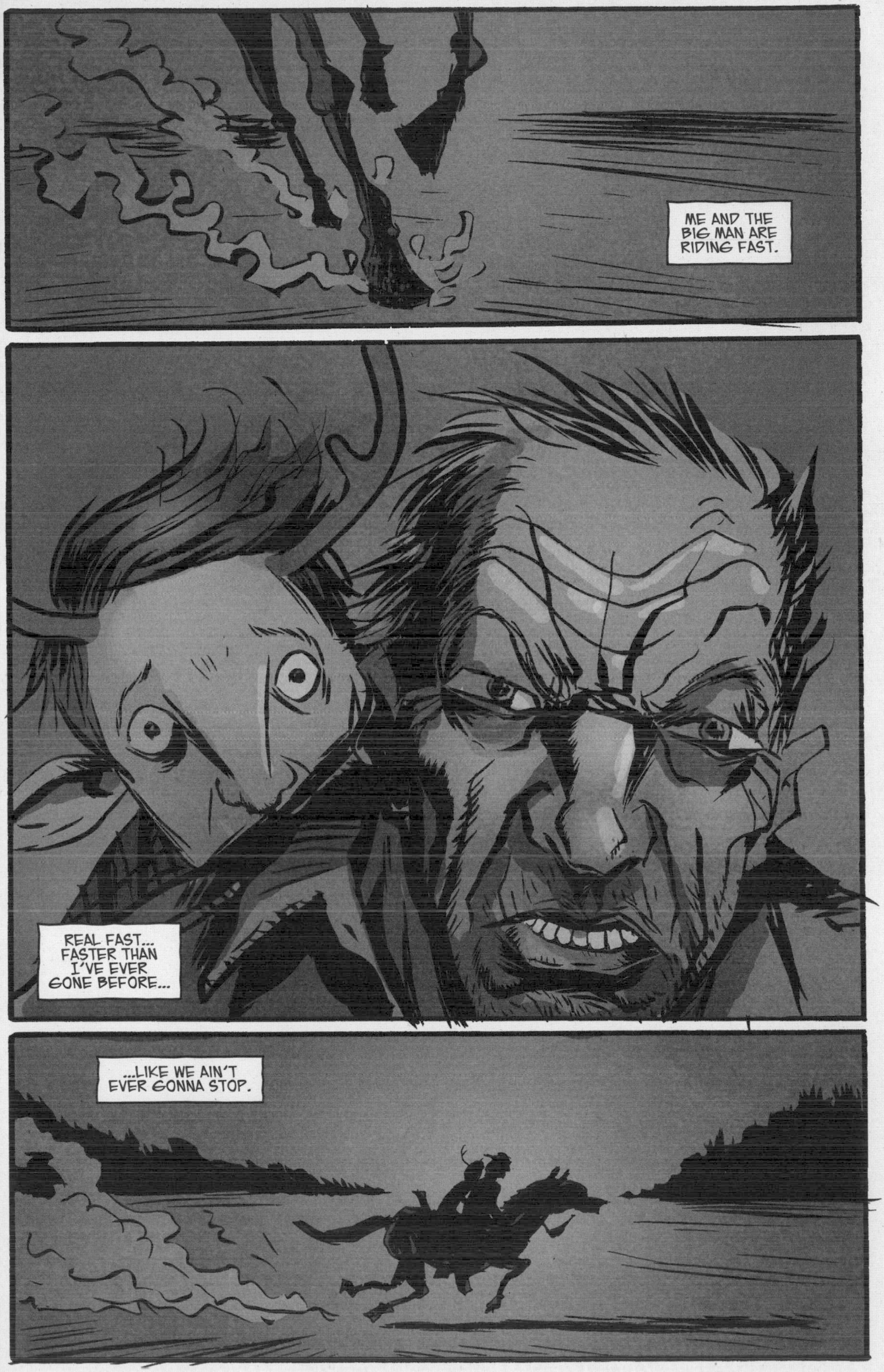
ME AND THE BIG MAN ARE RIDING FAST.
REAL FAST... FASTER THAN I'VE EVER GONE BEFORE...
...LIKE WE AIN'T EVER GONNA STOP.

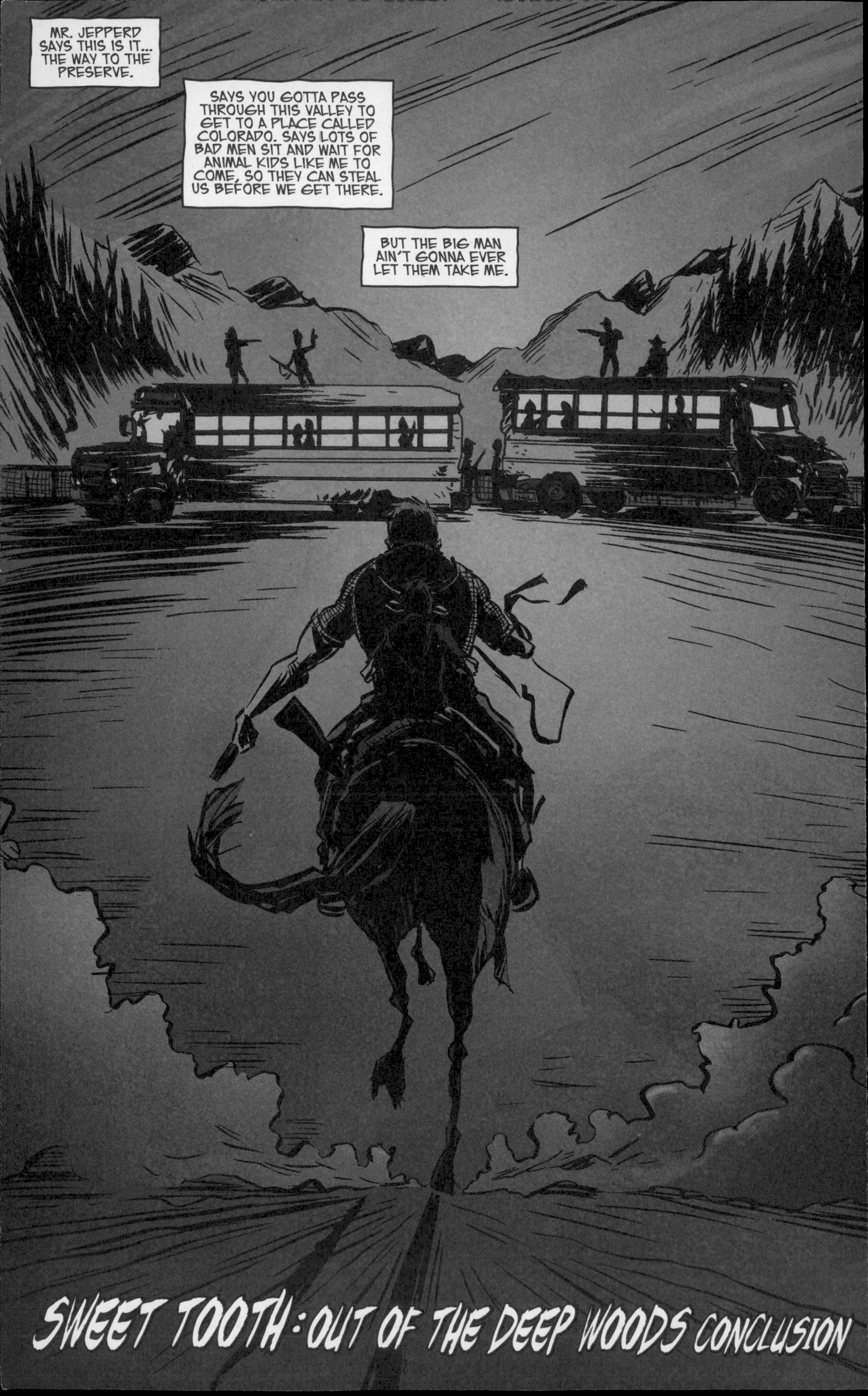
MR. JEPPERD SAYS THIS IS IT... THE WAY TO THE PRESERVE.
SAYS YOU GOTTA PASS THROUGH THIS VALLEY TO GET TO A PLACE CALLED COLORADO. SAYS LOTS OF BAD MEN SIT AND WAIT FOR ANIMAL KIDS LIKE ME TO COME, SO THEY CAN STEAL US BEFORE WE GET THERE.
BUT THE BIG MAN AIN'T GONNA EVER LET THEM TAKE ME.
SWEET TOOTH: OUT OF THE DEEP WOODS CONCLUSION

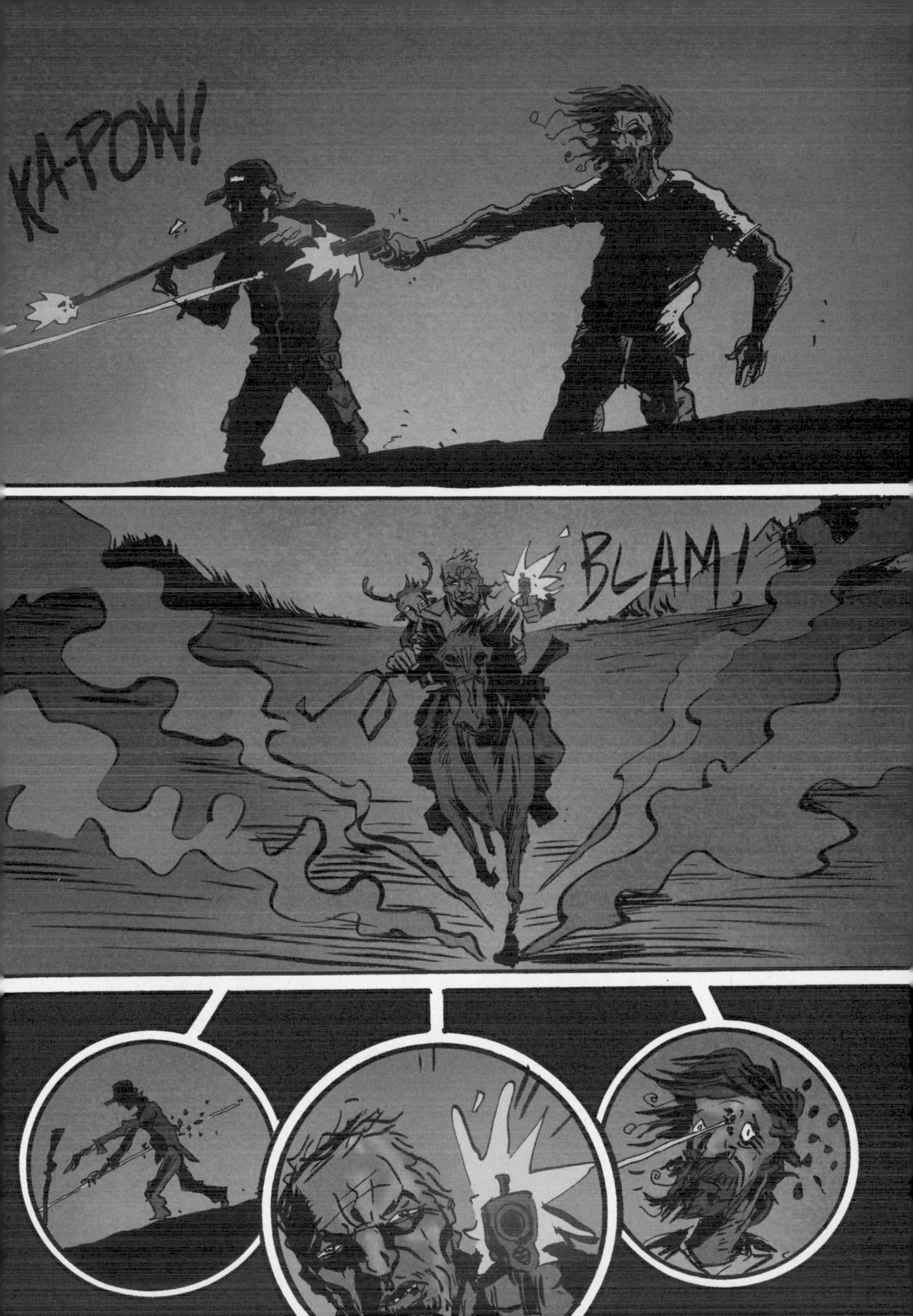
KA-POW!
BLAM!

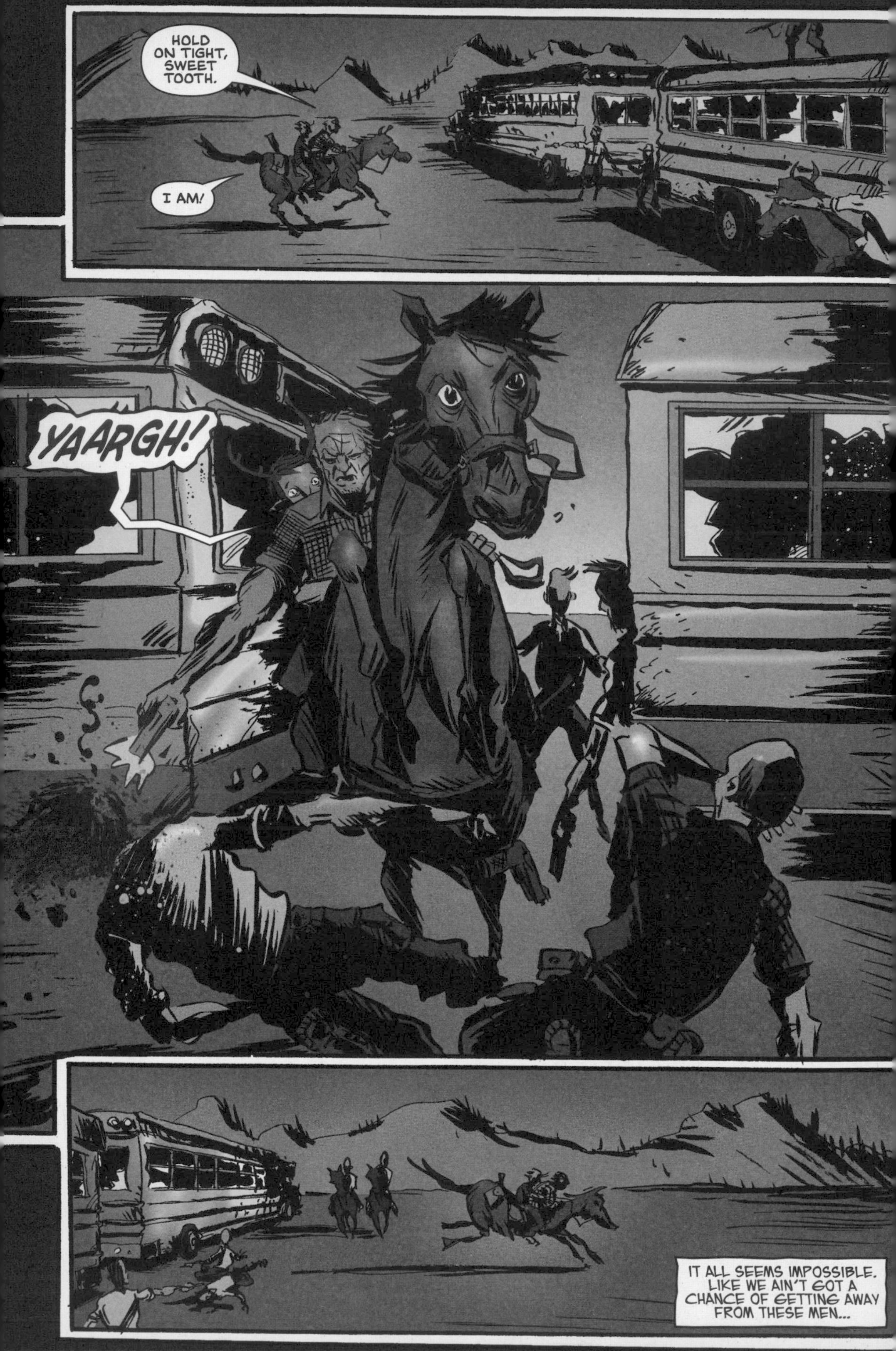
HOLD ON TIGHT, SWEET TOOTH.
I AM!
YAARGH!
IT ALL SEEMS IMPOSSIBLE. LIKE WE AIN'T GOT A CHANCE OF GETTING AWAY FROM THESE MEN...

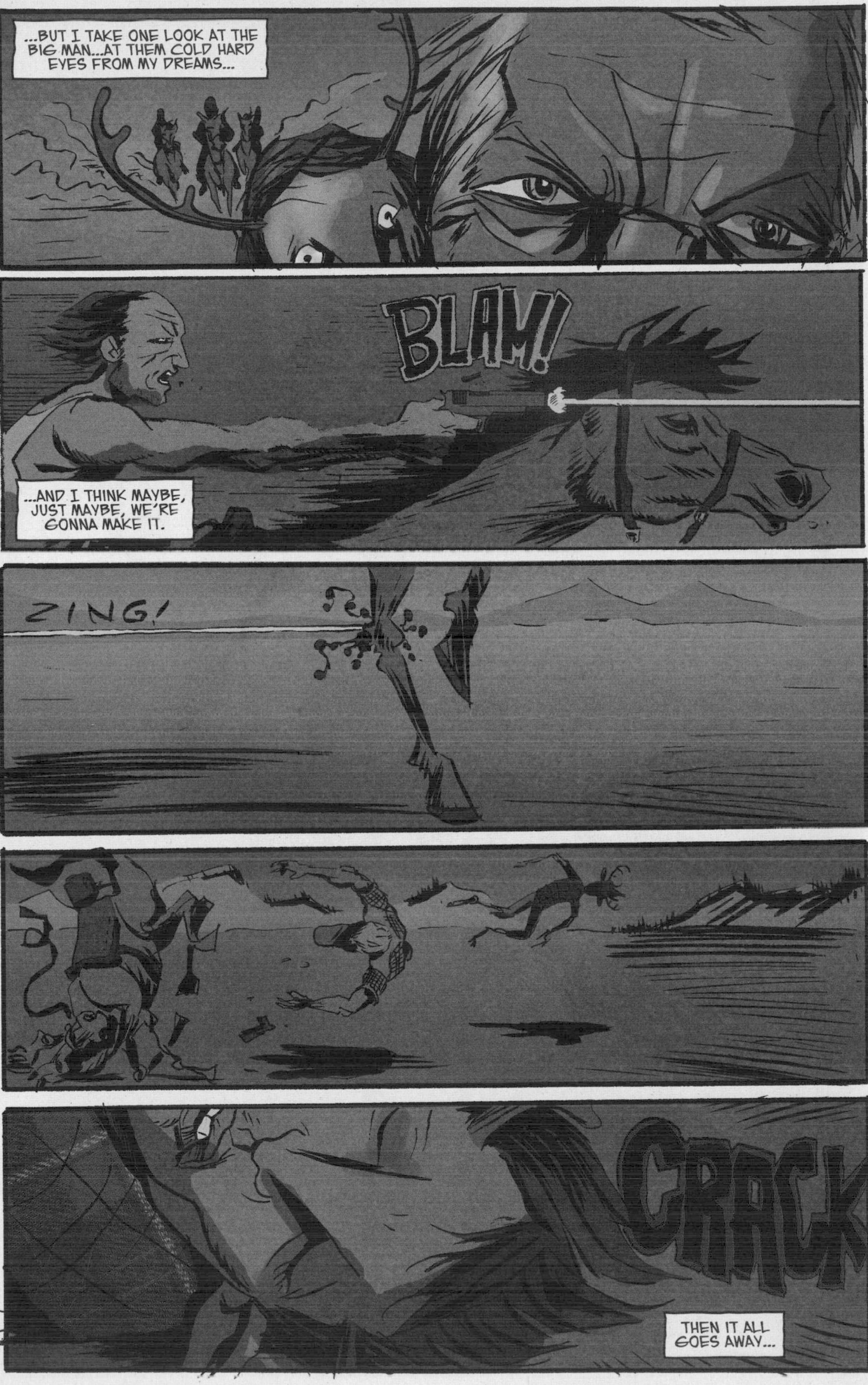
...BUT I TAKE ONE LOOK AT THE BIG MAN...AT THEM COLD HARD EYES FROM MY DREAMS...
BLAM!
...AND I THINK MAYBE, JUST MAYBE, WE'RE GONNA MAKE IT.
ZING!
CRACK
THEN IT ALL GOES AWAY...

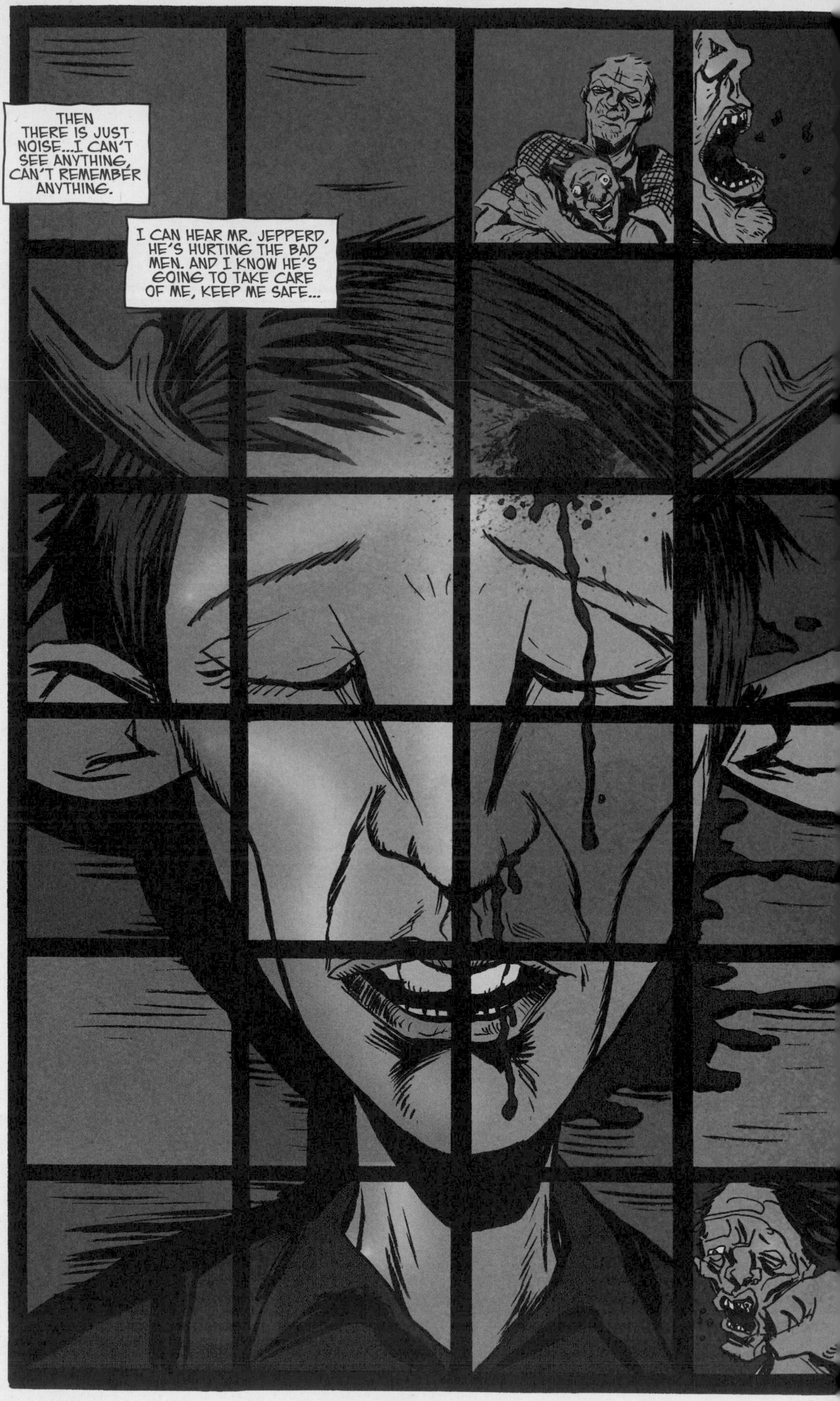
THEN THERE IS JUST NOISE...I CAN'T SEE ANYTHING, CAN'T REMEMBER ANYTHING.
I CAN HEAR MR. JEPPERD, HE'S HURTING THE BAD MEN. AND I KNOW HE'S GOING TO TAKE CARE OF ME, KEEP ME SAFE...

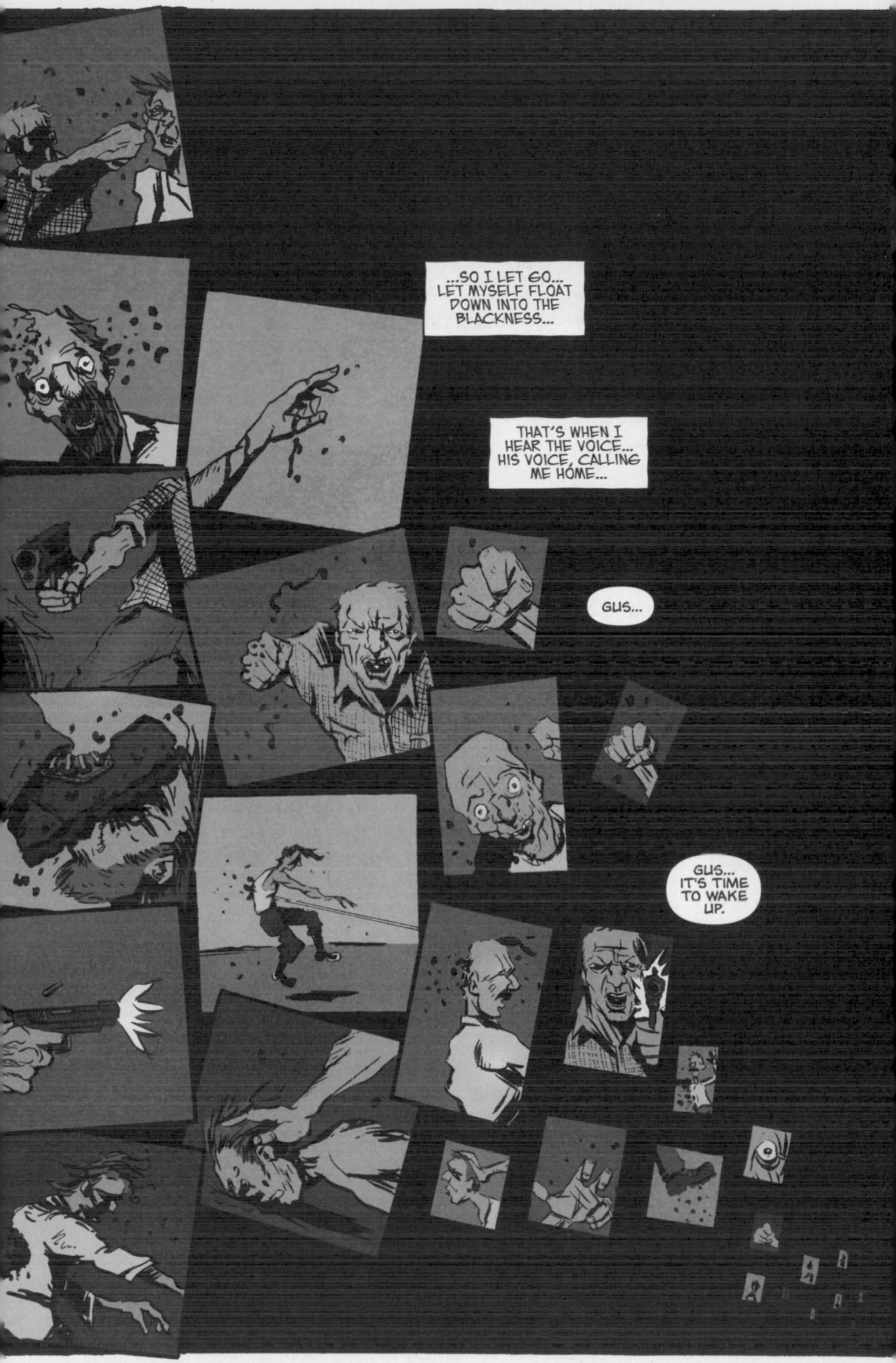
...SO I LET GO... LET MYSELF FLOAT DOWN INTO THE BLACKNESS...
THAT'S WHEN I HEAR THE VOICE... HIS VOICE, CALLING ME HOME...
GUS...
GUS... IT'S TIME TO WAKE UP.

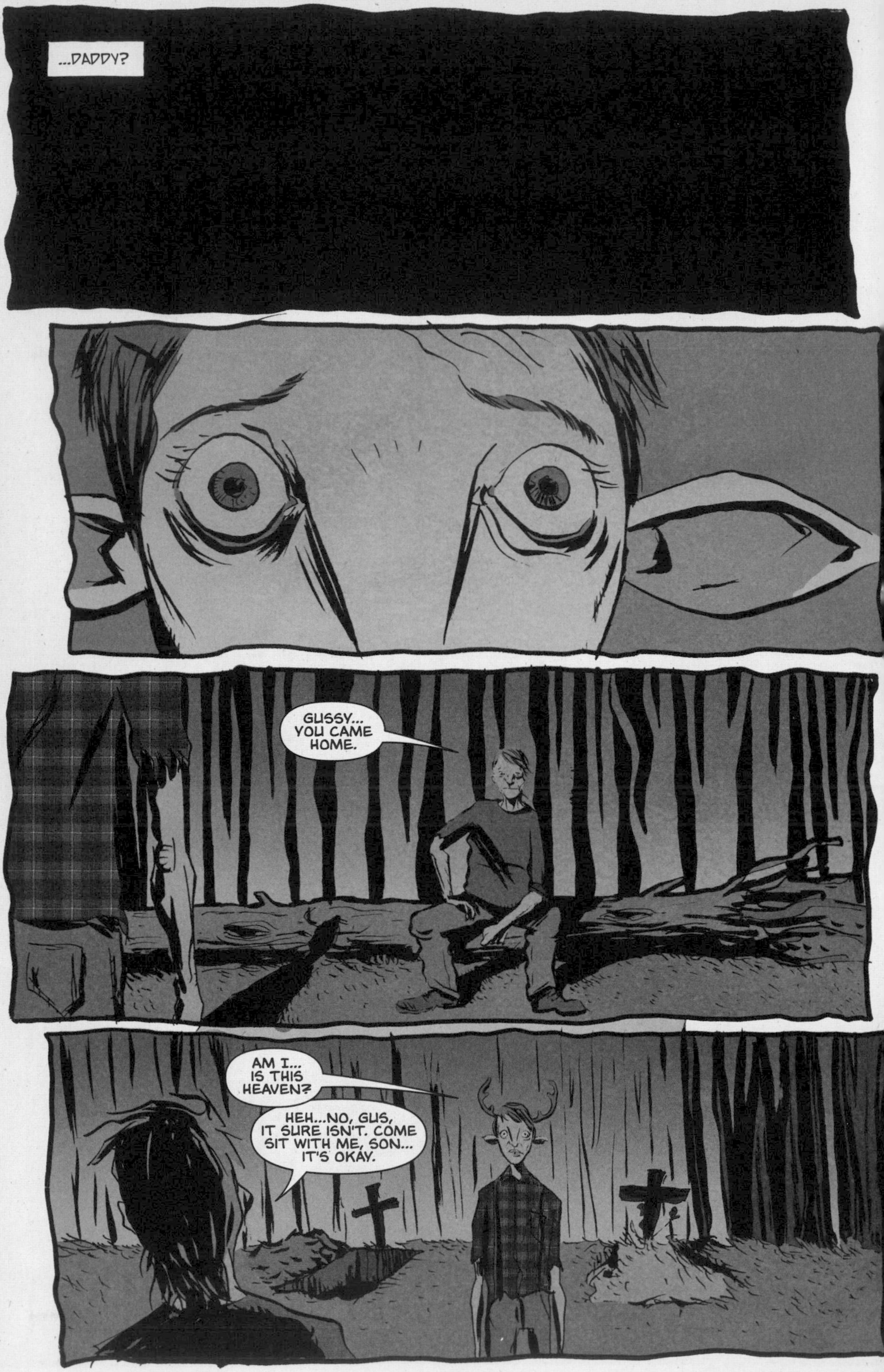
...DADDY?
GUSSY... YOU CAME HOME.
AM I... IS THIS HEAVEN?
HEH...NO, GUS, IT SURE ISN'T. COME SIT WITH ME, SON... IT'S OKAY.

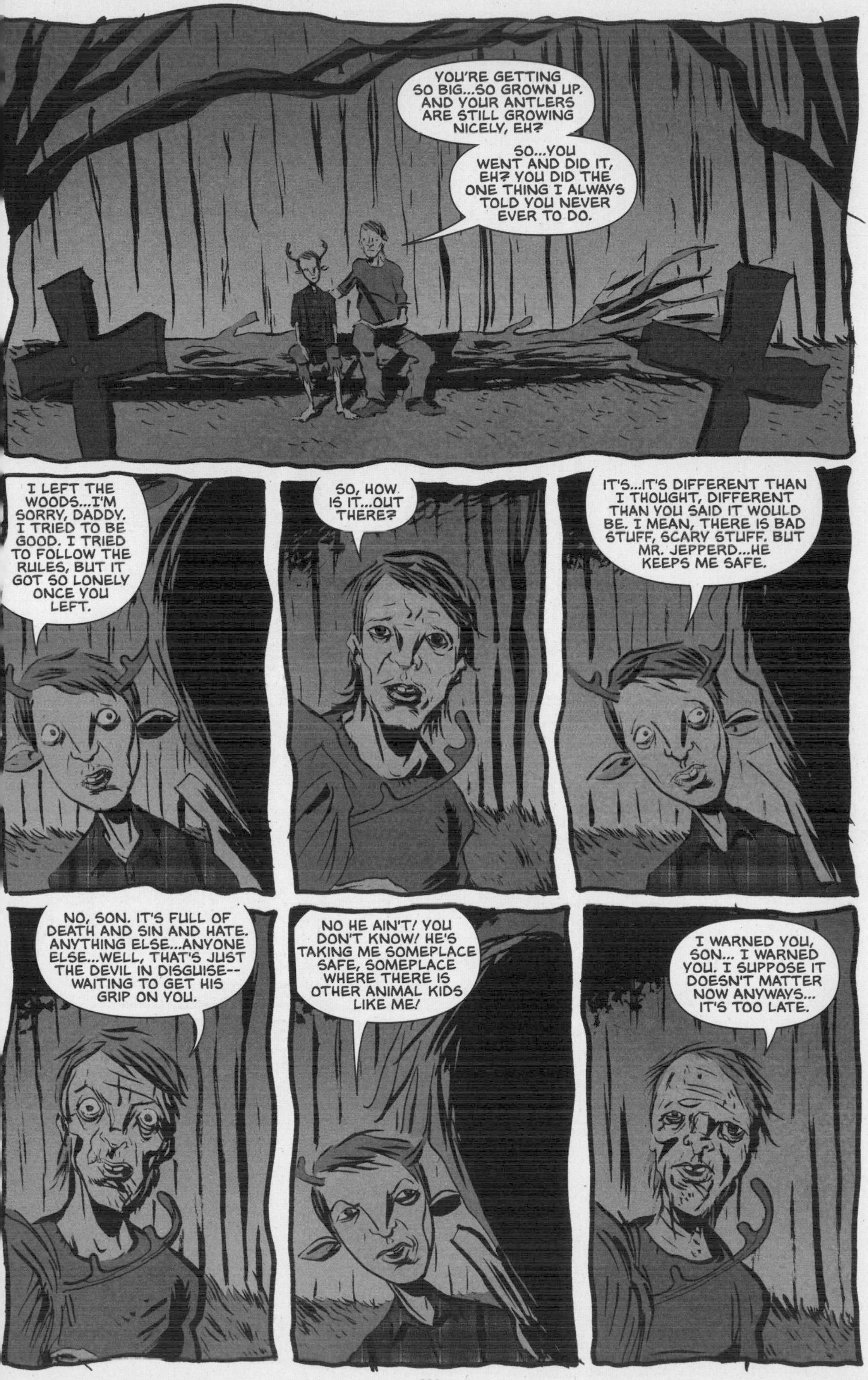
YOU'RE GETTING SO BIG...SO GROWN UP. AND YOUR ANTLERS ARE STILL GROWING NICELY, EH?
SO...YOU WENT AND DID IT, EH? YOU DID THE ONE THING I ALWAYS TOLD YOU NEVER EVER TO DO.
I LEFT THE WOODS...I'M SORRY, DADDY. I TRIED TO BE GOOD. I TRIED TO FOLLOW THE RULES, BUT IT GOT SO LONELY ONCE YOU LEFT.
SO, HOW IS IT...OUT THERE?
IT'S...IT'S DIFFERENT THAN I THOUGHT, DIFFERENT THAN YOU SAID IT WOULD BE. I MEAN, THERE IS BAD STUFF, SCARY STUFF. BUT MR. JEPPERD...HE KEEPS ME SAFE.
NO, SON. IT'S FULL OF DEATH AND SIN AND HATE. ANYTHING ELSE...ANYONE ELSE...WELL, THAT'S JUST THE DEVIL IN DISGUISE-- WAITING TO GET HIS GRIP ON YOU.
NO HE AIN'T! YOU DON'T KNOW! HE'S TAKING ME SOMEPLACE SAFE, SOMEPLACE WHERE THERE IS OTHER ANIMAL KIDS LIKE ME!
I WARNED YOU, SON... I WARNED YOU. I SUPPOSE IT DOESN'T MATTER NOW ANYWAYS... IT'S TOO LATE.

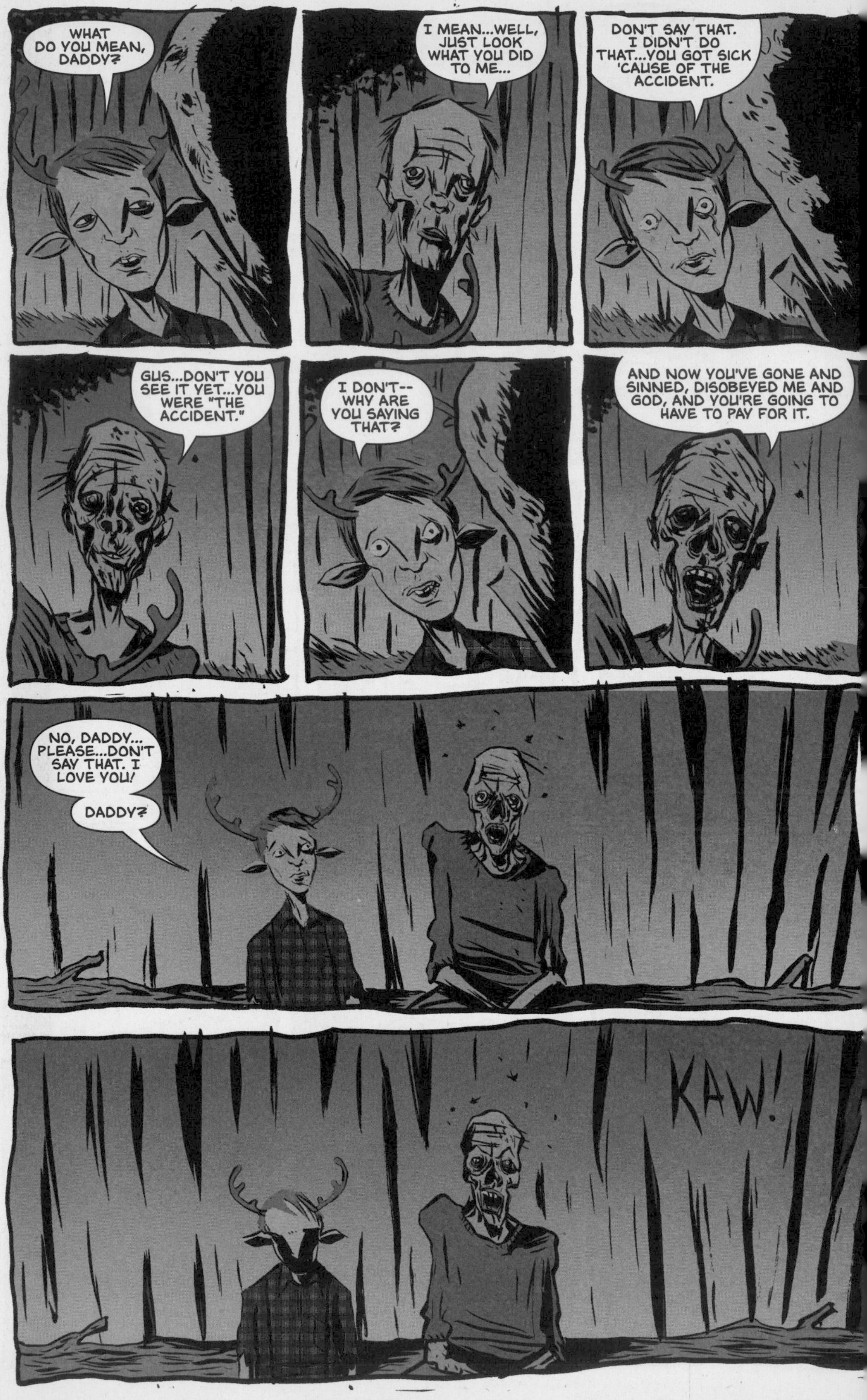
WHAT DO YOU MEAN, DADDY?
I MEAN...WELL, JUST LOOK WHAT YOU DID TO ME...
DON'T SAY THAT. I DIDN'T DO THAT...YOU GOT SICK 'CAUSE OF THE ACCIDENT.
GUS...DON'T YOU SEE IT YET...YOU WERE "THE ACCIDENT."
I DON'T-- WHY ARE YOU SAYING THAT?
AND NOW YOU'VE GONE AND SINNED, DISOBEYED ME AND GOD, AND YOU'RE GOING TO HAVE TO PAY FOR IT.
NO, DADDY... PLEASE...DON'T SAY THAT. I LOVE YOU!
DADDY?
KAW!

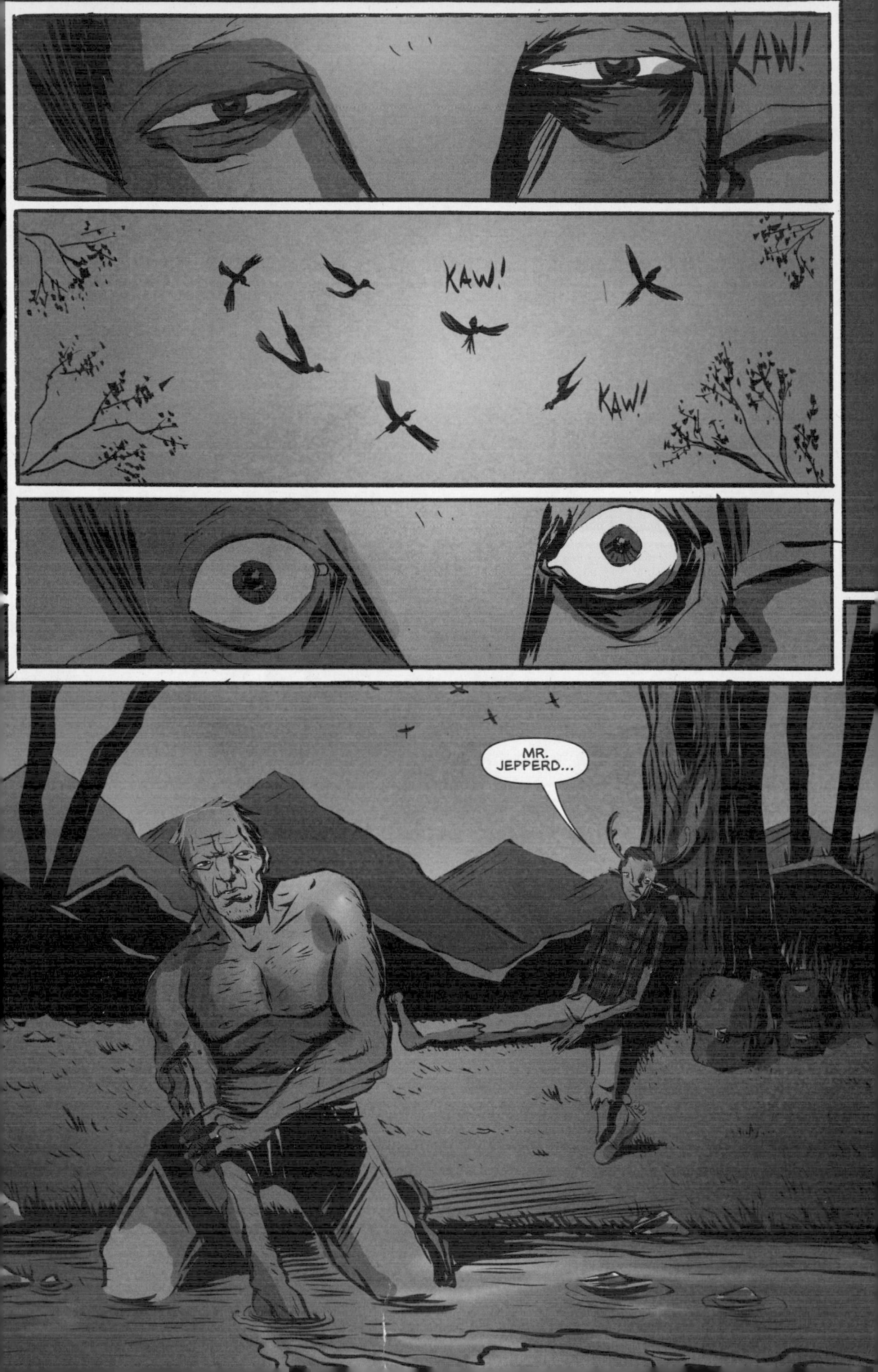
KAW!
KAW!
KAW!
MR. JEPPERD...

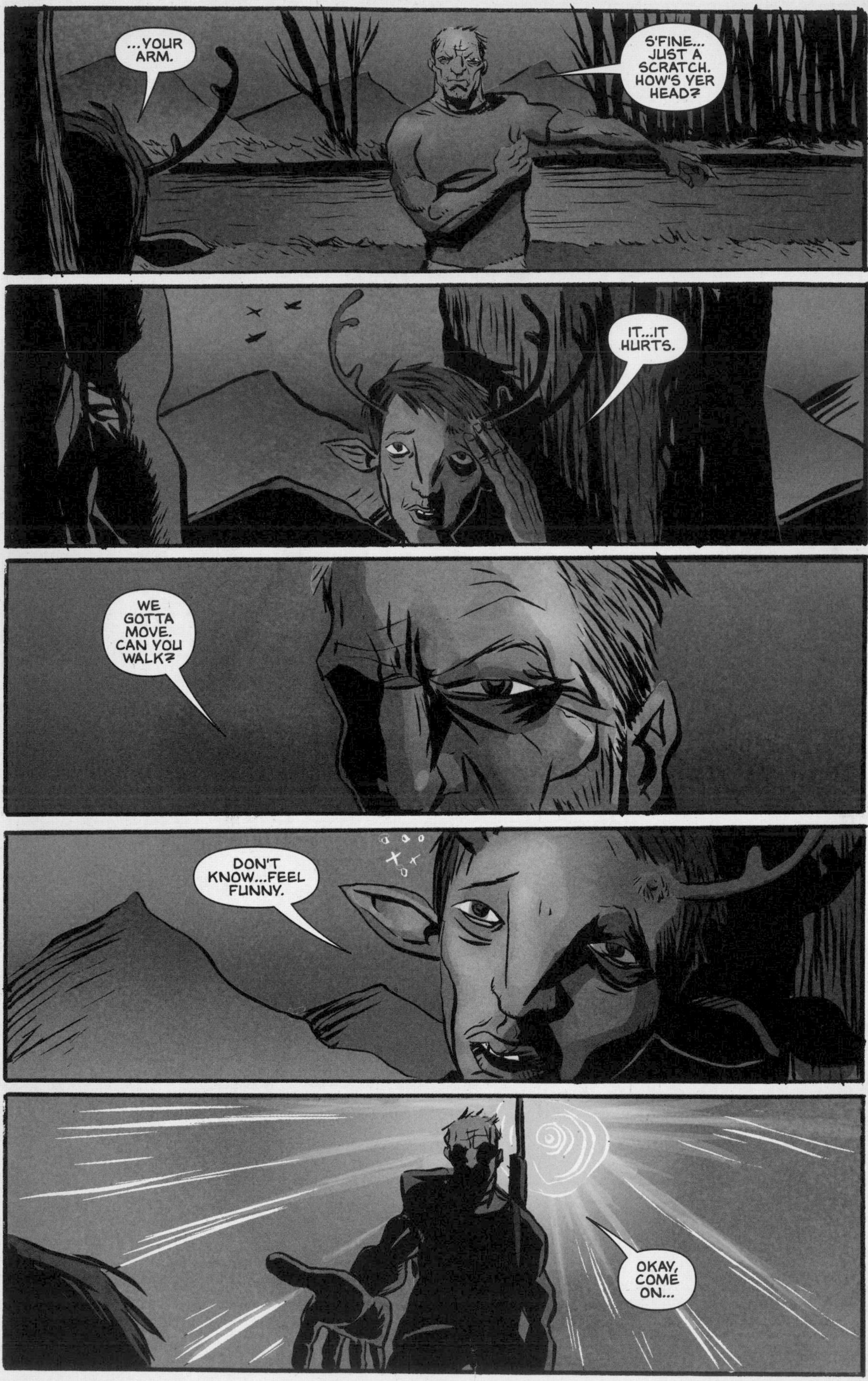
...YOUR ARM.
S'FINE... JUST A SCRATCH. HOW'S YER HEAD?
IT...IT HURTS.
WE GOTTA MOVE. CAN YOU WALK?
DON'T KNOW...FEEL FUNNY.
OKAY, COME ON...

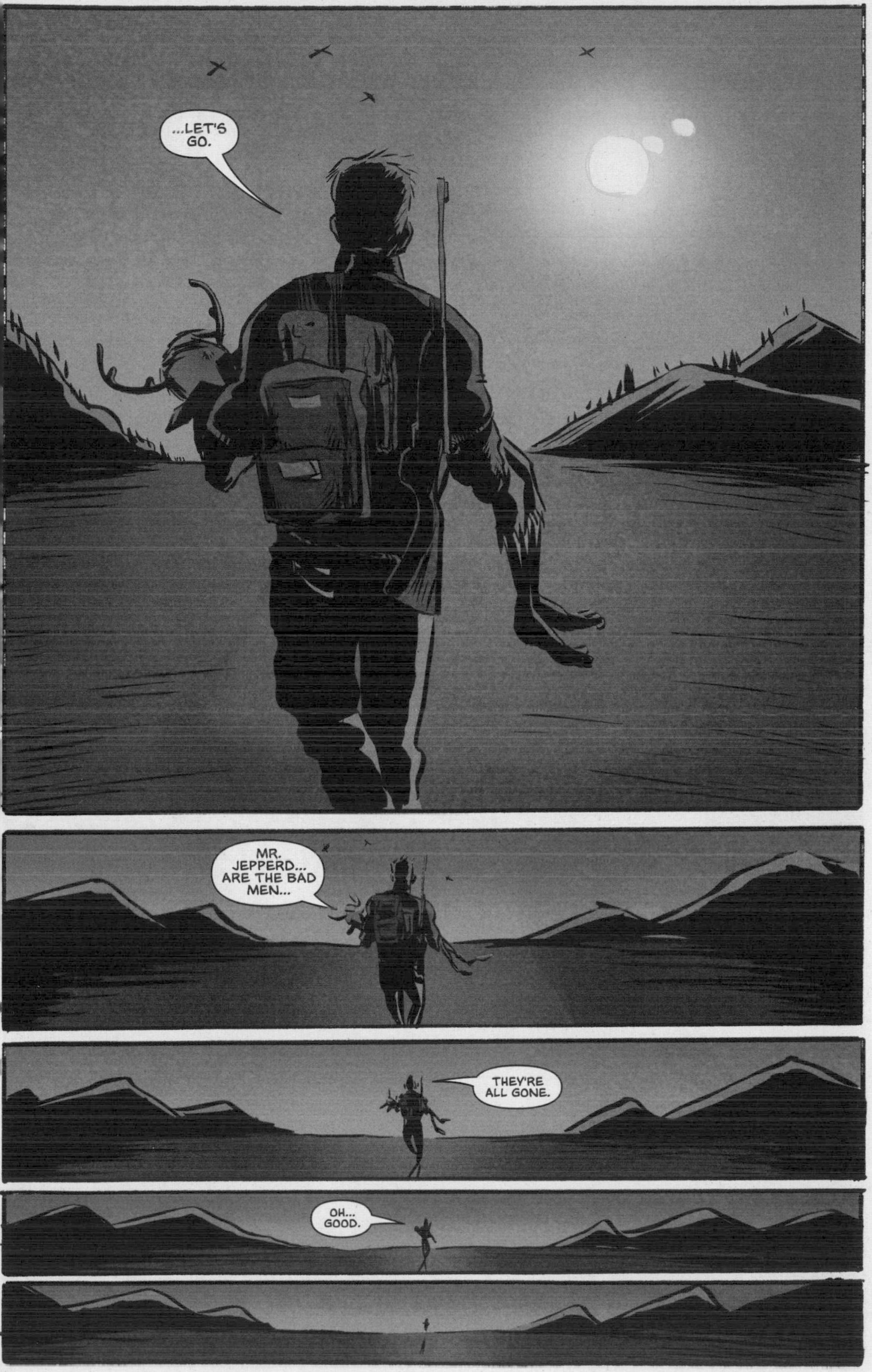
...LET'S GO.
MR. JEPPERD... ARE THE BAD MEN...
THEY'RE ALL GONE.
OH... GOOD.

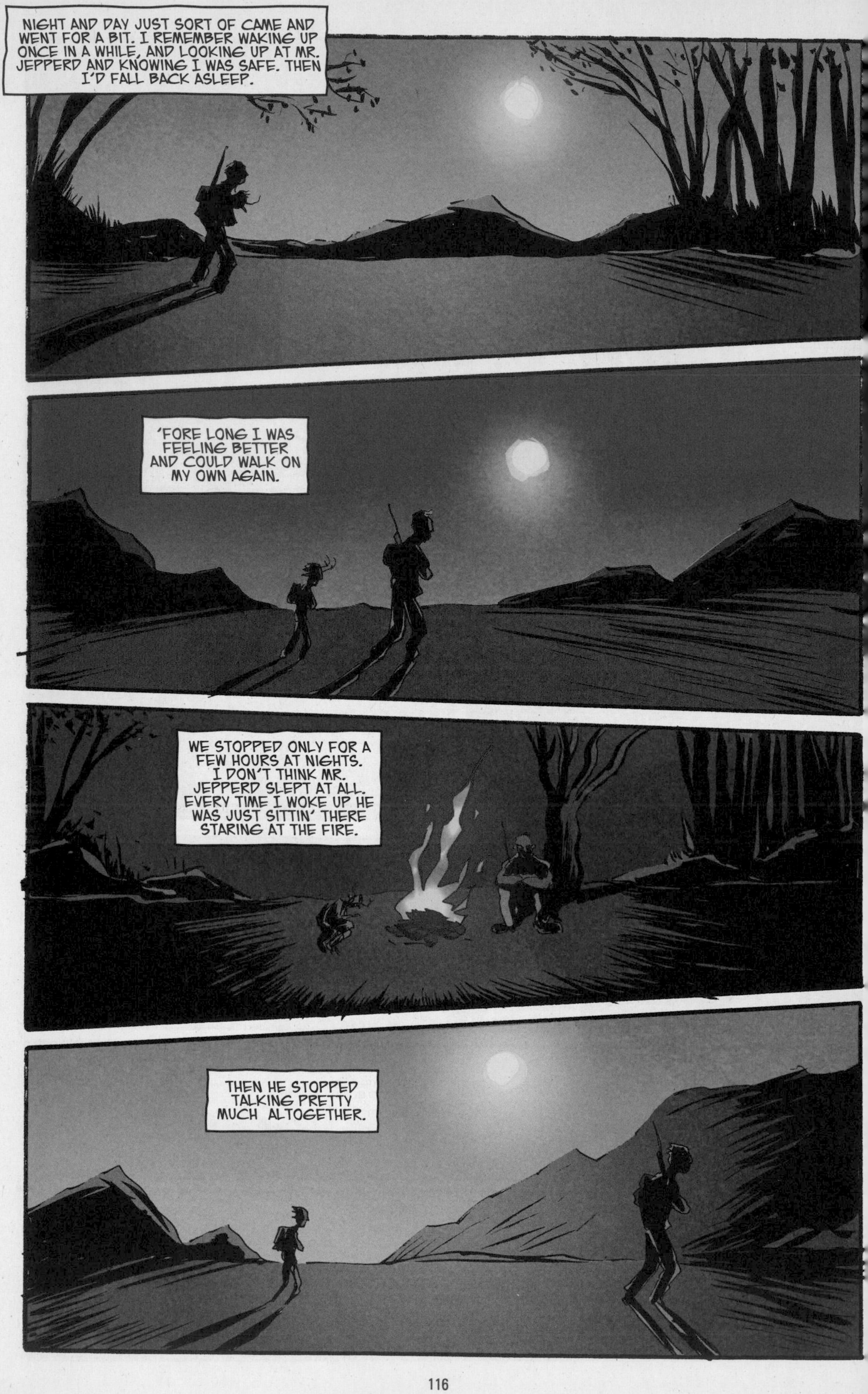
NIGHT AND DAY JUST SORT OF CAME AND WENT FOR A BIT. I REMEMBER WAKING UP ONCE IN A WHILE, AND LOOKING UP AT MR. JEPPERD AND KNOWING I WAS SAFE. THEN I'D FALL BACK ASLEEP.
'FORE LONG I WAS FEELING BETTER AND COULD WALK ON MY OWN AGAIN.
WE STOPPED ONLY FOR A FEW HOURS AT NIGHTS. I DON'T THINK MR. JEPPERD SLEPT AT ALL. EVERY TIME I WOKE UP HE WAS JUST SITTIN' THERE STARING AT THE FIRE.
THEN HE STOPPED TALKING PRETTY MUCH ALTOGETHER.

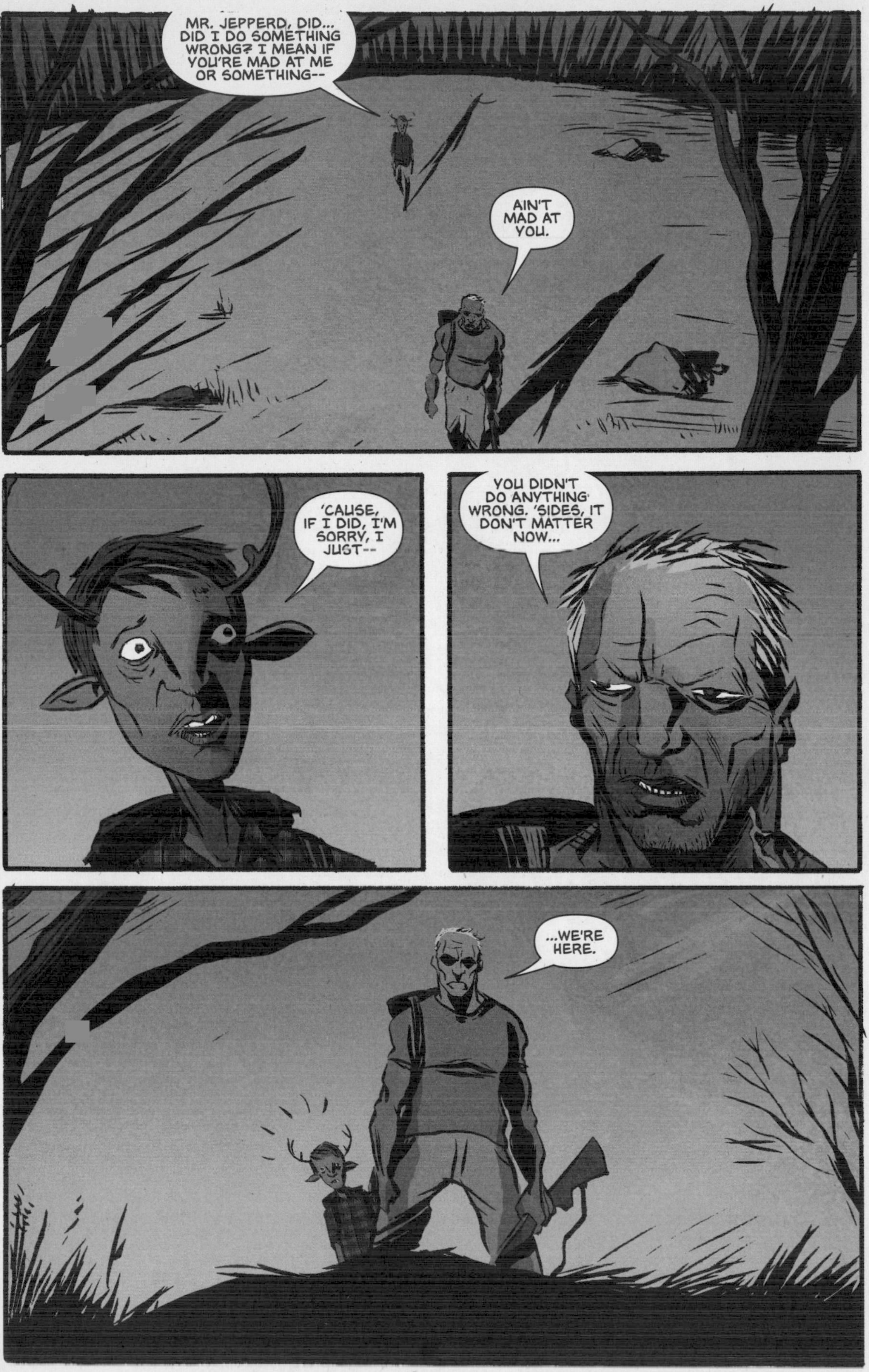
MR. JEPPERD, DID... DID I DO SOMETHING WRONG? I MEAN IF YOU'RE MAD AT ME OR SOMETHING--
AIN'T MAD AT YOU.
'CAUSE, IF I DID, I'M SORRY, I JUST--
YOU DIDN'T DO ANYTHING WRONG. 'SIDES, IT DON'T MATTER NOW...
...WE'RE HERE.

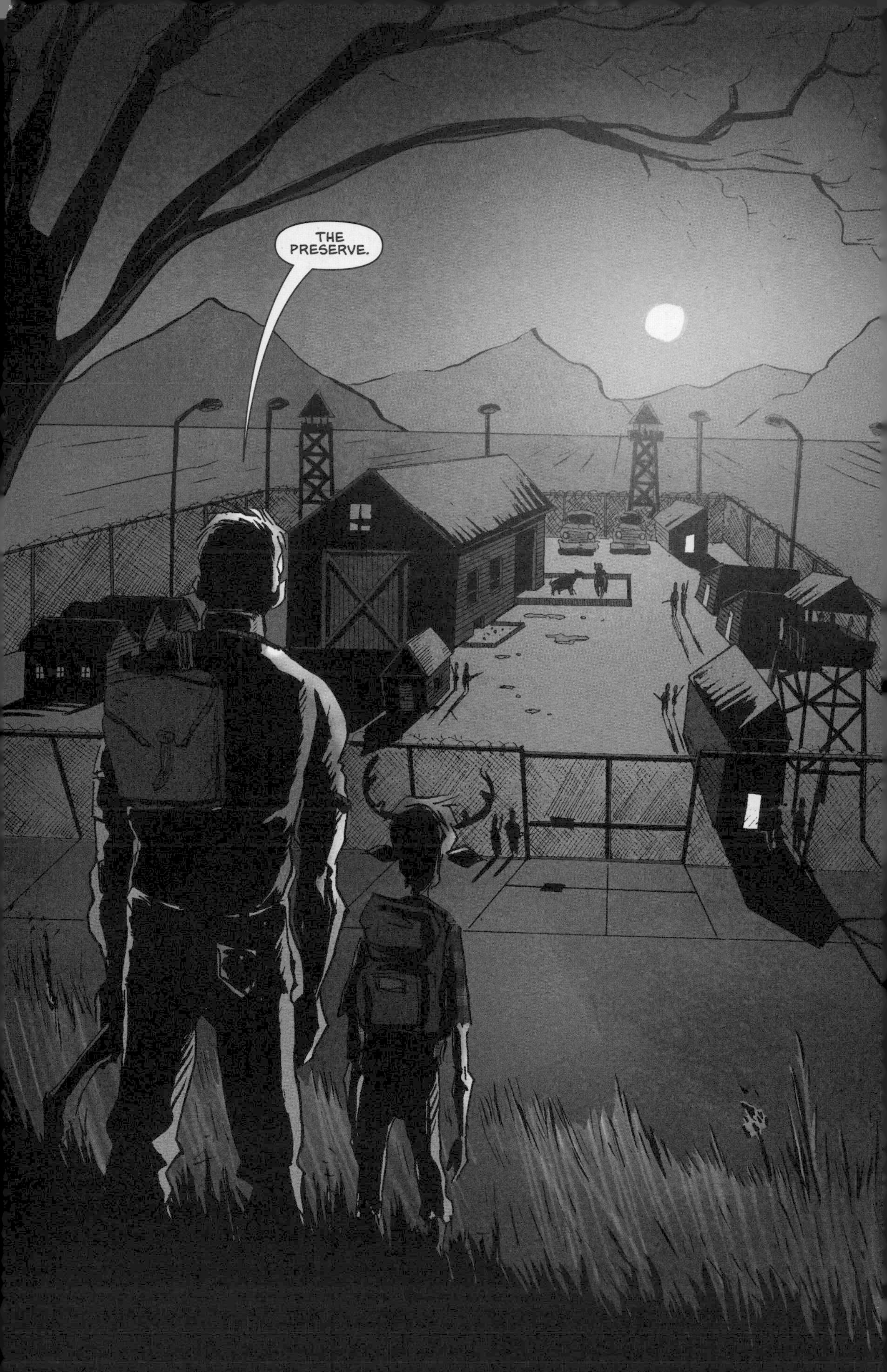
THE PRESERVE.

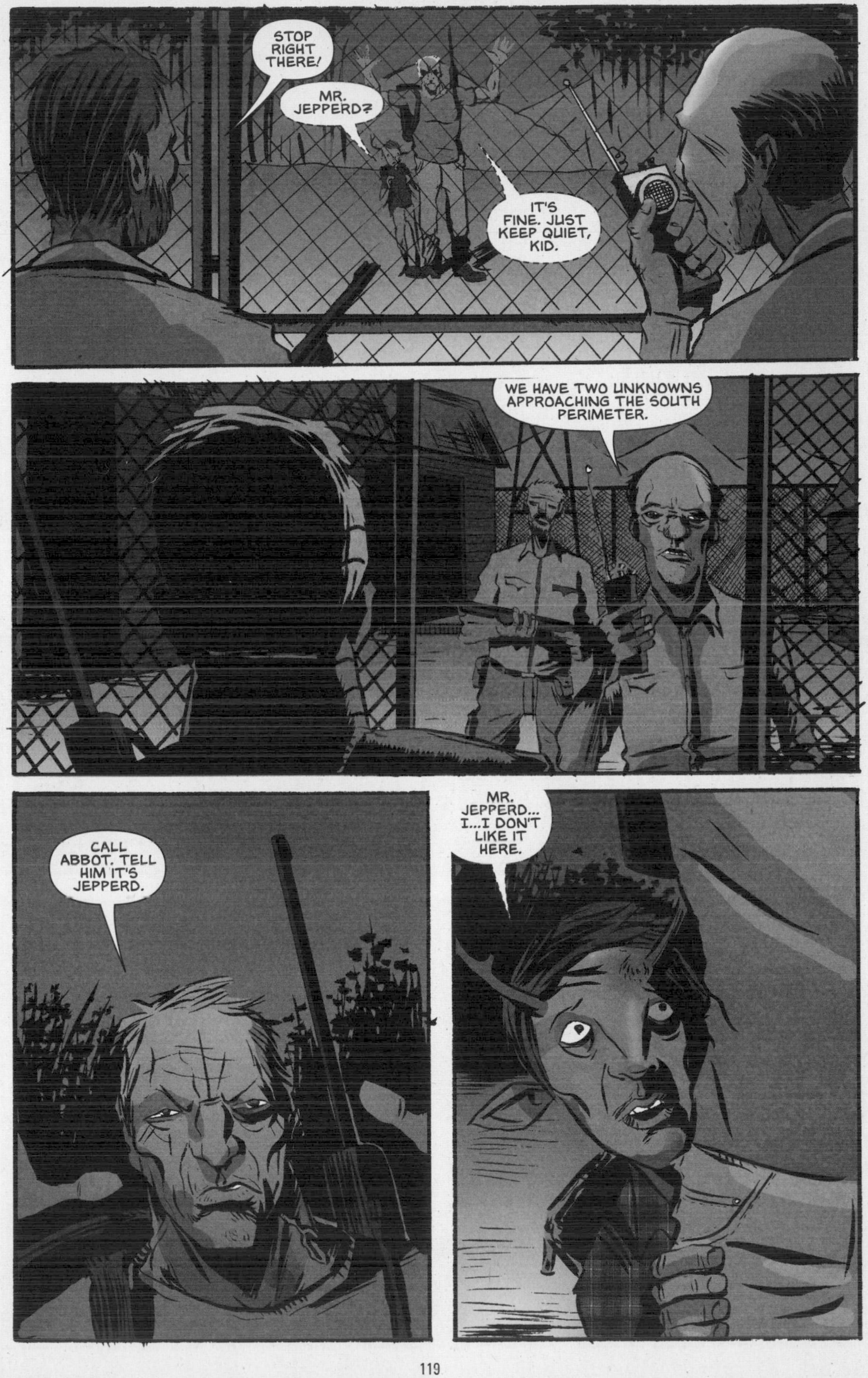
STOP RIGHT THERE!
MR. JEPPERD?
IT'S FINE. JUST KEEP QUIET, KID.
WE HAVE TWO UNKNOWNS APPROACHING THE SOUTH PERIMETER.
CALL ABBOT. TELL HIM IT'S JEPPERD.
MR. JEPPERD... I...I DON'T LIKE IT HERE.

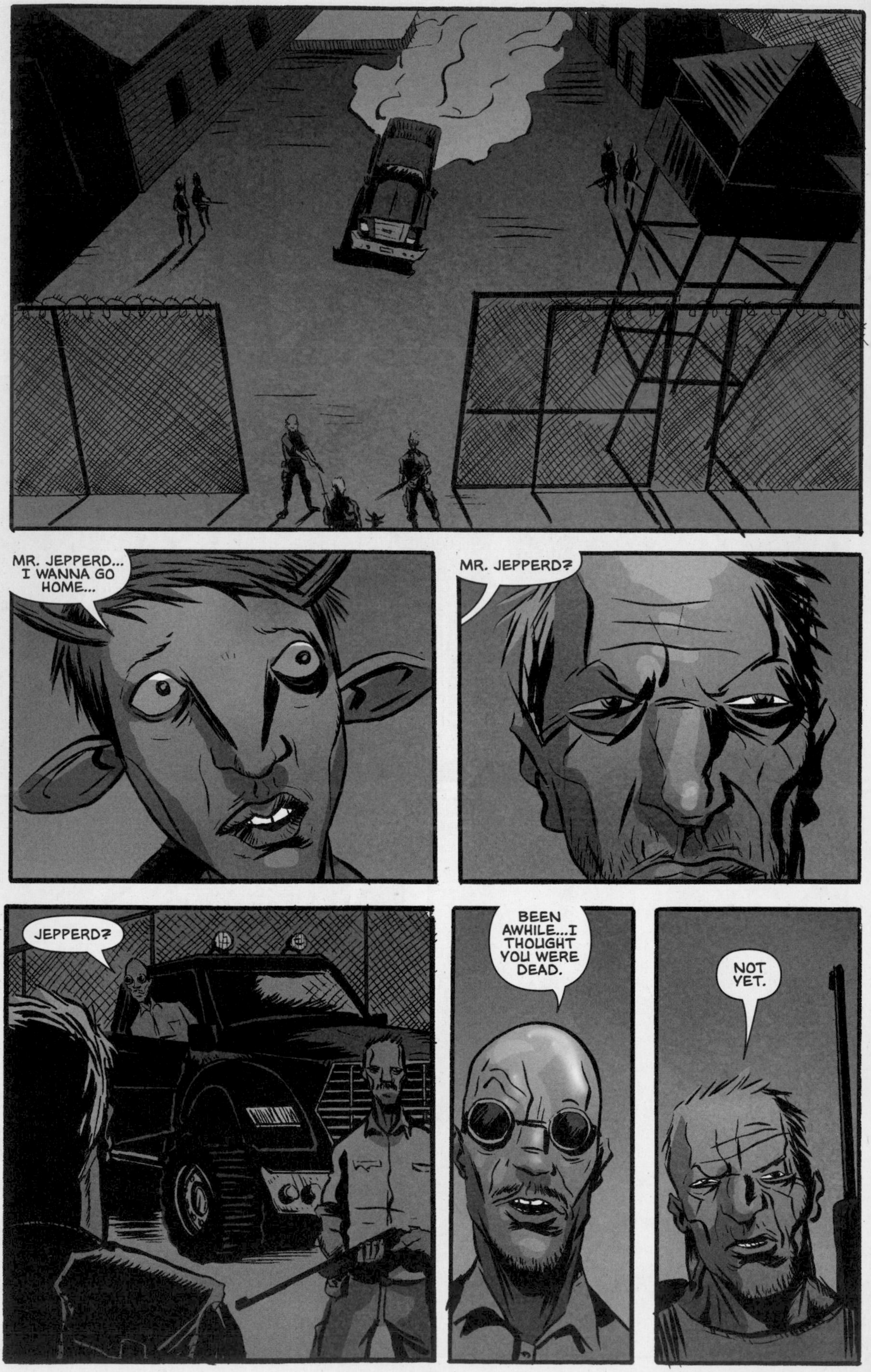
MR. JEPPERD... I WANNA GO HOME...
MR. JEPPERD?
JEPPERD?
BEEN AWHILE...I THOUGHT YOU WERE DEAD.
NOT YET.

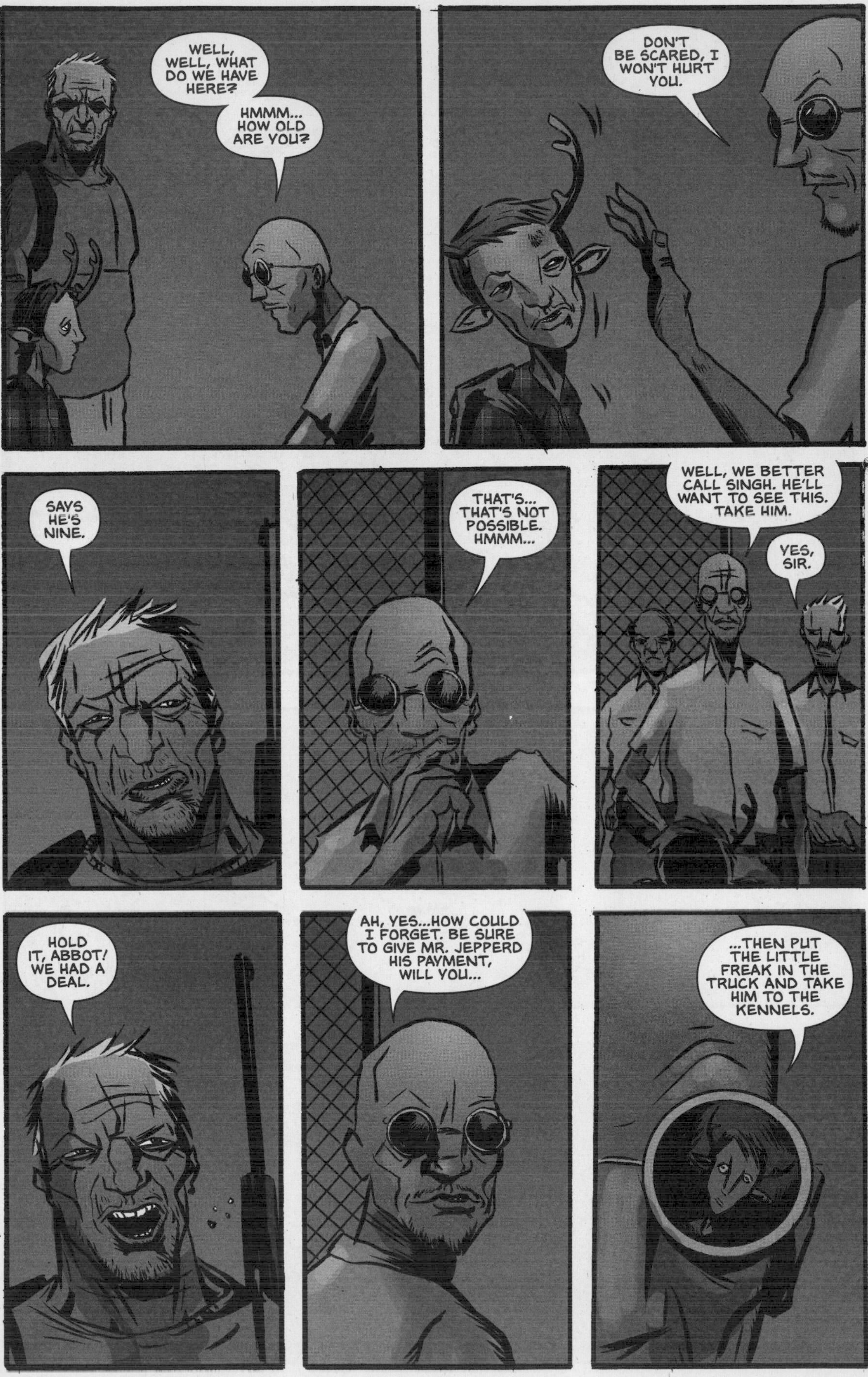
WELL, WELL, WHAT DO WE HAVE HERE?
HMMM... HOW OLD ARE YOU?
DON'T BE SCARED, I WON'T HURT YOU.
SAYS HE'S NINE.
THAT'S... THAT'S NOT POSSIBLE. HMMM...
WELL, WE BETTER CALL SINGH. HE'LL WANT TO SEE THIS. TAKE HIM.
YES, SIR.
HOLD IT, ABBOT! WE HAD A DEAL.
AH, YES...HOW COULD I FORGET. BE SURE TO GIVE MR. JEPPERD HIS PAYMENT, WILL YOU...
...THEN PUT THE LITTLE FREAK IN THE TRUCK AND TAKE HIM TO THE KENNELS.

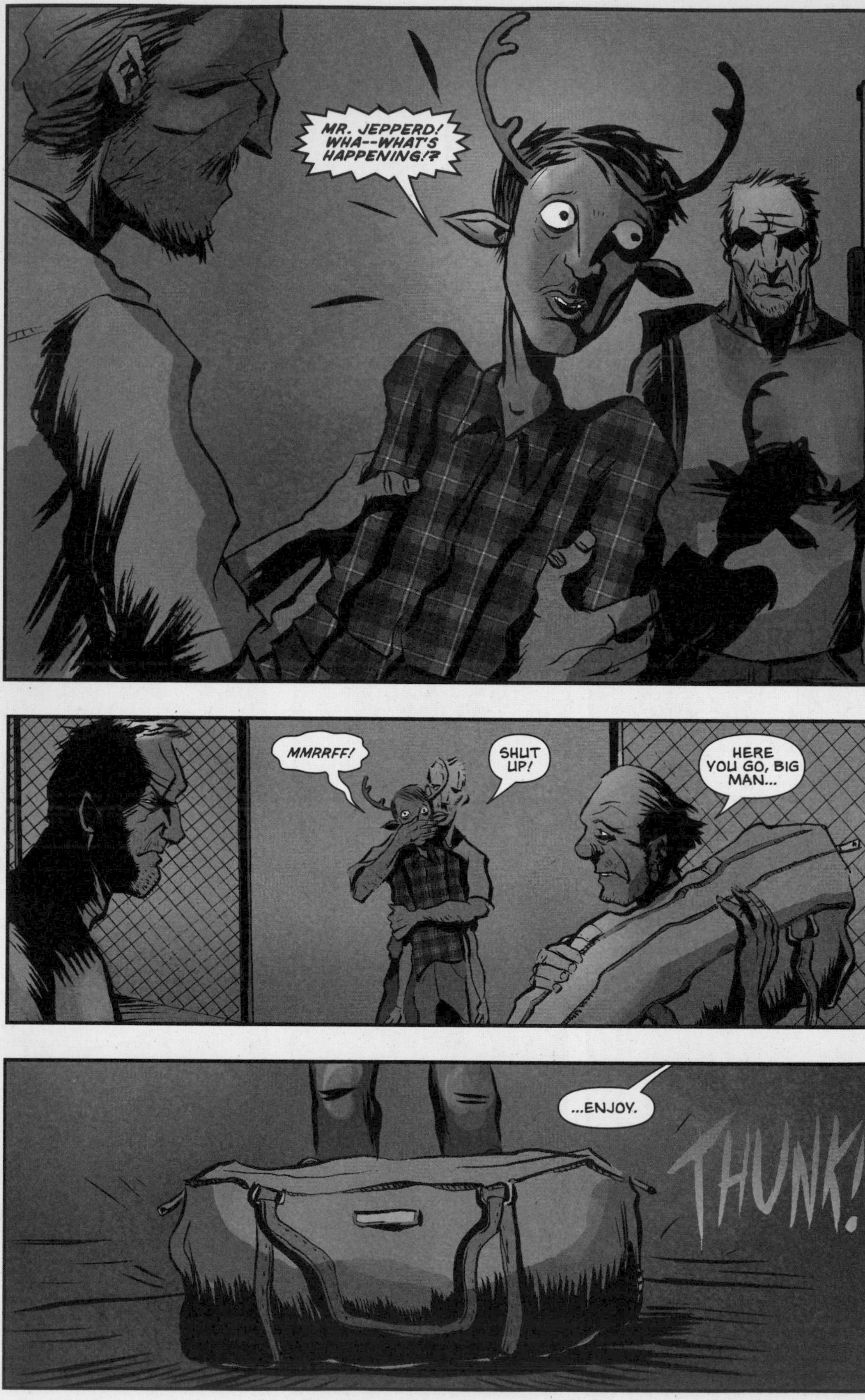
MR. JEPPERD! WHA--WHAT'S HAPPENING!?
MMRRFF!
SHUT UP!
HERE YOU GO, BIG MAN...
...ENJOY.
THUNK!

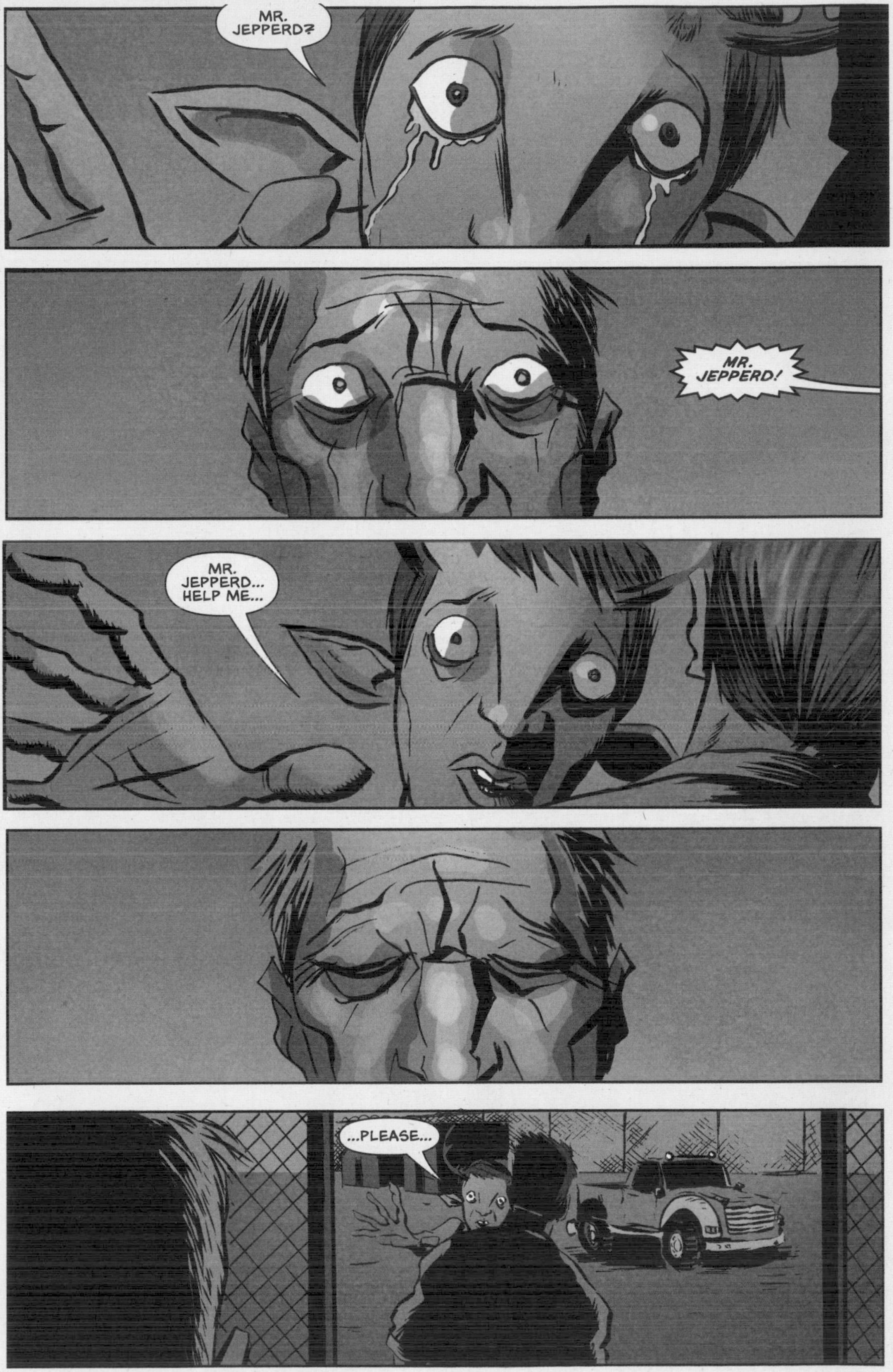
MR. JEPPERD?
MR. JEPPERD!
MR. JEPPERD... HELP ME...
...PLEASE...

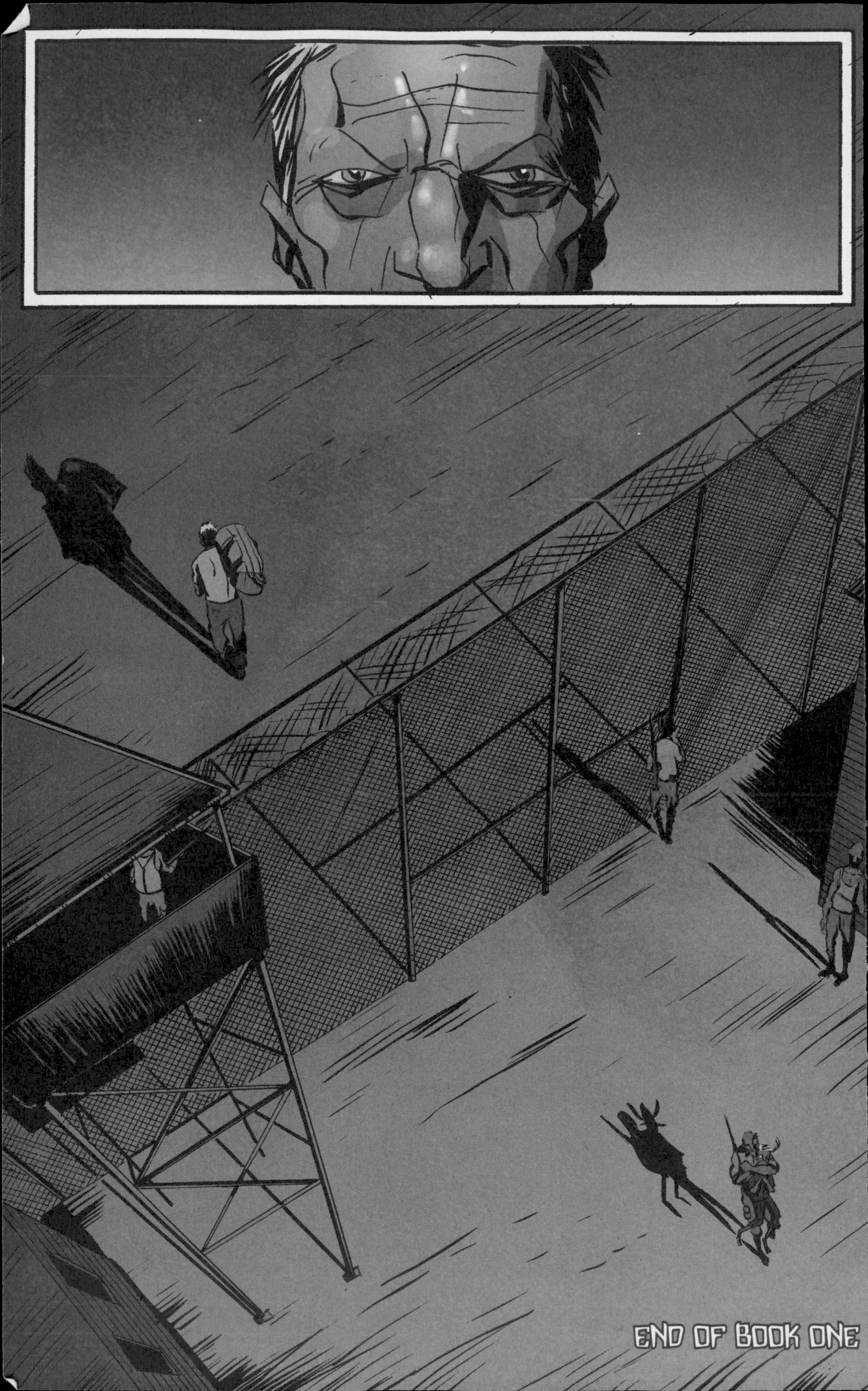
END OF BOOK ONE

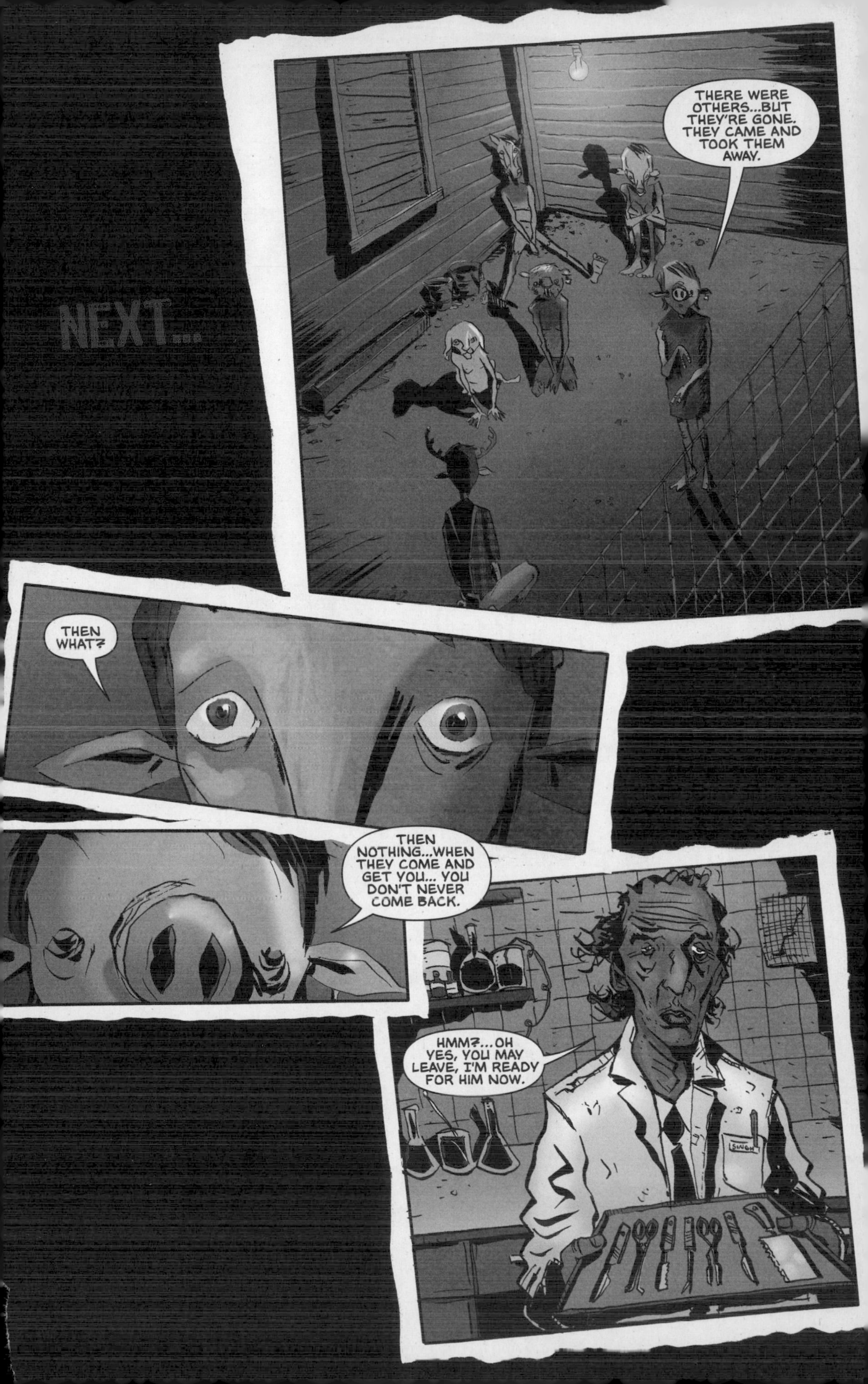
NEXT...
THERE WERE OTHERS...BUT THEY'RE GONE. THEY CAME AND TOOK THEM AWAY.
THEN WHAT?
THEN NOTHING...WHEN THEY COME AND GET YOU... YOU DON'T NEVER COME BACK.
HMM?...OH YES, YOU MAY LEAVE, I'M READY FOR HIM NOW.
SINGH

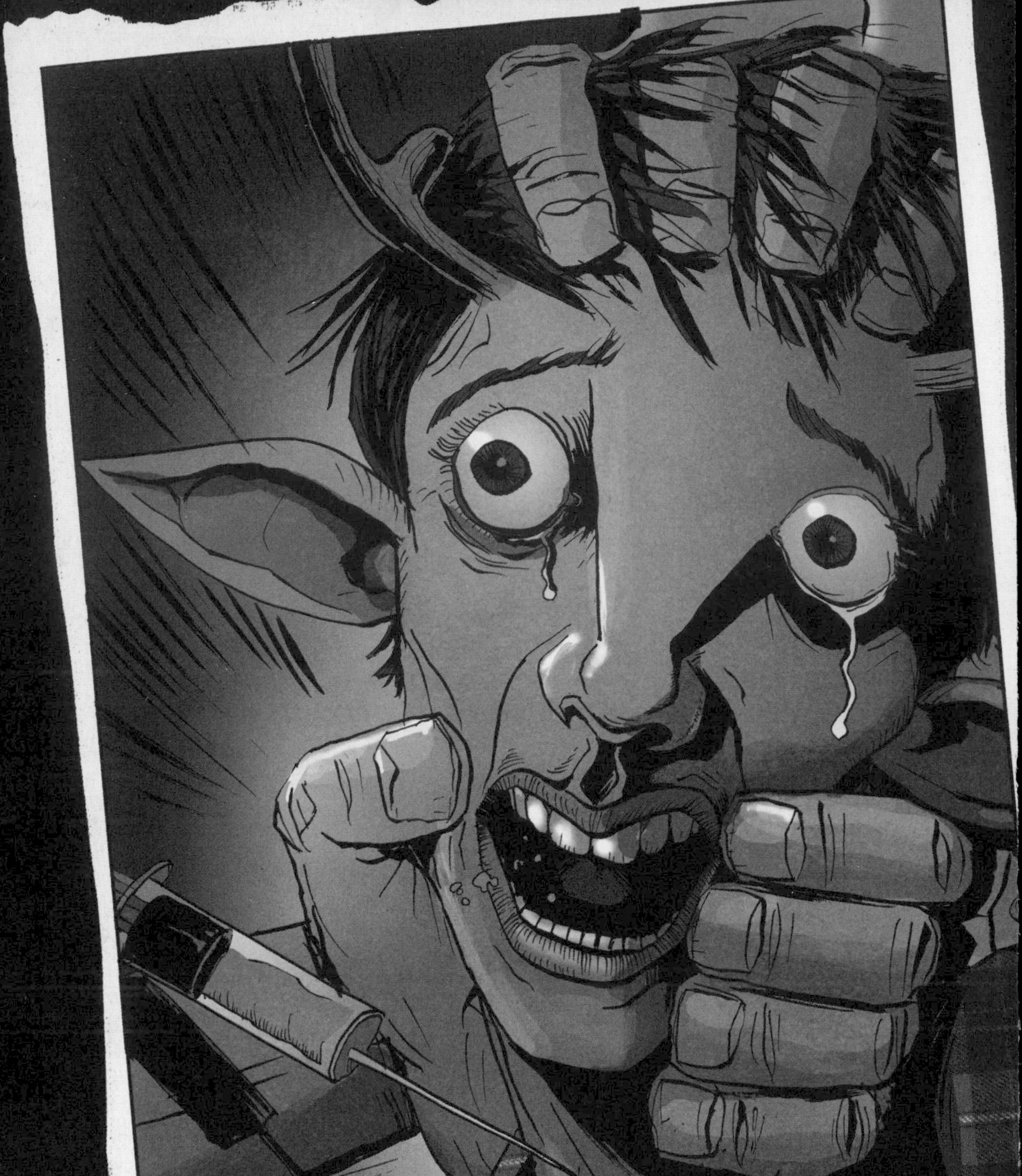

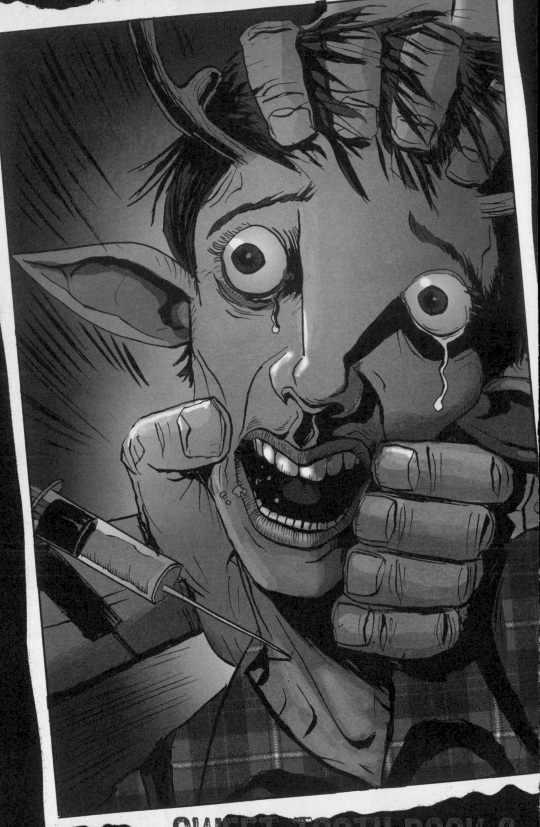

SWEET TOOTH BOOK 2

IN CAPTIVITY